EDUCATING AFRICAN CANADIANS

EDITED BY

KEREN S. BRATHWAITE
& CARL E. JAMES

An Our Schools/Our Selves Title

James Lorimer & Company Ltd., Publishers
Toronto, 1996

For subscribers to *Our Schools/Our Selves: a magazine for Canadian education activists*, this is issue #45–46, the Third of Volume 7.

The subscription series Our Schools/Our Selves (ISSN 0840-7339) is published six times a year. Publication Mail Registration Number 8010. Mailed at Centre Ville, Montreal, Quebec.

Canadian Cataloguing in Publication Data

Main entry under title:

Educating African Canadians

(Our schools/our selves monograph series ; no. 20)
Includes bibliographical references.
ISBN   1–55028–500–9

1. Black Canadians – Education – Canada.   I. Brathwaite, Keren.
II. James, Carl, 1952–   . III. Series.

LC2804.E48 1996   371.97'96071   C96–930290–8

Design and typesetting: Tobin MacIntosh.

Front Cover Design: Nancy Reid.

Our Schools/Our Selves production: Keren Brathwaite, David Clandfield, Lorna Erwin, John Huot, Doug Little, Bob Luker, George Martell, Claire Polster, Satu Repo (Executive Editor), Bairy Sium, Harry Smaller.

James Lorimer & Company Ltd., Publishers
35 Britain Street
Toronto M5A 1R7

Printed and bound in Canada by La maîtresse d'école inc., Montreal, Quebec.

For

Our Children

Wendy, Eddy, Tisha

and

Kai

&

Our Parents

Martha Williams

and

Milderine Tonge

Acknowledgements

We wish to acknowledge the support and encouragement of all those who contributed to this project. Most importantly, we wish to acknowledge the African Canadian children and youth in daycare, elementary and high schools, colleges and universities, and those who have been "pushed out" or dropped out of school, for providing us the inspiration for producing this book. We must also mention the students in the Transitional Year Programme, University of Toronto, for their unique inspiration. You have infused hope in us with your heroic struggle and relentless action to secure an education that fulfills your needs, interests and expectations. It is to you that we must also dedicate this work, for it is through your determination and leadership today, that inclusive and equitable education for African Canadians will be realized. We hope that this work will help to bring about the changes we need in education.

Sincere appreciation goes to our colleagues and friends who contributed chapters, comments and notes to this book. We have laboured with many of you for years in organizations and groups that have been dedicated to bringing about representation and equity in education for African Canadians students. We are very gratified to have been able to work with you to produce this book which represents our collective efforts, and our diverse and united voices in our struggle for equitable education. Also, thanks for responding to our requests and suggestions.

During the course of working on this book, we have been fortunate to have the support of the members of the Organization of Parents of Black Children (OPBC) with whom we have discussed many of the themes that appear in this book. We are aware that for OPBC this collection represents an important documentation of the issues on which we wish to see action that will bring about educational transformation.

Thanks to Lisa Codrington and Patrick Codrington who provided important insights into the education process of African Canadian students; and to Bob Davis who was a valuable resource. To Beverly Johnson, Philippa Brown and Collette Thompson we say thanks for your assistance in preparing the manuscript.

Very special appreciation goes to George Martell, Harry Smaller and the other members of the Editorial Board of Our Schools/Our Selves who invited us to produce this book. We are particularly indebted to Satu Repo, OS/OS Executive Editor, for her invaluable editorial work, advice, general assistance and confidence in this project.

Finally, to our families, our gratitude for your love and unfailing support: Clotilda Williams, Wendy, Eddy and Tisha Brathwaite; Gloria and Martha Williams, and Dorne Brookes and Milderine Tonge (Antigua), and Kai James. Thanks also to you for the education that you have afforded us. Peace.

Contents

EDUCATING AFRICAN CANADIANS

PART ONE

ASSESSING
THE EDUCATIONAL
EXPERIENCES
OF AFRICAN CANADIANS

Chapter One

THE EDUCATION OF AFRICAN CANADIANS
ISSUES, CONTEXTS, AND EXPECTATIONS

CARL E. JAMES AND KEREN BRATHWAITE

The education of African Canadians is one of the most contested areas of education in Canada today. Much of this contestation is due to the fact the education system has failed, and is failing, to meet the needs of African Canadians. As a result, there is a persistant and well-founded belief among African Canadians, especially the youth, that the formal education system cannot or will not accommodate itself to their needs. Some youth have been so disenchanted that they have given up on the system and dropped out (Dei et al., 1995; Brown, 1993); others remain in school, disengaged and displeased (see Dei, Chapter 2; as well as James, 1994; 1990; Yon, 1994; Solomon, 1992; Brathwaite, 1989). In response to what has happened to many of our young people, parents and members of the African Canadian communities have both initiated their own programmes and advocated consistently to the school boards and provincial government for changes to the education system, but with little result.

The contributors to this anthology explore the education issues and concerns of African Canadians in the 1990s. While most of our discussions make reference to Blacks in Ontario, and metropolitan Toronto in particular, we maintain that these issues and concerns are not unique to this region of Canada. Indeed, there is ample evidence to indicate that the experiences of African Canadians in other provinces such as Nova Scotia, Manitoba, Saskatchewan and Quebec[1] parallel those of Ontario (see Calliste, Chapter 5).[2] We see this anthology building on the research and writings on this subject in the seventies[3] and eighties. It is a response to questions such as: Has the educational situation for African Canadian students changed within the past two decades? What are the issues of the nineties and how different are they from those of the seventies? What programmes have been initiated over the years to address the educational needs of African Canadians? What roles have the schools, communities and governments played in attempting to make education accessible, equitable and responsive to the needs, interests and expectations of African Canadians? Is anti-racism a serious goal in Canadian education?

In this introductory chapter, we will explore the educational experiences and issues of African Canadians within the last three decades, with particular reference to our own Toronto/Ontario experinces and the research conducted in Ontario, and Toronto in particular.[4] Specifically, we will discuss the educational experiences and issues of the seventies, eighties and nineties, noting the similarities and differences and the implications they have for the Black community and students in particular. We highlight the seventies as a particularly significant and dynamic period in the struggle for representation and equity in education. It was also a period of much social and political activity. For instance, it was at this time that we saw a significant increase in the Black population in Canada, and Ontario in particular, the proclamation of the Canadian Multiculturalism Policy, the introduction of the provincial multicultural education policies and later race relations policies. It was also the period in which a number of community education projects were established, including the Black Education Project (BEP), the Black Liaison Committee (BLC) at the Toronto Board of Education, the Harriett Tubman Youth Centre (HTYC), African Canadian Heritage Programmes

(ACHP) and others. Community members also played a significant role in the establishment of the Transitional Year Programme at the University of Toronto (see Calliste, Chapter, 5;
and Allen, Chapter 14). We have been part of many of these initiatives and programmes. Since these experiences inform our
knowledge and understanding of the education of African Canadians in Canada, and Toronto in particular, they will be woven
into our discussion.

The Issues of the Seventies and the Eighties:
A Reference for the Nineties

Over many years, research has been done to assess the low
achievement or under-achievement of African students in Canadian schools. In the 1970's, for example, research was carried
out by some school boards in an attempt to understand the
adjustment problems and needs of Black Caribbean students:
Toronto (Schreiber, 1970), (Stewart, 1975); York (Roth, 1973);
North York (Fram et al, 1977). Independent researchers such as
Ramcharan (1975), Anderson and Grant (1975) and Beserve
(1976) also contributed to the understanding of the problems
Black Caribbean students were facing in the school system.
Without exception, these studies showed that the difficulties of
the students resulted, not only from their experiences of trying to
adjust to a new society (for those who had recently arrived), but
also from their experiences with discrimination based on race
and cultural differences.

For some time, this research was the major source of information about Black youth, primarily those from the Caribbean.
Evidently, the findings of these studies are reflective of the
social conditions of the 1970's, a time when Black immigrants
from the Caribbean were coming to Canada in large numbers
and their children were having intense difficulties in school.
Some school authorities at that time, maintained that the performance of Black students within the system was a result of
their adjustment problems. Other explanations tended to focus
on the pathological (see Christensen, Thornley-Brown and
Robinson, 1980). Many youth were labelled as having psychological problems, as being slow learners or being learning dis-
abled, as suffering from the attention deficit syndrome or

being hyperactive, and assigned to special education classes. These explanations satisfied educators because they helped to shift the responsibility of addressing the situation from the school to the parents and the community.

But these explanations could not account for the similar school experiences of Canadian-born Black youth, who were not doing well in school and had parents who supported their educational endeavours and aspirations. Indeed, during the 1970s, research on the educational aspirations of Black students showed that regardless of their social class background,[5] they tended to have high educational and career aspirations. Researchers have argued that Black students place a high value on education because they see education as making it possible for them to get ahead in this society (Calliste, 1982; Head, 1975; D'Oyley, 1976). As Calliste (1982) explained, education may be the most important, if not the only, mobility channel for Caribbean students. For this reason they were likely to be highly motivated and more achievement oriented and concerned about high grades than Anglo-Canadians. But the social construction of Black students as academically incompetent operated as a barrier to the realization of their educational goals.

The research of the seventies and eighties showed that Black students were regularly being streamed into lower level or vocational classes within Ontario schools. For example, Toronto Board of Education studies over the two decades showed that Black students were second to Aboriginals in being the most highly represented in basic level programmes of study (Wright, 1971; Deosaran, 1976; Wright and Tsuji, 1984; Cheng, Tsuji, Yau and Ziegler, 1987; Cheng, Yau, and Ziegler, 1993). Many Black community organizations (e.g. BLC, BEP, OPBC and CABE) and community members saw this placement of Black students into vocational classes, as a deliberate and discriminating practice of some school officials who tended to identify Black students, especially those from the Caribbean, as slow learners (Head, 1975). These organizations and members of the Black community advocated for a change in the practice of streaming. A 1988 report by the Consultative Committee on the Education of Black Students in Toronto Schools (CCEBSTS) also noted that stereotyping, streaming, educational assessment, inappropriate curriculum, and lack of role models — in short, discrimination — were responsible for the poor level of educational performance of many Black students in that Board. As one parent expressed it: "Students are forced into non-academic courses leading to dead-end jobs. The school expects the students to be low achievers. The school focuses on the failures of Black students" (CCEBSTS, 1988:Appendix p.1). And in the words of two students: "Black students with ability and ambition are discouraged and turned off by guidance;" and "Counsellors show us all the negatives" (CCEBSTS, 1988:20).

Evidently, this streaming of Black students has had a significant impact not only on their academic achievement, but also on how they perceive the educational and occupational possibilities that their schooling provided them (see Curtis, Livingstone and Smaller,1992). In fact, writers at that time indicated that Black students tended to become ambivalent and discouraged with the school system because they did not believe the reward system afforded them the opportunity to realize their educational goals (Head, 1975; D'Oyley, 1976; James, 1990; Solomon, 1992). Nevertheless, in struggling against their marginalization, some students actively resisted by challenging school authority and disengaging from the academic process (Solomon, 1992); but most were determined to hold onto their high educational goals, despite the system and their level of educational participation (Head, 1975; D'Oyley, 1976; James,1990).

Larter et al (1982) in their study of grade 8 students in the Toronto Board of Education found that Black and Caribbean students were the only groups who rated education as the most important to them; however, these were the two groups with the largest percentage (35% Blacks and 19% Caribbean) in special education classes. The researchers note that with the support of their parents, these students aspired to high levels of education because for them formal education was seen as an opportunity for self-realization (Larter et al., 1982: 53). It is the value that Black students attach to education that makes it difficult for them to drop out. As Oliver (1972:221) writes: 'The anguish that often accompanies the decision to drop out of school for the Black students is most excruciating. They face feelings of inadequacy and guilt on the one hand, and on the other, the realization that because they are Black their opportunities are far more limited.' It should be noted that Dei et al study (1995) shows that the high drop out rate among Black students persists to this time, in spite of the importance the students, as well as their parents and community, place on education.

That few Black students manage to attain high levels of education is related less to lack of parental encouragement, low educational aspiration or poor understanding of their situation in the society, than to other factors inherent in the structure of society and the school system in particular. Therefore, it is important to look at the school itself and the persons charged with educating students, since it is here that we find the evidence of the barriers to their achievement. Some of the evidence indicates that some teachers have been quite instrumental in discouraging students' interests, and in streaming Black students not only into vocational classes but also into athletic activities. For instance, one of the respondents in Head's (1975: 89) study reported that "when discussing his desire to become an engineer, the teacher commented that he was not suited to the field. 'You are a good basketball player and the school needs basketball players. Why don't you become a professional and forget about the engineering?'" Similar sentiments were expressed in the respondents' narratives in James' study (1990), and have also been expressed in many forums on education in and outside of the Black community. One well known Black educator (and former politician) often speaks to students about discouraging forces in her education that came from the school. She tells how her mother countered the limitations the school attempted to build around her, and thus assured her academic success.

Negotiating the Barriers to Education

Over the years, Black parents and students have always maintained that it is not "cultural adjustment" to the education system that was the cause of their low educational achievement. Rather, it was racism that was inherent in the education system as manifested in discriminationatory treatment by teachers, counsellors and administrators, and in curriculum and school practices that excluded Black students (Head, 1975; D'Oyley, 1976; Ramcharan, 1982; CCEBSTS, 1988; James, 1990). These practices included the streaming of Black students into vocational, technical and behavioural classes and encouraging them into athletic careers. Left unaddressed, systemic racism and discrimination, which inevitably contributed to the students' alienation from the schooling process, continued to have a significant impact on their education. In writing about what she calls "a Canadian dilemma," Keren Brathwaite, a member of the Toronto Board of Education Consultative Committee on the Education of Black Students, points out that

> in listening to the stories which Black students and parents tell about the school system, it is impossible to deny that racism is an active part of it. Indeed, racism is a theme of Black students' school experience and the source of their disenchantment with it. It is an integral part of the course content, classroom atmosphere, discipline procedures and the philosophy of streaming which sends our students in large numbers to inferior schools and programs. It is the most serious barrier to their progress in that it affects their self-esteem and sets up limitations around them in the form of expectations which, as self-fulfilling prophecy, they meet (Brathwaite, 1989:?).

But despite the seemingly insurmountable barriers that racism and discrimination posed for Black students, they continued to hold the belief that they would be able to negotiate the barriers and succeed. Their motivation was due to the fact that they perceived education as the most important vehicle for succeeding in Canadian society; and ironically, it is education that would help them to overcome racism and discrimination (Head, 1975; D'Oyley, 1976; Calliste, 1982; James, 1990). These sentiments were well represented in the research of the seventies and eighties. Take for instance the following comments as reported in Head (1975) and James (1990). In Head's study, a youth is quoted as saying: "With a university degree, options increase and the feeling is there are 'good' even 'very good' opportunities for employment" (Head, 1975: 97). James (1990) quotes two youth as saying:

> Greg: If you graduate from high school with good marks and get into a university and graduate from there you can pretty well get a good job, if you just keep on working hard.

Richard: I feel that I should go to university because without going I don't think I'm going to get too far in society. Without that piece of paper that shows that you have been educated you're not going to get far in the workforce. Like I don't want to end up working at McDonald's or Eaton's all my life. (James, 1990: 64, 65).

Ever conscious of racism operating as a barrier to their success, Black youth tended to believe that armed with their education, the significance of colour would diminish and "nothing will stop them if they are willing to try." Generally, they believed that individual effort, qualification and ability would ultimately help them to realize their goals in society. They tended to be determined that neither discrimination nor colour would be a barrier for them (Head, 1975; James, 1990). This determination of Black youth is likely a reflection of their understanding of their minority position in Canadian society, and a product of the encouragement they receive from their parents, many of whom are immigrants who wish to see their a children achieve upward social mobility (D'Oyley, 1976; Calliste, 1982; Brathwaite, 1989; James, 1990).

But not all the young people agreed that the avenue to success is through education. Some youth, albeit a minority and predominantly males, believed that sports and not education was a more viable option toward making it in Canadian society (Head,1975; James,1990). For these youth, sports was valued because it helped them to cope with an alienating and discriminatory school system through the recognition they received from teachers, coaches and peers, which in turn helped to "boost their ego," build their "self confidence" and develop "pride in themselves" (James, 1990). Referring to the Black student athletes in his late 1980s study who used sports (i.e. basketball) as a way of resisting the school system, Solomon (1992:76) writes: "For the Jocks, sports serve three main functions: it helps in the formation of Black culture and identity; it preserves machismo; and it is pursued as a viable channel for socioeconomic advancement." In reporting on the significance of sports to Black student athletes, James (1990:45) quotes one of his study participants as saying that a number of his peers cannot relate to school, and it might be hard for them, so they look to basketball, as a means of obtaining a "scholarship to universities. So you can say it is our ticket out of school because a lot of us do not have the money to pay tuition fees" (see also James, 1995: "Negotiating School through Sports").

Generally, studies of Black youth in the metropolitan Toronto area, show that during the seventies and eighties, most believed that education was important to their success in this society and that racism and discrimination were merely "obstacles" that they would be able to overcome through their high level of education. James (1990:113) notes that in addition to education, the youth in his study figured that they could overcome these obstacles through such strategies as proving themselves, working hard, being determined, relying on their own abilities and skills, having the "right" attitude, high career aspirations, a conviction that nothing will stop them, and the aspiration to become "the best," since it is only by being the best that they will be able to counter the obstacles. For those Black youths who were unable to effectively negotiate the white, Eurocentic, middle class school system, and therefore believed that racism and discrimination were insurmountable barriers to educational success, the studies (e.g. Head, 1975; James, 1990; Solomon, 1992) show that they became disengaged from the schooling process, believing that education offered little possibility for achieving in this society.

The educational experience of African Canadians in the 1970s and 80s parallels that of Blacks in Britain, most of whom share similar backgrounds in terms of being second generation Caribbean immigrants to Britain (Beserve, 1976; Fuller, 1982; Carrington, 1983; Lovell, 1991; Mirza, 1992; see also James, Chapter 15). These studies also draw our attention to the gender differences in terms of academic and athletic engagement and achievement. For example, with reference to the situation of African Caribbean young women, Fuller (1983:172) writes:

> Schooling and education provided them an alternative and less undermining possibility in their search for greater freedom and control. Concentration on education as a way out was something which all the Black girls whom I interviewed stressed, though ... as they pointed out this strategy had its drawbacks. In particular the vocational aspects of schooling and further

education were attractive and their achievement in these areas were thought to lead to better prospects of a 'good' job. Being aware of both sexual and racial discrimination the girls did not assume that good educational performance was the sufficient requirement for obtaining such jobs, but they did believe it was a necessary one.

From her study which reported similar findings, Mirza (1992) concludes that social class had an influence on the occupational choice of second generation Caribbean immigrant young women. Further, while the racially and sexually segregated labour market provided limited opportunities, "schools were seen to play an important role in both structuring and restricting Black female occupational aspirations and expectations" (Mizra, 1992: 192).

The Early Anti-Racism Movement

African Canadian parents and community members have always been dissatisfied with the notion that the low achievement and poor educational performance of African students were due to cultural differences. In challenging the conclusions of the various school boards' research,[6] parents and community members have argued that it is systemic racism,[7] rather than cultural adjustment that was at the root of Black students' educational problems. Their poor educational performance was due to their alienation from school, their low self-concept and feelings of being second class citizens (Oliver, 1972). This "psychological deprivation" of Black children, argues Jules Oliver (1972:221) is not a result of the fact that they live in an impoverished community, but rather, that they exist "in an environment which perpetuates white values and white dominance." With this conviction, parents and community members advocated for schools to identify race as a factor in the experiences of the students, and to identify systemic racism as a barrier to the students' participation in school, and with the consequence of academic underachievement.

In putting into action their convictions, a number of community organizations (e.g. BEP, HTYC, ACHP, CABE, OPBC) — working independently, and in collaboration with parental groups that were connected to various school boards — were

22

instrumental in seeking policies and programmes that would change the educational situation for Black students. One very important issue was streaming. It can be suggested that the tireless efforts of parents, students, educators and community members assisted in the dismantling of streaming in Grade 9 (1992/93) in Ontario schools.

Parents and community members have also maintained that the multicultural policies that were adopted by school boards following the establishment of the Canadian Multiculturalism Policy (1971) were insufficient in addressing the education needs and situation of African Canadian students. In the case of Ontario, the Ministry of Education initiated policies and programmes in the mid-seventies that were aimed at fostering sensitivity and relevance of school materials, respect for cultural difference, and "integration of the minority student" (McAndrew, 1991:135). With the help of federal funding, the school's "multicultural programmes" basically focussed on languages — heritage languages. This was based on the assumption that competence in their "heritage language" would help to build self confidence and a sense of belonging in students. Feeling less alienated from the society and school, students' learning would then improve and they would become successful. With these programmes, students were able to receive instruction in their mother tongue at school. African Canadians, particularly those who were not from the continent, did not fit the criteria, so it was left to the community to advocate for programmes for all African students. These Heritage Programmes were used to educate students about the contributions of Africans to Canadian society in particular, and to world development in general. It was a space also to teach students about Africa, to counter the negative "Tarzan and poverty images" to which African students had grown accustomed, and address the 'mentally genocidal' (Oliver, 1972) effects of racism. Continuous work by parents, students, educators and community members resulted in some schools incorporating these African Heritage classes into the school day or as a course in some high schools.

Needless to say, members of the African Canadian community were never satisfied with the federal Multiculturalism Policy nor the educational policies and programmes that resulted from it. They noted that the policies and programmes placed emphasis on cultural differences while failing to acknowledge race and racism as factors which were affecting students' achievement in schools. In fact, the Eurocentic curriculum which promoted conformity or assimilation to Anglo-Canadian values and norms, remained evident in the curriculum, teaching methods and materials and students assessment. It was understood that multicultural policies and programmes did not address the subtle, and sometimes blatant forms of racism, particularly structural and systemic racism, that are inherent in the educational system, and which affected the interactions of parents, students, teachers and administrators. The multicultural approach to education, according to parents and community members, also failed to meet the needs of Black students and address racism, because it provided information that focussed on "song and dance," stereotypes (or "museum culture"), and "other" Canadians — immigrants with a foreign culture (Consultative Committee on the Education of Black Students in Toronto Schools, 1988). As a prominent African Canadian anti-racism education expert Enid Lee writes:

> One can organize a unity and diversity club and deal with cultural holidays and host a Multicultural Week and yet not deal with racism. These events may present some information about cultural groups and focus on the exotic and leave many people with a nice feeling but do nothing to address the schools' response or lack of response to the languages and faiths of students of colour. They may leave intact the Eurocentric curriculum which students consume daily (Lee, 1994: 24).

In response to the criticism made by Black community members and others, some Boards of Education initiated Race Relations policies and programmes. In these cases, race was acknowledged, in terms of biological differences, but not as a political and social construct of society that resulted in low educational outcomes for racial minority students. Racism was seen to be a consequence of ignorance; and racial minority students' lack of success was seen to be the result of racial tension and lack of role models in the society generally, and in school and learning materials in particular. On this point, James (1995:37) in "Multiculturalism and Anti-Racism Education in

Canada," writes:

> To address this problem of racism, educators believed that students' experiences in racially mixed groups provided awareness of, and sensitivity to, each other. Understanding gained through such interactions would help to prevent racism, therefore creating a school and classroom atmosphere in which racial minority students could participate and become successful. For this reason, we would often hear teachers insisting that racial minority students must mix...; and racial minority "successful" role models would be brought into schools to demonstrate that success is possible in this society irrespective of race.

One very common "multicultural/race relations" activity that became quite prominent in the late seventies was the Black History Month programme. Althea Prince, in Chapter 10, interrogates the schools' initiatives and understanding of this programme and finds it a disjointed approach to the education Black youth.

Race relations and programs did little to arrest the educational difficulties of African Canadian youths. Essentially, as James (1995) argues, race relations programmes were in effect multicultural programmes, the only difference was that race was now acknowledged. This being the case, the multicultural approach to education continued to be the cornerstone of educational practices. Hence, for Black parents and community members, the changes for which they advocated during the seventies and the eighties have not materialized. Consequently, they would continue to advocate for changes in the 1990s, with the hope that the anti-racism literature, school boards' policies, teacher training and programmes would eventually result in educational action and changes that would speak to the systemic racism that is responsible for the situation of Black students in Canadian schools.

The Nineties: Is There Really a Paradigm Shift?

In recent years, many educators and school boards have developed policies and teacher training programmes in the area of anti-racism. In Ontario, in particular, the Ministry of Education of the previous New Democratic Party government, had initiated policies which required that all school boards in Ontario take an anti-racism approach to education. The Ministry document which spelt out the guidelines that should be followed in developing and implementing "anti-racism and ethnocultural equity policies" indicated that

> The intent of antiracism and ethnocultural equity education is to ensure that all students achieve their potential and acquire knowledge and information, as well as confidence in their cultural and racial identities. It should equip all students with the knowledge, skills, attitudes, and behaviours needed to live and work effectively in an increasingly diverse world, and encourage them to appreciate diversity and reject discriminatory attitudes and behaviour (Ministry of Education and Training, 1993: 5).

To oversee the implementation of this policy, the position of Assistant Deputy Minister was established and was occupied by an African Canadian educator. The lobbying efforts of African Canadian educators under the leadership of the Black Educators Working Group (BEWG) contributed to the establishment of this position.

The above is an indication of the continuing efforts of African Canadians to bring to the attention of government and official bodies the educational conditions of African Canadians which have been well established by research. The Royal Commission on Learning in Ontario whose report *For the Love of Learning* was published in 1994 was the most recent commission which was acquainted (one more time) with the extent of the education problem of Black students. The Stephen Lewis (Ontario)enquiry of 1992 was another study which solicited opinions on the state of Black students' education, as did the Consultative Committee on the Education of Black Students in Toronto Schools in 1988.

The Royal Commission on Learning which invited groups of Black educators, parents and community to address it in October 1993, was a recipient of several submissions on the education of Black students. These submissions converged on common themes. The written submissions would of course have their impact, but it was reported that on the evening of "Black" oral presentations, there was much electricity in the meeting room. There was much in-depth analysis presented on what is stifling Black students' attainment in the schools, and there was much unity among the various Black presenters, educators as well as parents. *For the Love of Learning* records our input thus:

> Black students, parents, and community leaders came to the Commission and expressed serious concerns about the achievement levels of their young people. They expressed frustration over lack of improvement over the years, during which time they have voiced their concerns to school boards and to the Ministry. They are concerned about the future of young Blacks who, without a secondary school diploma (let alone a college diploma or university degree), face limited job prospects, social marginalization, and personal defeat. These presenters argued forcefully that the education system is failing Black students, and that there is an *education crisis* in their community. *(For the Love of Learning*,1994:92; our emphasis).

The "education crisis" referred to here is a "crisis" African Canadians have been facing for many generations (see Brathwaite in "The Black Student and the School: A Canadian Dilemma," 1989; and George Dei,1995). The four-level Government/African Canadian Community Working Group which was established in 1992 after the "Yonge Street Incident" writes in their report:

> a review of a number of reports and of presentations before the Working Group makes it clear that, for at least one generation, the African-Canadian community has been crying out in anguish over the poor performance of its youth in the Ontario School system. The dropout rate, the truancy rate, the failure rate, the basic-streaming rate: all these pointed inexorably to the fact that, where Black kids are concerned, something is terribly wrong *(Towards a New Beginning*, 1992:77).

The duration of this "crisis" has led to the questioning of the capability of educational institutions in Canada to really educate Black students now, after failing to do so for more than a century. Should not the past twenty years have brought some change? Should not African Canadian parents, educators and community in general, expect more from the education system? Should not African Canadian students in today's classrooms feel more included and more hopeful than those of earlier generations? The answers to these questions are to be found in the research on Black students, and very importantly, in the lives they live, the stories they tell each other, their parents, and the various researchers and commissions who "study" their problem on a regular basis. To Stephen Lewis in 1992, Black students again voiced their disenchantment with their schooling. He writes in his official letter to Premier Bob Rae (Ontario's Premier at that time):

> Everywhere, the refrain of Toronto students, however starkly amended by different schools and different locations, was essentially the refrain of all students. Where are the courses in Black history? Where are the visible minority teachers? Why are there so few role models? Why do our white guidance counsellors know so little of different cultural backgrounds? Why are racist incidents and epithets tolerated? Why are there double standards of discipline? Why are minority students streamed? Why do they discourage us from University? Where are we going to find jobs? What's the use of having an education if there's no employment? How long does it take to change the curriculum so that we're a part of it?
>
> The students were fiercely articulate and often deeply moving. Sometimes angry. They don't understand why the schools are so slow to reflect the broader society. One bright young man in a Metro east high school said that he had reached grade thirteen, without once having a book by a Black author on the curriculum. And when other students, in the large meeting of which he was a part, started to name the books they had been given to read, the titles were "Black Like Me" and "To Kill A Mockingbird" (both, incredibly enough, by white writers!). It's absurd in a world which has a positive cornucopia of magnificent literature by Black authors. I further recall an animated young woman from a high school in Peel, who described her school as overwhelmingly multiracial, and then added that she and her fellow students had white teachers, white counsellors, a white principal, and were taught Black history by a white teacher who didn't like them. There wasn't a single non-white member of the staff.

The research, commissions and body of knowledge which have been generated around the performance of African Canadian students have been instrumental in heightening the awareness of not only the Black community and educators, but also institutions, governments and the general public to social and systemic conditions based on racial inequality which have been endemic in the history of African people in Canada. The Black Learners Advisory Committee (BLAC) report on Education titled *Redressing Inequity — Empowering Black Learners*, December 1994, is the most recent critique of the Nova Scotia profile of African Canadian education. In his introduction to the Report, the Chair writes:

> This report examines and illustrates major issues that persist in the education environment of Nova Scotia. From the African Nova Scotian viewpoint, this report demonstrates vividly the realities of the African Nova Scotian experience in a discordant education system that is devoid of any effective policies essential and sympathetic to their needs.
>
> Clear deficiencies that exist include the shortage of policies affecting race relations at the Board and school levels; the need for school curriculum and policies to accommodate cultural diversity; the need to realign the relationship between the home and the school; the lack of any development of creative and resourceful programs for teachers' professional training, maturation and growth in a multicultural and multiracial society; scarcity of Black role models in the systems, methods to respond to racial harassment and the assessment of students for placement; the lack of effective process to evaluate text books for bias and the absence of materials to engender more positive attitudes in the African Nova Scotian student. Programs to ensure early childhood education and access to post secondary education are also in short supply.

The introductory comments of Mr. Castor Williams go to the heart of the debate over the causes of the general poor performance profile of African Canadian students: curriculum concerns, teacher training, policies regarding "race relations"/anti-racism, bias in textbooks, parent involvement in education, early childhood education and post-secondary education.

The curriculum concerns are some of the most damaging elements in our students' schooling, and this is an area that has attracted much attention in the Black community and among educators. Annette Henry and others have critiqued the curriculum as a barrier to Black students' success. She writes:

Throughout my childhood, my school lessons never enabled me to make sense of my blackness in positive, affirming ways. My teachers never taught in ways that helped me critically understand a larger Black community.... As a young Black girl growing up in England and Canada, my school lessons were often acts of violence. (Henry 1994: 298)

These "acts of violence" must be eliminated from the education system. The schools with our input must provide resources that will truly educate Black students as well as others to survive in the complex global community of which we are all a part. The changes that are sought in curriculum cannot wait for another generation.

Conclusion

In this introductory chapter, we have highlighted the issues and approaches to African students education during the sixties, seventies and eighties, in order to scan the path we have travelled in the last generation. The evidence points to the continuing confidence that African Canadians hold about the capacity of education to provide them with the skills and knowledge to be able to fully participate and succeed in Canadian society. They hold this view despite their experiences, and the feeling that the education system has been unable to respond to the needs, interests and expectations of a large number of our students. The contributors to this collection provide a critical assessment of the current situation for African Canadians. We express the hope that education will help students triumph over the barriers of racism and discrimination which continue to prevail among African Canadians. The discussions that appear in this book should alert us not only to the problems, but also to the ways in which they can be addressed by all concerned.

NOTES

1 For example, there is the issue of language and schooling in Quebec (see Richardson, 1994; and Beauger, Dorsaint and Turenne; 1994 in V. D'Oyley *Innovations in Black Education in Canada*).

2 See also the BLAC Report on Education, 1994; D'Oyley, 1994; D'Oyley and Silverman, 1976.

3 We use the 1970s as our reference since in this period the significant increase in immigrants from the Caribbean brought a correspondingly large number of African students into the educational system.

4 Issues around Africans' successful participation in the education systems in Canada, has been a problem since our recorded presence here dating back to the seventeenth century. Ever since then, Africans have contested the ways in which education has been used in our marginalization, limiting our full participation in society.

5 Calliste (1982) suggests that Caribbean people in Canada, while characterised by low social class status, are less entrenched in their class position.

6 This research includes Schreiber, 1970; Roth, 1973; Fram et al, 1977; Wright and Tsuji, 1984; 1982.

7 Systemic racism is understood to be different from individual racism. It refers to established school policies, rules and regulations which systematically reflect and produce differential treatment and outcomes for students, in this case Black students. (see James, 1995 *Seeing Ourselves* p. 139.)

Chapter Two

LISTENING TO VOICES
DEVELOPING A PEDAGOGY OF CHANGE FROM THE NARRATIVES OF AFRICAN-CANADIAN STUDENTS AND PARENTS

GEORGE J. SEFA DEI

Introduction

In November, 1992, a multi-level government task force, the "African-Canadian Community Working Group," proposed, in a report titled "Towards a New Beginning," that one predominantly Black junior high school should be set up in each of the six metropolitan Toronto municipalities (see Working Group, 1992). The report suggested a five-year pilot scheme, establishing a Black-focused institution where Black history and culture would be taught. Such a school would have proportionately more Black/African-Canadian[1] teachers and administrators on staff than most mainstream public schools. The agenda would be to provide African-Canadian students with the choice of an alternative learning environment and to develop their sense of identity and belonging to a school. The hope was that, by teaching about the Black experience and African-

Canadian students' heritages, such a school would deal appropriately with the problems of isolation and frustration that many Black youths have in society.

Local community and parents' groups in the African-Canadian community, such as the Organization of Parents of Black Children (OPBC), in their submission before the Ontario Royal Commision on Learning supported the idea of 'African-centred' schools (OPBC, 1993). In fact, when the Ontario Royal Commission on Learning released its report, after an exhaustive study of the Ontario school system, this idea of creating an alternative educational environment for Black youth received some discussion. The Commission's report recommended that "school boards, academic authorities, faculties of education, and representatives of the Black community collaborate to establish demonstration schools ..." in jurisdictions where there are large numbers of Black students. (1994: p.78).

In the 1990s, Black/African-Canadian parents, guardians, caregivers, community workers, students and educators continue to ask questions about the ability of public schools to equip Black youth with the requisite tools and skills essential to their survival in a global community. It is generally acknowledged that one of the most crucial issues facing North American educational systems is the 'dropout problem' (see Conference Board of Canada, 1991; Cadieux 1991; King, et al., 1988). Dropout statistics are notoriously unreliable. But in Canada, currently, it is widely believed that at least 30 percent of students do not finish school and that at the present dropout level, as many as one million under-educated and untrained youth will have entered the Canadian labour market by the year 2000 (University Affairs, 1991:5, Statistics Canada, 1991, Youth Affairs Branch of Employment and Immigration, Canada, 1990).

In a 1991 high-school survey by one board of education in Toronto, it was revealed that African-Canadian youth were not achieving as well as other students in terms of credit accumulation. It was shown that 36% of Black students were 'at risk' of dropping out because of failure to accumulate sufficient credits to graduate within six years. This compared with 26% for whites and 18% for Asians (see Yau, et al., 1993; Cheng, 1995). This survey also confirmed "... that 45% of Black high-school students were enrolled in Basic and General level,[2] as compared to 28% of the entire student body placed in those two lower streams" (Cheng, 1995: 2; see also Cheng, et al., 1993; 15; Brown, et al., 1992: 13). In the most revealing statistics, the board of education's study of high-school students who enrolled in 1987 showed that by 1991, 42% of Black students (compared to the overall student population of 33%) dropped out of school (see Brown, 1993: 5).

Many factors have been suggested as influencing the dropout rate, ranging from streaming in the schools, poverty, Eurocentrism, white male privilege and structural discrimination (Ministry of Citizenship 1989; Pollard 1989). However, many of the analyses tend to over-generalize without delving into the specifics concerning various social groups in the educational system. Earlier efforts to understand the issue of school dropouts also concentrated on statistical tallies of dropout rates without in-depth analysis of students' perspectives as to why they stay in or quit school. In fact, studies of school dropouts have generally been structural accounts that offer little insight into the actors' points of view (see Weis, et al., 1989; Trueba, et al., 1989; Karp 1988). Few studies have attempted to explore the issue of dropping out from the point of view of students themselves (see Fine 1991).

Within the Canadian context, Cummins (1989), Radwanski (1987), Hargreaves and Earl (1990), Lawton, et al., (1988), Karp (1988), and Mackay and Myles (1989) have highlighted the specific problem of dropping out and underachievement among visible minority youth and looked at strategies for intervention. These studies agree that there are genuine problems in our educational system that need to be addressed for minority students. But while the authors provide recommendations for reforms in the schools, they fail to explore adequately the questions of class, gender, race/ethnicity, power and history in the discussion of dropping out, and particularly, how students' lived experiences and social reality have contributed to the decision to leave school early.

For three years (May, 1992 to June, 1995), with the assistance of OISE graduate students, I have been eliciting the views and experiences of African-Canadian youth and parents concerning school and the 'dropout' phenomeon. The study was guided by two objectives: first, to see if there are other issues involved in dropping out which the schools may not be aware of, and second, to find out what the students' and parents' views are of those issues which have been identified.

We have solicited individual and group responses from students to such questions as, what do they like about school, what do they dislike, why do they think some students drop out and why do others stay on to complete their education. We have asked students how the dynamics of social difference (race/ethnicity, class, gender) affect their schooling experiences. We have also asked them who is their favourite teacher, whether their parents help them in their school work and what changes they would want to see in the school system.

This paper provides some findings of the preliminary analysis of 'dropouts' and students' narratives of their experiences in the public school system. While these findings are by no means conclusive, they provide early insights into the school dropout dilemma and also illuminate why there is a debate about whether or not African-Canadian students should be educated in 'African-centred' schools. This debate is captured in public discourses about whether African-Canadian youths should continue to be mainstreamed or removed to alternative learning environments to ensure academic and social success.

Our current research points to the fact that much work needs to be done by way of re-theorizing and re-conceptualizing the whole phenomenon of 'school dropouts.' Educational researchers have to move away from simplistic cause-effect models of behaviour in which correlation implies causation. We need instead a grounded theory, based on students' articulation of their lived experiences and a good conceptual analysis about how the diverse experiences of students inside and outside the school system contribute to dropping out (Lawton, 1992: Dei, 1995a).

While we focus on students' subjective lived experiences, we are also interested in the role that social structure and culture play in shaping those experiences. By analyzing the 'subjugated knowledge' (Foucault, 1980) and discourse of students, and highlighting the statements of the main actors, I believe we can be provided with alternative perspectives of the dropout phenomenon. In providing alternative explanations of how and why the school system produces 'dropouts,' it may be necessary to focus on the power asymmetries of relationships structured by race, ethnicity, class, and gender that Black youth and other minorities experience in the wider society.

It is important to ponder certain questions critically. For example, what is it about mainstream public schools that creates many disengaged students who fade out? Are there some school policies and practices — as well as occurrences in the home — that place minority students in particular 'at risk' of dropping out? Do the institutional forms and practices of public education systematically function to keep Black and low-income students from staying in school (Fine 1991: 156)?

Methodology

This study focuses on interviews with over 150 African-Canadian students. This figure is made up of 22 school 'dropouts' identified through our community ties and 25 students from various Toronto high schools whom we managed to access over the summer holidays. A few of the 'dropouts' have actually dropped back into schools. In September 1992, we began a series of student interviews with African-Canadian youths in the four selected Toronto schools. Within each high school, students were selected to provide a representation of male and female students from general and advanced level programs, and to include Grades 10 and 12 students.

The criteria for selecting Grade 10 students at 'high risk' of dropping out include below-average marks, poor attendance or inadequate accumulation of credits (see Ziegler 1989; Waterhouse 1990). Grade 12 students are providing information as to why they stayed in school and how the system has worked for them. In a few cases, the difficulty of getting students from these two grades has led us to include students from other grades (i.e., Grades 9 and II). But we have generally focused on the total credits accumulated as an important criterion in the grade selection of students. I have also conducted three focus-group interviews with Black male and female students considered 'at risk' of dropping out. One group was in a program run by a school board for 'at-risk' students, and the other two groups were from a job program operated for youths in the summer of 1992 by the provincial government. Focus-group interviews with students in the selected schools are still being conducted. Group sessions have also been a way of cross-referencing individual student narratives.

Apart from these interviews with students, the project has also included an ethnography of selected schools (e.g., observations of school culture, work roles, gender roles, as well as student-peer and student-teacher interactions, and classroom activities). I have sat in classroom discussions, and hung around school compounds and hallways in order to observe the varied interactions that take place in the daily life of a school.

One hundred and forty five (145) of the students and the actual 'dropouts' interviewed also completed a survey which sought firm responses to certain basic questions (see Dei, et. al, 1995). We sought basic demographic information about ethnicity, gender, age, place of birth, occupation status of parents, language(s) spoken. Students and dropouts' responses were obtained prior to beginning the in-depth, individual interviews. Out of the 145 completed surveys, 80(55%) said they were born outside of Canada. Among them, 64(80%) were born in the Caribbean, 11(14%) in Africa, and 5(6%) elsewhere. Of the students born outside of Canada, 71(89%) came to the country after 1980. From the total 145 students surveyed, 97(67%) speak English only. Forty-three (33%) students speak additional languages. 65(45%) students took advanced level courses. The majority of the students and the 'dropouts' 93(64%), do not live at home with both parents. Among the students in the survey, the majority, ninety-five, said they knew someone who had dropped out of school. Finally, forty-seven students admitted they had considered leaving high school. The discussion of Black youth narratives about dropping out will focus on the actual 'dropouts' and those students considered 'at risk' of dropping out.

Theoretical Approaches to Understanding 'School Dropouts'

Lawton (1992) has synthesized the various theoretical positions, models and frameworks explaining 'dropping out.' He points out that Finn's (1989) *'frustration-self-esteem'* model views dropping out as a developmental process beginning in the earliest grades. The model argues that students who do not do well become frustrated early in school. With time, their frustration can result in a lower self-image, which eventually leads them to drop out. My critique of this model is that it does not adequately explain in the first place why some students do not do well in school. The notion of 'low self-esteem' could be used to blame the student and thereby mask the structural and institutional inequities and contradictions these students have to deal with that engender the phenomenon of dropping out.' Self-esteem' may not be a useful concept for understanding dropping out because it fails to acknowledge the individual self and cultural differences.

The *'Participation-Identification'* model, explaining dropping out, (Finn, 1989) postulates that involvement in school activities usually results in identification and social attraction to a group. Conversely, the lack of participation results in a lack of identification. It is argued that the likelihood of a youth successfully completing high school is maximized if the student "... maintains multiple, expanding forms of participation in school-relevant activities" (Lawton 1992: 20). Marginalized students can become isolated from the mainstream student body. They may feel alienated from the school system as a whole and consequently drop out (Finn, 1987, 1989). This model has some utility for understanding the impact of marginalization of racial and ethnic minorities in Eurocentric educational institutions. However, it does not adequately address how and why visible minority students, for example, become marginalized. It does not account for why even those students who identify with the school system could still fade out because of the way external structural conditions are mediated within the school system.

The *'deviance theory'* of dropping out (see LeCompte and Dworkin, 1991) argues that, by failing to support and respect the existing institutional norms, values, ethos and rules of the school, students stand the risk of being branded deviants. Consequently, these students may be denied privileges and rewards the institution accords to well-behaved students. With time, the 'deviants' internalize such institutional labels by redefining themselves in terms of their deviant behaviour. They drift towards behaviours that offer their own rewards rather than the institutional sanctions of the school. Students' oppositional behaviour acquires some legitimacy of its own. Because the school system would not tolerate such behaviour as frequent absenteeism, poor academic performance and truancy, their perpetrators are eventually 'pushed out' of school.

The deviance model is particularly relevant for steering attention to institutional structures and processes that rationalize school decisions to 'push out' students who are non-conformists. However, it does not problematize how 'deviance' is constructed in society. This is important if we are to make the connection between the school and its policies and the wider social setting in accounting for school dropouts. This connection is essential for understanding the school experiences of Black immigrant students. The policies of the school towards 'non-conformists' and those who act and look different from the mainstream are a reflection of the social forces of society. Society expects the school to legitimize certain hegemonic and ideological practices, while delegitimizing others.

Other theories explaining school dropout include those that hypothesize a link between structural strain on institutions and the behaviour and attitudes of their employees and clients. LeCompte and Dworkin's (1991) *'structural strain and alienation'* model, which argues that if societal changes reduce the fit between school and society, then teachers and students are likely to perceive their efforts and participation as purposeless. The outcome of such a situation is burnout for teachers, and alienation and dropping out for students. The relevance of this model lies in the introduction of key concepts such as 'alienation,' 'powerlessness,' 'meaninglessness,' 'normlessness,' and 'isolation' to explain why students give up on school when their lived realities do not match the expectations society and schooling has promised (Lawton 1992: 21). Other studies such as Manski (1989), Stage (1989) and Bickel and Papagiannis (1988) have utilized economic models of *cost-benefit analysis* to try and explain the causes of dropping out. Stage (1989) and Bickel and Papagiannis (1988) focused on local economic conditions, arguing that high-school students will more likely stay in school and graduate if there is a good chance of gaining employment and improving their incomes with completed education. On the other hand, if students feel local conditions make employment unlikely regardless of education level, then there is a good chance of students leaving school prematurely. These theories provide additional insights into students' decisions to stay or leave school. There are students who leave school when they realize they could be better off economically doing something else. But even here, the narratives of the lived experiences of these students reveal the complex web of social structural, cultural and institutional factors that come into play.

For African-Canadian youth in an inner, multi-ethnic city, a grounded theory for understanding the etiology of dropping out builds upon the insights provided by earlier theoretical approaches. By analyzing the subjugated knowledges and discourses of students, and highlighting the statements of the main actors, we begin to uncover how social difference, based on such dynamics as race, ethnicity, socio-economic class and gender, restrict the educational and life opportunities of some students. We also learn how public schooling privileges and engages certain groups, whilst disengaging and disempowering others.

The African-Canadian student population is not a homogenous group and students' concerns vary to some extent. For example, Continental African students have concerns about the broad issues of language, religion, and culture. Students who have been schooled in the Caribbean complain about the "social labelling" of Black students as "trouble-makers." There are also complaints about the attempts by schools to place them in English skills development (ESD) classes. Questions of identity are raised by students born here in Canada and, particularly, to mixed parents. Students who speak with distinctly different accents and dialects point to intragroup discrimination and prejudices among their peers. However, it is noted that certain common themes and concerns do emerge from the analysis of the Black students' narrative discourses.

Understanding of 'Dropping Out' of School

We begin with African-Canadian students and parents' view of 'dropping out' of school. Marlo was a participant in a summer jobs program for students when interviewed. He indicated at the time that he was dropping out of school. He did not mince his words when he spoke about 'dropping out,' and besides, was not a student one could claim as lacking in self-esteem:

> When I hear that (dropout), it just means the person couldn't cope with all the hassles that they're getting from school. The first thing that comes to mind is ... yeah, that they couldn't cope with it — couldn't handle it and said, forget it. And try something different.... Yeah, that tells me, yeah, that's the end. They're not going back again, period.... That's because they hate the school they're going to — a lot of bull (I can say that?) shit. A lot of bullshit. To find somewhere where they can be comfortable. If they can't find it — too much bullshit there — they can find it somewhere else. Until they can find ... you know; somebody can get along with the people there. My school — the first school I left was because of the reason of people — the teachers and stuff that was going on was the reason I left. Too much bullshit. (08/06/92).

Steffan, 19, another participant in the summer job program views 'dropouts' as:

> Very brave and courageous. They decided to make a move to benefit themselves. It may not be the right move for me but they see it as the right move for them and they do it! ... Right now it's rough (at school). I can admit that. But in time we'll be able to appreciate everybody's needs. (13/08/92).

Generally, African-Canadian parents and community workers point out that it is easy for their children to drop out of school, given the way the system is set up to function. Amma, a parent, who has worked with a number of youths and parents, is concerned about the young people who no longer see education as a tool to achieve their dreams or, as she says, "... kids who just don't feel like they have a place in the school system, or that it (school) speaks to their needs or their interests." She points out that education is "... not just about making the big grade, it's also making sure that they (youth) have the social skills to succeed. (Education) ... is learning how to interact with other people, and building, learning, working with them to make them feel good about themselves...."

Unfortunately, she thinks the youth today feel "there's some-where else that you can go and be made to feel important and loved and special." She is concerned about the disengaging aspects of school and views 'dropouts' as youths who cannot translate their dreams into reality within the school. They are students who may be in school in body but who are really not there in spirit:

> When I think about that person I think about someone who is just sort of, someone who is alienated, somebody who is disillusioned, somebody who is just frustrated, somebody who has just basically given up in believing that the school system can work for them or that it can make a difference.... (8/11/93).

For students who admit they have considered dropping out of school at one time or another, such revelations are usually followed by a recognition of the importance of staying in school. This is articulated in terms of a desire to learn, an awareness of the state of the labour market and the economy, parents' desire that their children fare better in life, a need for some structure in their day, and an awareness of the need to succeed as Black/African Canadians. Students admit that, by dropping out, the student places himself or herself at a social disadvantage. However, criticism of the decision to drop out is muted by the knowledge of someone who actually dropped out of school.

Black students' narratives suggest that when the student is considering leaving school it is often the existence of one caring adult in his or her life that makes the difference. Students include in their reasons for considering leaving school, teacher disrespect, being turned off by a teacher, a sense of being over-ly-visible (i.e., targeted) for misconduct by school personnel, teacher inaccessibility for help, a depersonalized school environment, absence of adult encouragement and expectation that they will succeed, a sense of invisibility (thinking that no one would notice or care if they dropped out anyway), teenage pregnancy, a need to help the family financially which places schooling as a lesser priority, pressure to succeed at home and a feeling of inadequacy in terms of school work.

Many times conditions at home compound student's problems. Elaine, a Grade 12 student, was born in the Caribbean. Today she lives on her own. Her parents have long been divorced and she explains that the last time she saw her father was when she was "little." She has an older brother who dropped out of high school. She points out that conditions particularly at home were ripe for her to be a 'dropout statistic.' She is still unsure how she managed to pull through the cracks. When she was growing up she lived with her mother "… for a while then got kicked out of the house," she says. She situates her understanding of 'dropping out from school' in the context of the home experiences:

> Well, I look at it this way, like, I'm in, like — a year and a half, then out. I probably would have been one of those statistics that says so many people dropped out, because I'm on my own, and no support from family or anything, just myself. And, when, when I got kicked out from my house, the first thing that dawned upon me was 'how am I going to get to school?' I cried and I was like, I called my house and I don't know how I'm going to get to school, instead of worrying about where I'm going to live. So, I came to school the next day, I don't know how I managed to get here, and, umm, I got help…. But, I could have been one of those, somebody who's out there too, but I choose not to. You see, if I drop out I have nowhere to go. I mean, I look at it that way…. Like, it's … the future's whatever I make of it, and, if I find if I dropped out, I would probably be somewhere I don't want to be, or I don't think I should be. That's the way I look at dropped out. (25/02/93).

The Economics of Schooling for African-Canadian Youth

Many students are reluctant to admit that they or their parents come from working-class backgrounds. They do acknowledge, though, the impact that economic hardships have on schooling. Students feel the school environment 'favours' rich students and that rich and powerful parents have some influence at school. Not being wealthy makes many things inaccessible to students. But economic background and hardships do impact on students' motivation and school achievement in both negative and positive ways. Dorothy, a Grade 10 student discusses her personal economic hardships:

> At least, I don't consider myself rich, I'm, I'm surviving, let's just put it that way, like right now I'm scrambling for money, believe me. I walk to school because I can't afford to have TTC bus tickets. Yeah. I do. And sometimes, I ... amazing, I don't know how come I didn't fall down as yet, or faint I should say, because I don't have a well-balanced diet. Because, yesterday was perfect, I had night school yesterday, and all I had was cereal and I went to school. And that was like, an eight-hour day. Day school full-time, plus night school, and then went home and do homework and wake up and then come to school today. It's the same routine, and I didn't, I didn't fall as yet. I guess I'm strong, I don't know why. (6/12/92).

For Nisha, 17, an OAC student who is characterized as 'gifted' by the school system, the desire to improve upon home conditions can have a 'motivating' impact on the student:

> Well ... even though sometimes I hate school and I don't want to go, I would say, "oh I'm going to drop out," but I'd never actually do it because of, I guess, the way my parents raised me. Like, I just think a person with an education is better, right, and I want to do something with my life. I want to get a good job and I want to make good money so I can get good things and go to nice places.... (15/06/92).

Julian, 17, a Grade 10 and 11 student, struck me as a student who had done quite a bit of reading. But he also epitomizes the deep inner conflicts of African-Canadian students in the inner city coming to grips with economic hardships while still at school. I will always remember his powerful response to my question as to where he got his ideas from. He simply told me: "I live it."

> Sometimes I think about leaving school, because really what's the point? You can go to college and get educated — I know people like that — and they don't have a job. So sometimes they just want to go and make money, you know, but ... I don't think I'm serious about leaving school. Sometimes I say, yeah I'm going to quit school when I get pissed off at my teachers or something. But I don't think seriously about it.... 'Cause all the time we're in school, we're not making any money. And just because you're in school it doesn't mean that you stop eating

while you're going to school. So you know? If people were paid to go to school, a lot more people would be in school right now. Because they wouldn't have had to leave school to find a job so that they could take care of themselves and so on. A lot more people would still be in school, you know. (27/08/92).

Current harsh economic realities mean that students who find jobs want to hang on to them and continue to work while going to school. It is very apparent that, unless economic conditions change for the better, the problems of schooling are going to get worse for many of these youths. While it is possible that the current unfavourable economic climate may influence a few students to stay in school longer or drop back in, there are other students who find deplorable economic conditions as legitimate grounds to question the relevance of education.

African-Canadian parents talk about the expectations that children from disadvantaged and low socioeconomic backgrounds have to face in school, and the consequences for our understanding of student disadvantage. In Dena's case, she shows how economic factors are mediated in the school system:

> I think that in a lot of cases you find students who are — who do drop out, do come from poor neighbourhoods, but in speaking to a lot of these students and working with them, I find that they don't drop out because they feel that they have to go make money. They drop out in a lot of cases because of the prejudices that are associated to them because of their socio- or economic status. The administration, the school knows that they come from a poor background, whether it be from Metro Housing, and the expectation of these kids is generally lower, the attitude towards these kids by the teacher is one of negativity, and the students themselves know that, so you do find in a lot of cases in working with these students that they are the students who have a tendency to drop out more. (24/07/92).

Dealing with Low Teacher Expectations

Students generally express the opinion that a small number of teachers exist in their school who make attending and learning worthwhile. The most favourite courses of these students tend to be the ones which are taught by these teachers. Clearly, if there is one area in which students show much emotion and anger when discussing unfavourable school experiences, it is the low expectations of some teachers about Black students' capabilities. Students explain such low teacher expectations as part of the deeply-held beliefs about people who are non-white. In interviews, students would cite particular teachers making fun of students and making students "… feel dumb." Low teacher expectations add to the bitterness that students feel about the negation and devaluing of their experiences, histories and knowledges, as well as the contributions they bring to the school:

Marlo introduces the issue of student relationship with a school teacher as the most unpleasant experience of his school life:

> … being … judged by a particular teacher … that was the most (unpleasant experience).… I mean that I wasn't expecting that I mean you look up to your teachers they're supposed to be … there for you and they're not supposed to judge you and I was judged by this particular teacher and it wasn't to say it wasn't done behind my back. It was done in front of my face and I wasn't expecting that so that was a big letdown to me — it was unpleasant. (08/06/92).

Jami was born in North America and has been in Canada since the late 1970s. She dropped out of high school and later dropped back in. Today she is attending university, and has a son in the public school system. In discussing the experiences that led her to drop out of school, she critiques the conventional explanations of why students drop out. She questions the narrow interpretations offered in terms of 'boredom' and 'lack of motivation' because these explanations only serve to locate the individual student as the 'problem.' She wants schools and teachers to be critical of their pedagogical practices and other school processes that feed on students' sense of alienation and disengagement from school. She calls for a deeper interrogation of the conventional explanations of students' disengagement as due to a lack of personal motivation.

> Students, if they're not motivated, again it's not necessarily the fault of the student. Teachers have to accept some liability in that instance, so I think that has to be something they have to not be afraid to find out what it is. I see it in university too you know. So I think it's just a personal thing with teachers that the stu-

dent's bored. They think, well, that's just that. You know they don't see that it could have something to do with them or the environment or anything you know. But any time that their (students') behaviour deviates from what they've known of them in the past should be an indication for concern. (19/05/92).

Robina, a divorced mother and university student, says she is concerned about the 'high dropout rate' among Black youth, and insists no single factor can explain students' disengagement from school. She is convinced that the reasons lie somewhere between "... the school, society and maybe ... the home." She questions attempts by some educators and school administrators to locate the 'dropout problem' strictly in the home when teachers know that the youth are in school for a greater part of the day than they are at home. She points to an apparent contradiction and paradox she sees in the attempts to blame the home for the problems that Black-African-Canadian students face at school. In response to how she sees the 'home' implicated in youth disengagement from school, Robina questions educators' refusal to examine critically how their prejudices, conditioned by the structures of schooling, can have the effect of disengaging some students from school:

> ... I think when certain people are talking about Black students dropping out and it's because of the home, they need to take a look within their own system, within their own institution that they're perpetuating on our own Black youths before they blame the household.... You know, I see some households are religious, family-oriented people who send their children to school and as soon as they get to school, because of peer pressure, teachers' prejudice, students' prejudice and all kinds of other little things, they change. They're not the same anymore. Some of them, they're doing "A" student work, they're doing "A"s and they're not getting the marks they need.... (18/11/93).

Like Jami, Robina thinks that schools do not push students hard enough and that some teachers unwittingly use the family background and socio-economic, cultural experiences of students to discourage them from achieving their life dreams. When this happens, students lose interest in school and opt out. In suggesting ways for the schools and parents to work together, Black parents insist that what is needed are new attempts at facilitating the social-structural context of the inter-actions of school-parent/guardian/caregivers. Black parents want the school to start from the strengths of parents and build up their confidence so that they can be 'involved.' Julie, a single parent, brings an interesting perspective to the on-going debates about the roles and responsibilities of parents in the education of their children. She argues that, instead of questioning Black parents' commitment in the education of their children, school administrators should devote their energies to listening to those who are speaking out on the problems of schooling, and the necessity for educational change. For example, she is critical of those who identify immigration as presenting challenges for the school system:

> ... these same parents that everyone is criticizing and blaming were the parents who came here in the seventies and were fantastic citizens, of the kind who worked in the factories and their jobs and everything was fine and people didn't have any problem with them. So therefore, if they were people who were law-abiding citizens, working and everything was fine, why is it now that their kids are in school, everything is falling apart? Because most of the children who are having the problems are not the new immigrants within the school because we don't have that many coming in. Most of them were actually born here and they have been referred to as immigrant but they are not, they are Canadians. Therefore, the main fact that they are being referred to as immigrants is saying something right there. (08/11/93)

Racism, Sexism and Gender Bias at School

Students are generally reluctant to talk about racism and discrimination because they are sensitive to the accusation of 'having a chip on their shoulder.' They acknowledge some of the efforts schools are making to address systemic racism and discrimination. Nevertheless, students generally do not think much has been done so far and they are not confident their schools will ever be free of all forms of racial prejudice and discrimination. When asked about what they want to see changed about their schools, they point to discriminatory and sometimes racist practices of a few teachers and school staff and other colleagues (and sometimes discriminatory behaviour of students 'within their own group,' intra-group racism). In fact, students often cite racist behaviour and attitudes as reasons for disliking particular teachers.

Nisha laments what she sees as racial prejudice of some white teachers:

> ... lot of them (teachers) are and I mean you figure they're so well-educated they won't show it but it doesn't make a difference no matter how many degrees you have or whatever, it still shows and I mean the way they treat you the way they talk to you it's just different than how they talk to other students like white students and that.... (27/06/92).

Elaine, a Grade 12 student born in Guyana, also laces her discussion of low teacher expectations with instances of sexism at her school:

> I think in our school ... especially, where the other ... where the field is more dominant in men, and when a woman goes in and tries to succeed, it's pretty hard. Because I, I experienced it (male teacher bias against female students) when I was in Grade 10 math, and there was — I probably, if I recall correctly, I was probably the only Black girl in this math class, advanced. And, I used to always put up my hands to ask the teacher a question, because I don't think whatever he did was correct. And, I would have my hands up for like five minutes, and somebody else at the back of the room would have their hands for, like, [snaps fingers] just a minute or so, and it's a male, doesn't matter whether it's Black or white, but he would prefer going to that person. (25/02/93).

Deborah, the designated 'at-risk' student, also talks about sexism being "... subtle in the school system ..." and that "not all students may be aware of it." She talks of one particular incident involving a fellow Black student:

> Jokes towards women ... well, I never got any. Well, I did get one and I thought it was really rude. And I just looked at him, I guess funny, because people say I have this look, [laughter] and when I give them the look, they mean, you shouldn't try it or something like that, and he said something to me. It was after school, and I was working on a presentation for physics, and he goes, 'Hey babe,' and he said something like 'I want to

sex you,' and I was like.... (29/01/93).

Nisha, the gifted student, points out that there is sexism in the schools, most often directed against female students and particularly Black females, through name-calling and sexist jokes from their male peers. She also talks about the enormous pressure to live up to a macho image in which Black male youths find themselves. What these instances of prejudicial and discriminatory treatment on the basis of race and gender do is to further alienate students from the school system. They are also sources of emotional and psychological stress for students. Unfortunately, these issues are hardly discussed in the discourse about race, gender and class discrimination in the schools.

Negotiating Self and Group Cultural Identities

African-Canadian students want their schools to reflect the communities in which they live. They are desirous of 'bringing the school into the community' and vice versa, and are very frustrated because this is not happening. Added to these pressures and frustrations with the school system is the constant struggle of Black students to maintain their individual selves and group cultural identities. Sometimes their actions do come into conflict, not only with school authorities but even with their peers. Nisha's is a case in point. She cannot understand Black students who are prejudiced and make negative comments about other students, particularly their Black female friends. Her observations point to the enormous pressures that the young female student experiences, which could possibly lead to a student disengaging from the school. She focuses on an aspect of the myriad forms of racism, one which has to do with distancing between *self* and the *other*, and between *us* and *them*. This form of racism is influenced by the specificity of students' locations in the school. In response to a question about who her best friend is at school, she reveals some inner pain that perhaps some students think she may not be 'Black' enough:

> ... my best friend is Filipino actually but I used to have a whole bunch of Black friends but I just noticed a lot of my Black friends it's like I can't keep my Black female friends. I mean

one minute they're my friend and the next minute they're all talking about me and everything so that's one thing about me. (*Int: What do they say about you?*) ... well I found out because of Michael (boyfriend) ... he hangs around with the Black guys, and the Black guys and Black girls stick together. After I leave with my best friend after school, they all talk and he told me like they talk I used to have green contacts, oh you know and (long) black hair (or) ... hate people who think they're white and ... try to have their contacts and everything ... and they used to write on my locker oh you green eyed so on and so on, or they might say oh she's showing off her hair it's in that you know or she's so cool you look good you know ha ha and stuff. So I had my hair back and then they say she thinks she's so sophisticated with her hair back ... so it's really stupid. (27/06/92).

Students attribute the difficulties they have in negotiating their individual self and group cultural identity to a very narrow school curriculum. They complain about schools not linking questions of identity with schooling. They point to the importance of history in the formation of social identities, as well as the relevance of identity to knowledge production. The month of February is set aside for activities marking the achievements of Black and African peoples in history. Students appreciate the chance to show and tell about their cultures and to express their identities as peoples of African descent. But there is also a wide acknowledgement that this is not enough and that for much of the time their existence is marginalized. Students define their marginalization in the context of both the formal curriculum and the unwritten code of acceptable behaviour and practices in the public school system.

The Absence of Black Teachers

Students interviewed want to see more Black teachers in the school system. But a few students are quick to add that having Black teachers would not necessarily make a major difference. In fact, these few talk about ".... Black teachers who are not really Black." These students engaged in essentializing what it means to be '... really Black.' The students feel it is important to have a teacher who has the interests of Black students at

51

heart and who would encourage them to do well at school. While many see the Black teacher as an important role model, a few speak about the likelihood of the teacher having a social perspective they can identify with.

Jean-Brenda, a Grade 12 student-activist, in the advanced program in one of the selected schools, carefully expands on the difference it makes to her if there is a Black teacher around. She is worth quoting at length:

> ... I can even take it so far ... I've never had a Black teacher and I've been able to make it. But I think it would really help on perhaps not the educational level, because I'm sure that a person who is white or a person who is Black I mean they are both able to learn the same amount and teach the same amount to students and they can both teach very well or whatever. But I think just having someone who's Black up there who can share like some of my experiences with me ... like a lot of white teachers I don't think would be able to share more personal things like you know oh if I have a trip, my family's from Guyana, so I went down to Guyana and you know came back and started talking about all the things that I did down there, I think a Black teacher would more understand than a white teacher depending on you know where the Black person is from also. So just, I think, little things like that. And also ... I have a tendency of developing good relationships with my teachers or at least a few of them anyway and so if I were able to develop a relationship like that with a Black teacher I mean myself wanting to become a teacher um I think it would be wonderful for me to do well. You know I'd be able to learn how hard or how easy it was for that person to become a teacher and the experiences that they went through maybe in terms of racism they had. Some instances occur and they'd be able to tell me how to deal with it and I'd be able to learn in that aspect. I think that would help me a lot.... (05/02/93)

Discussions about the need for Black teachers usually lead to students expressing some desire for a 'Black school.' Not all students, of course, share this idea and some are actually vehemently opposed to it. However, some of the ambiguities in students' views on 'Black school' are very evident in their narratives. For example, those students who oppose the idea, rather than challenging the academic merits, fall back on mainstream perceptions of the school. They raise questions about what the larger Canadian society would think of a Black-focused school. They also raise concerns about the potential for violence in such a school in a manner that gestures to their internalised racism. I would like to devote the final section of this chapter to examining why some African-Canadian students 'want their own school.'

Discussion

Three primary concerns pervade student narratives about their school experiences: First, there is the problem of differential treatment by race. Second, is the inadequate curricular content, communicative and pedagogic practices that do not reflect the diversity of experiences, ideas, and events that have shaped, and continue to shape, human growth and development. And third, is concern over issues of representation, that is, the absence of Black and minority teachers in the school system.

The examination of African-Canadian students and parents' narratives clearly points to the need to address the inherent structural problems of public schooling in Canada. Many of these problems and issues of African-Canadian youth education have been identified in such works as Sium (1987), Brathwaite (1989), James (1990), Solomon (1992), Henry (1992, 1994), CABE (1992); BEWG (1993); Calliste, (1994), Lewis (1992), Little (1992) and OPBC (1993). A critical interrogation of voices reveals that African-Canadian students and parents like everyone else want schools that all students can identify with. This means we must intensify the struggle to make Canadian schools more 'inclusive,' governed by a set of principles that stress power-sharing with all stakeholders in the educational system. Canadian schools must speak to, and act on, the diversity of experiences, histories and knowledges that have shaped, and continue to shape, human growth and development. Students link their personal and group identities to schooling in complex ways. But the continuing educational crisis for African-Canadian youth demands that alternative and additional strategies be pursued to bring academic and social success for the youth. While mainstream schools strive to be more inclusive, additional action on several fronts can be embarked upon to tackle the problem of educational underachievement. Else-where, (Dei, 1995b) I have discussed the idea of 'Black-focused/African-centred' schools in a Canadian context, as originally proposed by the Working Group (1992).

The marginality felt by some African-Canadian students in the mainstream schools cannot be lost on the astute, critical educational researcher. There are students who are completely 'tuned out' of school. They are there in body and not in spirit or soul. While an approach to 'inclusive schooling' can assist these youths, I also believe that the idea of alternative focused schools should be a valid option. This is not a contradiction at all. We should interpret the existence and success of Black-focused/African-centred schools as a challenge to mainstream schools to live up to the ideals of genuine inclusion. While all steps are purportedly being taken to make our schools inclusive, African-centred schools can be instituted for those parents who wish to send their children to these schools and those students who wish to go to such schools. The success of African-centred schools will bring an added pressure on the current school system to respond to the needs and concerns of a diverse student body. This is because most parents want their children to stay in inclusive schools.

The notion that having African-centred schools simply means going back to the days of segregation needs to be challenged. Segregation refers to more than physical space and location. The act of segregating a group always takes place in an economic and political context. The economic and political aims of those segregationists of the first half of this century were certainly meant to exclude Blacks from full participation in society. Segration was to show bias and to discriminate. It was not meant to improve the lives of Black people. These aims must be distinguished from the needs of those who wish their children to be schooled in an environment free of bias in the 1990s. This distinction between forced segregation and segregation by choice (if indeed this is segregation at all) should mean something. Those concerned about segregation could assist by developing mechanisms to promote working partnerships/relationships between African-centred schools and mainstream schools. I believe that there is enough talent in our communities to develop these stragegies and practices that would ensure that students and staff of all schoools can co-operate and learn from each other. This should be read as the challenge and should serve to allay the fears of those who argue that our pluralistic society requires youth of all races to interact and learn from each other at school.

Other questions persist in public discourse about African-centred schools as alternative educational environments. To a large extent some of these questions are fostered by misinformation. For example, there is a concern that academic credentials from African-centred schools may not be highly appreciated by main-stream society. This is internalised racism and follows from a twisted logic that just because it is an African-centred school the curriculum would be watered down. An African-centred school strives for high academic excellence. Students do not only learn about African culture and history. They learn about everything else but from an African-centred perspective. These schools would be subject to the same provincial testing and evaluation standards as other schools.

There is also concern that 'giving in' to the Black communi-ty raises the issue of where do we stop. That is, do school administrators and public officials give in to every social/racial group that demands a school for its youth? For me, the answer is simple. Society must consider seriously the concerns of those groups with a demonstrated educational disadvantage (Burnett, 1995). Studies repeatedly point to the 'crisis' of Black youth 'with respect to education and achievement' (RCOL, 1994; Dei, et.al., 1995). The dropout rates reveal that the problem is consistently acute for Black youth (Brown, 1993). For those who merely see African-centred schools as *separate* schools, one could ask how different are the religious schools and the emerging push for all girls schools? Or, is it that segregation only comes up when it is seen along the lines of race?

The call for African-centred schools is not asking for all Black youth to be pulled away from mainstream schools. Far-rell (1994) has pointed out that the concepts of "alternative" and "choice" are significant in debates about African-centred schools. Students should have the right to be exposed to alter-native learning environments and parents should have choices in the selection of schools for their children. The African-centred school should be a school for those who want to go there. The cause of Canadian democracy and social pluralism requires that African-centred schools be not defined as same race schools. An African-centred school should be seen as a school different in its fundamental organizational structures from the way mainstream schools. As I have argued elsewhere in this book, African-centred schools are defined more by a set of principles than by who attends the school or teaches in the school. There is an understanding that racial identity will not in and by itself guarantee academic success for African-Canadian students. In other words, the issue is not racial solidarity so much as cultural solidarity. However, given that the situation is serious for Black youth, it is fair to *expect* that the majority of students, staff and teachers in an African-centred school would come from the Black community. In fact, I see the African-centred school as a more open school than some of the schools in the system. I am talking about those schools that have a constitutional requirement that at least one parent must meet an established criteria and/or appear before an admission board before the child is admitted.

The issue of funding for an African-centred school is often raised in discussions about the implementation of the idea. If we accept that education is not only for self improvement but is a common good, then the question of whether Canadian taxpayers should fund these schools at all is simply dishonest and hypocritical. We live in a democracy but we do not always have the right to determine where and how our tax dollars should be spent. We should consider those who send their children to African-centred schools as taxpayers. There are religious schools that receive public funding in Ontario. Also, it is often asked if African-centred schools are to be seen as a permanent feature of the Ontario educational system. The valid question is not whether these schools should be permanent but rather when would mainstream schools be truly inclusive to deny a justification for African-centred schools. There is no reason to expect students of an African-centred school to ask for re-integration into mainstream schools if these schools continue to take issues of inclusivity lightly.

In conclusion, I will reiterate that indeed we live in a complex world and we should always be looking for multiple solutions to problems and concerns. Some of the educational solutions may not sit well with mainstream thought but we should have the courage and the political will to do what is right for the youth, especially when the issues/concerns being raised have been on the table for a lengthy time.

Acknowledgements

I would like to acknowledge the assistance of the many graduate students at the Ontario Institute for Studies in Education (OISE), University of Toronto, who worked on the longitudinal study of African-Canadian experiences in the public school system. I am particularly grateful to Deborah Elva, Josephine Mazzuca, Bobby Blanford, Thato Bereng, Elizabeth McIssac, Leilani Holmes, Lianne Carley and Jasmine Zine. Financial support for this project has been provided by the Ontario Ministry of Education and Training (MET), and the Social Sciences and Humanities Research Council of Canada (SSHRC).

NOTES

1. In this paper I use the terms 'Black' and 'African-Canadian' interchangeably to refer to Canadians of African descent and who also describe themselves as such.

2. Until recently, the Ontario public school system placed students entering Grade 9 into three different course levels, based on ability: the *basic or vocational* level, the *general* four-year level, and the *advanced* level, which includes courses leading to university entrance. This is a process referred to as 'streaming.' In September, 1993, the provincial government destreamed Grade 9 classes as part of the reform measures intended to address the school dropout rate.

Chapter Three

CONFRONTING A HISTORY OF EXCLUSION
A PERSONAL REFLECTION

Nancy A. Hoo Kong

Research indicates that students are often required to read Canadian history textbooks that either exclude or provide minimal coverage of Black Canadians (Klein, 1985; Walker, 1980; Bristow et al, 1994). In general, textbooks tend to present the perspectives and experiences of white, upper-class, Anglo- and French-Canadian males (Burnet & Palmer, 1989:3). Consequently, many textbooks do not acknowledge African Canadians as active participants in the shaping of our nation's history. As Peggy Bristow et al explain in *We're Rooted Here and They Can't Pull Us Up: Essays in African Canadian Women's History* (1994), "The educational system has maintained and perpetuated the common perception that Black people were either nonexistent in the development of Canada, or only arrived in Canada through recent migration from the Caribbean and Africa" (p.3). Given the absence of African Canadians from Canada's documented past and the Eurocentric nature of the dominant interpretation and depiction of Canadian history, the purpose of this paper is to awaken educators to the horrific impact that an exclusionary curriculum can have on their students. To achieve this objective I shall share my experiences with the Canadian history curriculum I encountered from elementary school to university. In doing so, I hope to not only reveal how exclusionary history marginalizes Black students, but to also raise other questions that educators need to address. It is important to stress that these queries are not limited to history teachers. On the contrary, these questions are important to any educator, regardless of the subject area [s]he teaches, who is trying to construct a curriculum congenial to diversity. I shall define exclusionary history as the conscious and/or unconscious omission of historical perspectives that conflict with Anglo-Canadian males' interpretation and representation of past events and people, as well as the omission of ethnic or racial groups, such as Black Canadians, from history textbooks.

I grew up in a suburban community in North York, Ontario, during the 1970s and 1980s. The neighbourhood was mainly composed of white European-Canadians. I attended a predominately white public school, which had a few students from racial minorities. Apart from the few times that a classmate called me 'nigger,'I was not a victim of many openly aggressive acts of racism, such as being physically attacked or being denied entrance into a mainly white school. As a matter of fact, the verbal incidents of racism that I experienced in public school were never as painful as the subtle and blatant forms of racism I had to deal with from some of my teachers and from the history curriculum that rendered my racial group invisible. Racism, according to Carl James (1995), "is the uncritical acceptance of a negative social definition of a colonized or subordinate group typically identified by physical features.... These racialized groups are believed to lack certain abilities or characteristics, which in turn characterizes them as culturally and biologically inferior" (p.137).

I remember my grade three teacher and the teacher of the other grade three class calling me up to the centre of the two adjoining classrooms. About sixty grade three children, all dead silent, stared at me as I stood in the middle of the classroom To my knowledge I had done nothing wrong. I was known as an obedient student. There I stood looking up at two teachers, wondering why they were singling me out. They loudly informed me and the other students that I would never amount to anything. I cannot remember if they explained their criticism more fully or precisely. What I do recall thinking, is that as teachers, they knew what they were talking about. After all, I believed that teachers were the custodians of knowledge, and thus, students went to school to learn from them. Consequently, rather than challenging my teachers or questioning why they felt the need to tell me, the only Black student in the two grade three classes, that I would not succeed in life, I accepted their assessment as the truth. Thus, my teachers managed to not only single me out from my white peers, but to also make me feel insignificant and inferior. Their words and actions caused me so much pain and confusion, that it was not until years later, when I was excelling academically, that I disclosed to my parents what my grade three teachers had told me.

Just as my teacher unjustifiably singled me out as a failure in the classroom, I felt singled out by the pioneer unit that she taught. My first formal instruction in Canadian history occurred when my grade three teacher taught a unit on pioneer life. I learned how fleece was cleaned, how houses were called log cabins, and that the early settlers were of European descent. I do not remember anyone telling me that there were no Black pioneers, but no-one ever told me that there were people of colour who helped build this nation. As part of the learning experience, my teacher took the class to Black Creek Pioneer Village. All of the people re-enacting the early pioneers were of European decent. This mono-racial representation of early pioneers reinforced the messages I received from the history texts I read in school: the racial identity of Canadians is white.

Regretfully, critical thinking was not encouraged by my teachers during this period of my life. Without knowledge of African-Canadian history or critical, analytical skills, I was unable to challenge the messages I received about pioneers in Upper Canada by asking questions, such as: Whose knowledge is being taught? Whose knowledge or voices are being silenced? What issues are not being addressed? I was under the impression that what my teachers told me and what the textbooks or museums presented was the truth — the only version of our nation's history. This reality left me vulnerable to racist and distorted interpretations and representations of Canadian history.

I left grade three feeling insignificant and inferior for two reasons. First, my teachers had verbally informed me that I would never amount to anything, thus marginalizing me and shattering my self-confidence. Second, by not learning about Black pioneers, I left grade three feeling as if I were living in a society which rendered me, a Black person, as a non-contributing intruder. To make matters worse, I was not even aware that the experiences of African Canadians in Upper Canada were being excluded. As Gillian Klein (1985) asserts, "The most dangerous aspects of omission is that books may very effectively conceal what was left out of them, or even that anything has been left out" (p.30). This omission of information led me to buy into the misconception that Black Canadians are recent immigrants who did not play an active role in the building of this nation. In this respect, although I was born in Canada, the history curriculum did not permit me to identify myself as a Canadian. Moreover, the absence of Black Canadians from the pioneer unit reinforced my teacher's perception of my status in Canada; I did not and would not 'fit' into 'their' community. Looking back, I learned that I had *no history* or *future* in Canadian society. This was the understanding that I had from being educated in one of Ontario's public elementary schools.

My earlier encounter with an exclusionary history curriculum was repeated in junior high school. In my grade 7 Canadian history class I was handed a course text, *Flashback Canada* (1978), which did not acknowledge African Canadians. Even when the authors of *Flashback Canada* (1978) dedicated three pages to Canada's involvement with the civil war in the United States of America, the issue of slavery and the existence of Canadian and American abolitionists were not mentioned. For example, the text states, "From 1861–1865, the Americans had been fighting a bloody Civil War. It was a battle between the States of the North and the South. The issue at stake was whether North and South should remain united together or separate into two countries. By 1865, the South had been defeated, and the United States remained one country" (Cruxton, 1978: 52). The chapter continues by discussing Canada's role in the war and its effect on Canada without referring to African Americans or African Canadians. I do not recall being given any supplementary reading material that incorporated the history of African Canadians or of being informed of the subjective nature of textbooks (see Apple, 1994; Osborne, 1995). I was required to read and to memorize the information presented in this text. Thus, my understanding and knowledge of my country's history were mainly shaped by a course text that omitted the contributions of Canada's Black community.

While writing this article, I mentioned my junior high school experience to a colleague. In disbelief, he questioned my recollection of the course text. He found it difficult to accept that there was no reference to Black Canadians, not even in the index. After reviewing the text, which I was able to obtain at a library, I explained to him that my memory was accurate. In fact, out of the hundred plus photographs that were published in the text, not one of the faces can be clearly identified as Black. Consider the chapters on women, "Women Get the Vote" and "Only the Beginning" (pp. 332–356) There are eleven photographs that show immigrant women arriving in Quebec in 1911, females working in a clothing factory in 1918, women settling out West, women nurses and secretaries as well as women working in a munitions factory during World War I. None of these pictures, however, shows African Canadian women. The contributions of Black women, such as the hundreds of African Caribbean women who immigrated to Canada between 1904 and 1932 to supply domestic labour, are not mentioned (Calliste, 1994: 145). By ignoring or omitting the faces and experiences of African Canadians in a society where race is often used to define people, the history curriculum (ie. the themes and concepts I was taught), not only alienated me from what I was supposed to believe was the history of my country, but also rendered me, a Black female, as a non-contributing 'newcomer' (see James, 1995). In *A History of Blacks in Canada: A Study Guide for Teachers and Students* (1980), James Walker notes, "In the Anglo-dominated schools they [Black students] have been taught that the heroes are white, the accomplishments have been attained by whites, the nation was built by whites, all of which leaves blacks as intruders, or at best hangers-on in a flow of history that ignores them" (p. 5). Therefore, by not receiving an accurate historical understanding of the cultural and racial diversity of Canadian society, I was under the erroneous impression that only Canadians of European heritage built this nation.

Around grade 9 or 10, I began to encounter information that conflicted with what I had been taught in school. For example, I learned about the famous Underground Railroad, which led hundreds of Black Americans to Ontario during the early 1800s. This information led me to conclude that Blacks have resided in this country well before the 20th century. Armed with this historical knowledge, I was now in a position where I could begin to refute any argument that suggested that Black Canadians are recent immigrants, and thus did not participate in the construction of this nation. Moreover, my relationship with African Canadians from Nova Scotia provided me with knowledge about Black Nova Scotians' long historical struggle for social, political and economic equality. While my historical knowledge of the challenges, struggles, losses and victories that African Canadians had faced was limited, I gradually became aware of Black people's strong Canadian heritage. Unfortunately, what I learned from family members and friends about Black Canadians, was not fully discussed or represented in the textbooks I was expected to study in school. As a result, I became unsettled and angry with the way in which the dominant historical narrative discounted and ignored the experiences and accomplishments of African Canadians.

However, my dissatisfaction with Canadian history courses did not discourage me from taking another class in my senior year. In trying to graduate a year in advance with the grades I needed to make me eligible for university entrance, I enrolled in an OAC Canadian history class when I was in grade 12. My decision to take this course was not out of personal interest, but because I was good at memorizing text-book information and writing historical research papers.

As for the curriculum, I found it to be similar to what I was taught in junior high school. The only difference I can recall is that more attention was given to the feminist movement in the 1970s, and Black Canadians were briefly acknowledged by the course text, *Challenge and Survival: The History of Canada* (Herstein et al, 1970). In comparison to *Flashback Canada* (1978), this text does refer to Black Canadians. In the chapter on Loyalists' migration to Canada after the American Revolution, one sentence mentions the existence of Africans. After spending two pages describing why some 'English men' in the thirteen colonies remained loyal to the British Crown, the authors state: "Among the arrivals were many Arcadians who returned to their former homeland, and several thousand Negroes" (p. 115). The issue of why Blacks would fight for the British as well as their experiences in Nova Scotia, however, were never dealt with. In fact, African Canadians were dropped from historical consciousness in succeeding pages.

I do not remember being overly concerned with the way in which the curriculum continued to place more emphasis on the experiences of white, Anglo-Canadian males. At this point in my educational career, I had figured out that if I were to survive in a school system that omitted the stories of African Canadians, it was best not to challenge the curriculum. To do so may have cost me the grade I needed to get accepted into university. Therefore, in order for me to cope with a curriculum that rendered Black Canadians insignificant, unimportant and powerless within Canadian society, I had to separate myself emotionally from the material I was expected to learn and believe to be the truth.

While the Canadian history curriculum refused to deal with African Canadians' quest for social, political and economic equality, the OAC American history course I took that year embraced issues around slavery, institutional racism, and civil rights. My American history teacher encouraged me to critically analyze the American Civil War, the Civil Rights movement and other events, such as the Vietnam War. In all, I found that American history not only acknowledged the existence of people of African heritage, but also discussed how they played a role in the construction of American society. While emphasis was still placed on the memorization of 'facts' and the course textbook tended to emphasize Anglo-American males' experiences and perspectives, I found the course to be, in many respects, liberating. The way in which my teacher presented the course material and structured the assignments and class-room environment, gave me the opportunity to voice my concerns and queries about classism, racism, and sexism within the discourse of history. It was at this point in my life that I began to take more pride in my African heritage and to openly discuss with family members and close friends the negative messages and perceptions of Black Canadians I learned and internalized as a child.

I began university the following school year. As an undergraduate I majored in history, concentrating on American and Caribbean history. My decision was influenced, in part, by my positive experiences with the OAC American history class I took in grade 12. But more importantly, I chose American and Caribbean history because of the sparse coverage Black Canadians receive in Canadian history courses, specifically in the class I attended one summer with my sister Michele. After class, on our long drive home, my sister and I would discuss the course material. One recurring theme that we often talked about was the Eurocentric representation of Canada's past found in the course materials. In other words, Anglo- and French-Canadian males, such as Lord Durham, were given centre stage. All others, in my opinion, were poorly dealt with. Take for example the way in which First Nations people were described and how their stories were told. In *Readings in Canadian History: Pre-Confederation* (1990), the articles in the first section, "The Native People and Early European Contact" (pp. 1–48) depict First Nations' People as nonprogressive 'tribes.' "But they [First Nations' People] had no concept of a pan-Indian identity. Each tribe spoke its own language and regarded its own members as 'the people.' This *lack* of perceived common identity contributed to *their failure* to resist the Europeans (p.1). The text states that the "Europeans' arrival both *improved*, and at the same time *fatally* weakened, the native societies" (p.1). As I scan the notes I made in my text, I had sarcastically written "Indians' Failure" beside the above statement. I recall talking to my sister about the way in which the text portrayed First Nations peoples as being responsible for European domination of Canada. We also noted how the text conveniently begins the history of Canada with the arrival of French and

Anglo-Saxon males, thus sending the message that Canadian history is the history of Europeans' 'discovery of Canada.'

As for people of African descent, I do not remember learning very much about their participation in Canadian history. The only reference to Black people that I can recall, is the brief coverage, in one of the articles, of Black Loyalists in Nova Scotia. Other aspects of Black Canadian's experiences, such as the enslavement of African people in Lower and Upper Canada and their contributions and fight against discrimination in the military during World War I and World War II, I can not recall being discussed. To my disappointment, the Canadian history curriculum at university continued to distort and omit stories of African Canadians. Therefore, I learned that if I was to acquire knowledge about the history of people of African descent, I had to take topic-specific American social history courses and Caribbean history courses. Only these courses seemed to provide me with some of the information I had been denied since my entry into Ontario's school system. I should mention, however, that an African Canadian history course is currently being offered at the university I attended.

Besides my acquiring knowledge about the experiences of African Americans and African Caribbeans, some of my professors, particularly my Caribbean history professor, instilled in me the importance of questioning what I read and developing my critical writing and reading skills. For example, while discussing a historiographical paper I was labouring over, my professor made a statement that has had a lasting effect on me and my work: "Due to the blatant lies that have been recorded as the 'truth' about African Caribbean history, it is imperative that students know how to critically analyze what they read and to question what the historian relies upon as his/her evidence." His comment and my personal experiences made me increasingly conscious of the ethnic, gender, cultural, racial, and class biases of historians. Therefore, by developing critical reading and writing skills, and by being in an environment that fostered critical analysis, I acquired the necessary tools to question, identify, and attempt to challenge pervading misconceptions and misrepresentations of Black Canadians in history texts. More importantly, I was finally able to overcome the negative messages that I received from my earlier schooling.

Some people may interpret being critical as a negative and destructive approach to studying history. I disagree. Being critical means that as as Canadians from any ethno-cultural minority, we have the right and duty to seek equal representation of our collective experiences and perspectives in the history of this country. It also recognizes the subjective nature of history and how it can undermine and oppress individuals and social groups who are not aware of its biases. As Michael Apple explains, criticism is a "profoundly important way of saying that I am not 'just passing through.' I (we) live here. Criticism, then, is one of the most important ways we have of demonstrating that we expect more than rhetorical promises and broken dreams, because we take certain promises seriously" (1993: 5). Apple also argues that "being critical means something more than simply fault-finding. It involves understanding the sets of historically contingent circumstances and contradictory power relationships that create the conditions in which we live" (1993: 5). By teaching students, particularly racial minority students, critical reading and writing skills, enables them to become the "subjects not the objects of [their] own existence" (Osborne, 1995:27). Rather than having students read history texts, which are often written by those who belong to the dominant cultural group, they should be told how to perceive or understand Canadian history. Then they will be able to think for themselves about historical issues and events.

After reflecting on my experiences with the Canadian history I was taught in school, I am convinced that the messages that students receive from their texts will affect the way in which they see their racial group and how they fit into Canadian society. In the words of the American historian, Pinar (1993), "We are what we know. We are however, also what we do not know. If what we know about ourselves, our history, our culture, our national identity is deformed by absences, denials, and incompleteness, then our identity — both as individuals and as Americans — is fragmented" (p. 61). Pinar defines identity as a "genderized, racialized and historical construct" (1993: 61). While Pinar speaks of an American experience, his observation can also be used to understand the current situation in Canada. Since history plays an important role in shaping an individual's identity, Black students are marginalized and made to feel unimportant by the texts educators use to instruct their classes about Canadian history.

As my story illustrates, the messages I received from a history curriculum that neither recognized my ancestors' existence nor their accomplishments, had a negative effect on my racial and national identity. Exclusionary history instilled in me the feeling that I was invisible, inferior, non-existent, non-Canadian, in short, powerless. As historian Ken Osborne points out, students are often led to internalize that only a "handful of exceptional men," mainly upper-class, white Anglo-Canadian males, "challenged the course of history — leaving ordinary people, meaning the working class, people of colour and women, powerless" (1995: 153). This brief account of my experiences, raises a number of questions that need to be addressed if we, as educators, are to construct courses that respect and reflect the diversity of our students. Some questions I consider important are:

1. Why teach Canadian history?

2. Why are the experiences of African Canadians omitted or distorted in many of the Canadian history textbooks educators use to instruct their students?

3. If identity is a social, historical construct, how does exclusionary history affect students' racial identity and identity as Canadians?

4. How does the exclusion of Black Canadians affect the way in which white Canadians perceive the role of Blacks in our nation's history?

5. Given the effects of an exclusionary curriculum, how can we change the school curriculum so that it becomes more inclusive?

6. Is it possible to construct a curriculum that includes all of the different perspectives and experiences in Canadian history? In other words, is it possible to teach a polycentric curriculum? If so, how?

7. Is critical pedagogy part of the solution? If so, how can we teach students critical reading and writing skills?

8. What messages do we send to students by creating 'special topic' courses so that certain voices can be heard?

Chapter Four

EFFECTS OF EARLY MARGINALIZATION ON AFRICAN CANADIAN CHILDREN

GLORIA ROBERTS-FIATI

Early Experiences of Marginalization

A number of factors work together to undermine the school achievement of African-Canadian children. In this chapter I will examine the impact of early marginalization and discrimination on their learning and achievement. Marginalization in this context refers to the under-representation of the child's racial group in the culture of the child care and school environments, and the relegation of its members to the periphery of the mainstream society. Discrimination[1] is the differential treatment or expectations of the child on the basis of a set of values associated with his or her racial group membership.

It is the contention in this chapter, that children's experience of discrimination and marginalization exert a significant impact on their perception of themselves. When these experiences occur in the early years, children begin to internalize the negative values assigned to them and to their group, and may later organize their behaviours around these values. The high percentage of Black youths aspiring to make careers in sports or in the entertainment field, may be seen as a concrete example of how societal expectations can become group values, shaping behaviour. By the same token, learning and achievement are compromised when children begin to understand that diligence in these areas is not expected of them by those who evaluate their success.

Research from the mainstream culture on school achievement has identified a number of factors that are related to this outcome for students (Radwansky 1988; Toronto Board of education 1995). Primary among these are parental support for learning; expectations for achievement; and children's self-esteem.[2] I have chosen to examine the area of self-esteem and achievement in greater detail as it is the one area that is shaped by early experiences and is most susceptible to influences outside the home.

While the traditional literature looking at these variables has identified several antecedent conditions which influence children's self-esteem (Coopersmith 1961), there has not been the context for addressing the impact of racism and marginalization on children's developing sense of self, because the populations with whom such research has been conducted have been predominantly white.

In this literature the main influences on the child's self-esteem are seen as the amount of nurturance the child receives for learning efforts and the quality of his or her early relationship with significant others in the home. For African-Canadian children, however, experiences of racism and marginalization in school undermine the quality of their early home experiences no matter how positive these experiences might have been. Unlike white parents, the parents of African-Canadian children must battle against these external forces to support their children in maintaining healthy self-concepts and positive aspirations for learning.

The Impact of Marginalization on Children's Self-Perception

The following scenarios will serve as examples of some of the ways in which exclusion of children's culture from the learning environment sets the stage for the early development of self-doubt and a diminished sense of self.

The non-inclusive child care environment

Centre Street Day Care encourages new parents to introduce their children to the centre gradually over a period of a week or more. During this time parent and child may visit the Centre for a few hours at a time, before the child begins full time in the program. Alternatively, the parent might stay with the child for an hour or two on the first few days, then leave. During this introduction period, the parent and the child have an opportunity to explore their new environment together.

Nzinga and her mother were on their first day at this Child Care centre. It seemed like the perfect setting for Nzinga. The rooms were neatly arranged with child-sized chairs and tables. There were low shelves with a variety of toys, blocks and "lots of neat stuff" just within Nzinga's reach. While she was excitedly going from one shelf to another, Mrs. Miti began to look around the rooms, casually checking out the surroundings.

It soon became evident that this centre was very different from the centre Nzinga had been attending previously. It somehow felt like "foreign territory." The pictures on the wall were mostly from magazine cut-outs and portrayed people and children, all white, engaged in various activities and dressed for the different seasons — Summer, Spring, Winter and Fall.

Mrs. Miti went to select a book to read to her daughter. The characters in the books were the same as those on the walls - children and adults from the mainstream culture. She tried to find a book with characters that Nzinga could identify with, and failing to do so, she decided to let her play in the drama centre instead.

The drama centre reflected the same Eurocentric theme as the decor and the books. There was a variety of clothing here, but nothing that Nzinga could put on to simulate the way her mother or the other women in their community dressed at home, or on special occasions. Mrs. Miti was well aware that dramatic play should allow the children to simulate the attire and activities of their families and community as well as the larger society. But here, her daughter didn't have that choice.

The teachers, the decorations on the walls, the ceiling hangings, the books and other material in the play centres gave no clue that the children attending the centre were from a variety of racial and ethnic backgrounds.

Mrs. Miti left the Centre after her first visit feeling very uncertain about whether this was the place she wanted her child to spend the next three or four years of her life, in a period of growth when children actively filter information from their environment in developing their identity and a sense of who they are in the society. As a child of African heritage, she wondered how her child could be supported in developing positive feelings about herself in this environment.

Mrs Miti's concerns are very valid. In the early years of life children need a sense of belonging in order to experience optimal psychological and emotional growth. When they are brought up in environments where the self is negated, where they do not see any representations of themselves or their group, or where such representation is negatively stereotyped, they begin to develop a diminished sense of who they are.

I will now look at the mainstream literature on the development of self-esteem, and at more recent literature on the development of self-esteem in minority children, to show how some of the core conditions for the development of positive feelings about themselves are violated by experiences of marginalization. It is important to place such experiences in the context of achievement, because when a child's sense of self is diminished, his or her motivation for learning and achievement becomes compromised. This paves the pathway for later disenchantment with school. Disenchantment is identified as one of the factors related to the high rates of drop-out and school failure reported in recent articles on the school achievement of African-Canadian children (Dei 1994; Royal Commission on Learning and Education 1995). The seeds of the problems that crystallize in Middle School and early High School are sown in earlier experiences of discrimination and marginalization.

Relationship Between Self-esteem and Achievement

The work of Felker (1973) describes a number of core conditions that are necessary for the development of positive self-esteem in children. These include: a sense of belonging, feelings of worth, and a sense of competence. Children's aspirations and achievement are in turn affected by each of these factors. For the African-Canadian child, however, experiences of marginalization at school undermine rather than support the child's need for optimal development in any of these areas.

For children to view themselves in a positive way, it is necessary for them to feel that they belong and are competent and worthy. It is therefore important for caregivers and teachers, especially in the early years, to ensure that the learning environments provided for minority children are supportive of these developmental needs. Mrs Miti's concerns after visiting the Centre Street Day Care were therefore very well founded.

The work of Abraham Mallow (1980) identifies *belonging* as a fundamental human need in the development of our psychological selves. Because we are born and nurtured in social communities, human beings as a species have a need to belong. The attachment relationship that children form in the very early months of life is an indication of the developmental importance of our belonging needs. In the earliest stages of life, this need is met in the caregiving experiences and within the family. As the children's life extends beyond the family setting, it is the responsibility of those who care for them outside the home to provide the conditions for these needs to be met. To fail to do so constitutes a violation of the authority invested in them.

According to Felker to *belong* in the context of self-esteem means that an individual is part of a group and is accepted and valued by the other members of that group. To belong requires a mutual sense of oneness. For self-esteem to be operative, it is not only necessary that the group regard the individual in this way but that the individual regard himself/herself as belonging. He or she must see himself/herself as an accepted and valued member of the group.

Messages of exclusion work to create feelings of isolation, making it nearly impossible for children to feel a sense of affiliation. The emotional outcomes of acceptance are the development of a positive sense of self, motivation and pride, whereas exclusion creates very negative emotions like self-doubt and shame. It also interferes with both learning and and motivation.

Self-esteem of Minority Group Children

This brings us to the literature on self-esteem in minority children(Martinez and Dukes 1991; Ogbu 1988; Phinney 1989; 1990). Since African-Canadian children experience marginalization in several of society's arenas — in the Child Care setting, in the school environment, in the curriculum, and in the media, are we to assume that they generally have poor self-esteem? The work of Phinney (1990) and Martinez and Duke(1991) challenges this position. Phinney's work shows that the way Black children feel about themselves is very situational. In the company of their peers where their activities are supported and valued, they experience very positive sense of themselves. In those environments, however, where they do not feel valued or supported in their aspirations, they will demonstrate behaviours typically associated with more negative self-esteem.

When we consider that the majority of reports about low self-esteem of African-Canadian children come from the school environment where their primary experiences are those of marginalization — and stereotypic expectations for not achieving academically — it is not surprising that the generally held view of them is that they lack self-esteem. It must be reiterated, however, that the demonstration of high or low self-esteem for these children is situation specific.

The lack of representation of the African-Canadian child's culture in the Child Care environment is repeated in the school environment. The administrative units, the teaching personnel and most critically the curriculum, all negate the presence of African Canadian children in the culture of the school. The area of sports and athletics is the area where their presence is acknowledged. Ironically however, this is often to the detriment of their academic achievement.

Impact of Discrimination on Self-worth

Children's experience of discriminatory treatment erodes their sense of self in the same way that marginalization does. Discriminatory treatment does not only come from the adults in the environment who relate to children on the basis of preconceived notions of their capabilities. It also comes from peers and could have similar impacts on longer term motivation and achievement.

Mark is in the Second Grade class at Melville Public School. He is the only Black child in the class and started school here two months ago when his parents moved to the neighbourhood. His family is excited about their new home, and is working on getting settled in their new community. But all is not going well for Mark at school. For the first month Mark mostly worked alone at his desk and didn't seem to "join" any of the group activities that are so much a part of school life in the early years. By the end of the second month the situation had not changed and the teacher was becoming concerned about his "adjustment" problem. She started making plans to contact his parents to discuss this situation. Before this appointment was scheduled, an incident happened in class that placed a different perspective on Mark's "withdrawal."

The children had to pair up to do an exercise which they had not completed the previous day. As the teacher casually observed them getting ready for this activity, she realized that no-one had chosen Mark as their partner. There was one boy left who should naturally have been Mark's partner, but he scooted off and attached himself to an already formed pair rather than join Mark to do the exercise. Mark looked around to see if there was anyone he could team up with and seeing everyone already paired up, he went off to work on the task by himself as he had been doing for the past two months.

This observation provided the teacher with fresh insight into why Mark withdrew from his peers. She intervened and paired up the odd boy with Mark for the exercise. The message of rejection, however, was clear to Mark. Over the past months he had become the isolate of the class.

This incident may seem relatively innocuous to the casual observer, but when children are repeatedly exposed to such experiences, they begin to question themselves and develop self-doubt about their value in the community of their peers. Without proper education about the permutations of racism, they will eventually begin to question their worth as individuals and as members of their society.

Teachers of young children *must* therefore deal with issues of rejection in the school environment as part of their everyday responses to the psychological well-being of the children in their care. In the case illustration given above, it was not only necessary for the teacher to regroup the children to include Mark, which she did, but there is an additional responsibility, on the part of the teacher, to address the racial overtones in the incident with the children, in a way that is developmentally appropriate for them. They have to learn about valuing human differences.

If teachers are to nurture positive self-esteem in children from ethnic and racial minority groups, it is critical that they learn how to treat these differences as normal conditions rather than as deficiencies. They have to teach the children in their class about valuing differences. The extent to which children's differences are acknowledged and integrated into their daily experiences, is the extent to which they will see their differences as normal rather than a sign of deficiency. This unfortunately is not the case for African-Canadian children.

In Canadian society, as in the school system, differences between people are often treated as deficiencies. When children learn to see themselves as deficient, they inevitably feel less capable and frequently lose the motivation to strive to be the best they could be. This is one of the most corrosive effects of racism at the level of the individual and it is related to the difficulties Black youths experience in defining a place for themselves in society.

Validating Differences

For schools and care settings to fulfil their mandate of attending to the psychological well-being of all children in their charge, they *must* find ways of validating these children's realities in the social, cultural fabric of the curriculum.

Several Boards of Education have developed policies for the introduction of multicultural material into their school curriculum as a way of acknowledging the growing diversity among their student population. This is recognized as a significant achievement which must be commended. Two additional steps need to be put in place for the intent of these policies to be operationalized in the classroom. Firstly, funds need to be made available for the development of the necessary curricular material to foster more inclusive teaching, and secondly, provisions need to be made for teacher training to cultivate a philosophy of inclusiveness that would encourage them to move beyond the Eurocentric focus of the traditional curriculum.

Teaching to promote inclusiveness and positive self-regard

There are several ways in which teachers could foster a sense of belonging, competence and worth in the children in their charge, in the absence of funds to make the necessary larger scale transformation.

Simply giving validation to their world in the classroom or child care program can have a positive impact on children. When they see their lives reflected before them, whether in music, art, cooking or reading material, they come alive, they feel that sense of belonging and acceptance that are such fundamental conditions of learning.

There are many opportunities in the child's day that could be used to provide these validating experiences. Most classrooms in the early grades and in child care centres are organized around learning or interest centres. If there are children from different ethnic or cultural groups in the class, the teacher should make a conscious effort to incorporate some material that reflects the lives of these children into the theme of the centres. When children use the centres, they could relate at a deeper meaning level with the materials they are interacting with. Similarly, the decor of the environment should be representative of the lives of the children in the school or centre.

Language Arts and Social Studies

Children's learning experiences can easily be categorized into areas reflective of the domains of functioning. If one looked at their daily experience from that standpoint, many opportunities will be found to incorporate culturally relevant content in every aspect of their learning. Here are some suggestions as to how this could be achieved:

In the area of Language art activities, teachers could include stories, poems and historical material from the culture of children outside of the dominant societal group, to complement the material available from the educational publishers and Boards of Education which often do not reflect the non-mainstream groups.

Including a social-studies flavour into the language arts activities would be seen as a "developmentally appropriate" practice in these early years. Organizing trips to selected ethnic communities and gathering collectibles from their outings would provide the teacher with natural material to address issues of cultural diversity at a level that the children could learn from and appreciate. The first step could be visits to communities that are reflective of the non-mainstream children in the group or class. This would enable all children to see themselves as part of a world of diverse people.

The Inclusive Child Care Environment

Child care personnel could also begin to make their programming more inclusive. By contrast with Centre Street Child Care program, a more inclusive environment, socially and physically, will have much more positive impact on both children and their families.

The Centre that Nzinga attended before her family moved to the present neighbourhood had several features representative of inclusive programming. At that Centre her mother remembered how pleasing it was to watch Nzinga play in the drama Centre. She was always happy to try on different outfits. One day she was a Mexican lady, another time she was a Polish dancer, or an Indian child. She even asked if she could bring one of her older sister's dresses and her dad's dashiki to put in the drama centre. Mrs Miti thought of the wonderful opportunities this provided her child to learn about the peoples of the world. Coming from Africa where she had no exposure at all to some of these groups, it was reassuring to Mrs Miti that although she was away from home, her child could see herself as one in a world of diverse people who all dressed in unique ways.

The concept of inclusiveness was not only limited to the drama centre. Rather, it embraced several dimensions of the child care program — staffing, diet, the decor of the physical environment and its outreach to parents for their contribution to the program activities.

A note of caution is needed here least teachers and care-givers confine themselves to the restricted concept of "multi-cultural education" that focuses on artifacts, material and the celebration of festivities. The practice of inclusive education must address issues of racism (and classism although this is not the main focus of the present discussion), and attempt to help children understand its manifestation and the effects on its victims and perpetrators.

Marginalization in the Popular Media

The media serves as another source through which African-Canadian children see themselves and their group marginal-ized and stereotyped. For the most part African-Canadians are excluded from the public media. Past experience with media coverage in the community, has shown that as a group we are given selective publicity when there are opportunities for sen-sationalism or for reinforcement of negative stereotypes assigned to the group. When young children see primarily neg-ative images of members of their community portrayed in the media, not only will they begin to evaluate themselves in this light, but they will also aspire to the images of their group that they see portrayed.

Their sense of what is not attainable is equally conditioned by what they view. Smart and talented kids are the predominantly white child heroes of film or the stars of Television shows. The portrait of successful white businessmen are the white models that look back at them from the pages of brochures, posters, magazines, and TV screens across the nation. No teacher has to tell children of minority cultural or racial heritage that their capabilities are limited. The media send this message powerful-ly and devastatingly by the process of omission, whether this is intentional or coincidental. The unattainable is directly defined by the media through its portrayal of who the successful figures in our society are.

Conclusion

From the foregoing discussion, it is evident that children experience marginalization in many areas of their lives. These experiences impact negatively on their perception of themselves and frequently influence their educational attainment and career aspirations. Parents of African-Canadian children must fight an intensive battle against the impact of these external influences in their children's lives and continue to advocate for inclusive education and the dismantling of barriers to their children's success that are imposed by discriminatory treatment and exclusion from the culture of the school, and those areas in society which support educational attainment.

School success for Nzinga and Mark and many other African-Canadian children rests as much with parental nurturance and encouragement for success as with the dismantling of the obstacles to success imposed by racism and marginalization at school.

NOTES

1 The term *racism* is used interchangeably with *discrimination* throughout this discourse as discrimination is being used in this context to mean differential treatment and expectations on the basis of race.

2 *Self-concept*, *sense of self*, and *self-esteem* are likewise used interchangeably.

Comment

OUR EXPECTATIONS OF THE EDUCATION OF AFRICAN CANADIANS — NOW AND IN THE YEARS AHEAD

Keren Brathwaite

Evidence points to African Canadians' continuing faith in education, in spite of the failures of formal education systems to advance our group goals of upliftment, community development and future security for our children. Education is now more valuable for any group in Canada than it was a generation ago due to the skills and knowledge which are necessary for survival in the advanced Information Age into which we have moved. African Canadians are very aware of the new occupational and career challenges, and must continue to place value and priority on equitable and quality education. In order to face the social, economical and technological challenges of this period and the future, it is important for African Canadians to be even more vigilant about education than we have been in the past.

Our parents have taught us that education is the most important ticket to the future for us as Black people due to our historical experience of racial discrimination and limitation, against which we have always struggled. We also instruct our children and Black youth in general about the necessity of getting a sound education. Ironically, some of our young people are now critiquing this notion because of the poor employment prospects and discrimination in the work place, which many of our university graduates have experienced. Since we continue to transmit a belief in education to our children in our homes, our community centres and our churches, it is incumbent on us as educators and parents to ensure that they receive in public institutions what we think good quality education should deliver to them: critical knowledge of self and society in a global context, with language, mathematics, science and communications content to provide them with the skills necessary for future employment, personal development and contribution to their community and society.

We need to ensure *now* that when we teach our children and youth the value of education, they will in turn be instructed in institutions that value them and give them the quality of education that they deserve. To achieve this, we will need to place more emphasis on *our students as the centre of the learning process* and the main reason for the existence of the schools. In this regard, more attention will need to be paid to helping students develop their *voice* and express more how they view their connection to education and what they expect from it. Some of our students have already been using their *voice* in African Canadian students' clubs, in Students of Toronto Against Racism (STAR), in African Canadian Heritage Programmes, Saturday schools and in community and church settings. These locations have been providing a venue for our students to learn and practice leadership skills, and to increase their self esteem and confidence which for some have been undermined by the experiences of their regular schooling. Mentoring programmes such as those offered by Jamaican Canadian Association and Each One Teach One will continue to be needed in our community to support and strengthen our students.

In addition to the above, to achieve our goals, we will need to increase our activities around curriculum development, thus producing more of the resources which should improve the instruction of our students. Resource development will have to be connected to teacher preparation, for ineffective pedagogy tied to the stereotypic expectations some teachers have of Black students, have been recognized among Black educators and organizations as contributing to our students' underachievement.

Our vision for the future of education for our students is one in which our expectations of equity and academic attainment will be realized. We will need to continue to critique the education institutions when our expectations remain unfulfilled and our vision unrealized. It is important that we provide ideas and recommendations, if we believe that in good faith they will be implemented. However, at this time, we need to consider some alternative methods and settings for educating those of our students who are dropping out of school, failing in it, or who are excellent students who do not receive the support they deserve.

As African Canadian students, parents, educators and community members, the years ahead demand that we take some bold new approaches now if we are to realize our vision/our expectations even in a partial way.

PART TWO

PARENTS, SCHOOL AND COMMUNITY LINKAGES
A Critical Assessment

Chapter Five

AFRICAN CANADIANS' ORGANIZING FOR EDUCATIONAL CHANGE[1]

Agnes Calliste

Introduction

In discussing the 1994 *Black Learners Advisory Committee Report on Education*, a colleague told me that it was time for African Nova Scotians to help themselves and stop depending on the government to redress educational inequity. Other ethnoracial and ethnoreligious groups (such as the Chinese and Jews) helped themselves by organizing Saturday schools. My colleague's comment reminded me of the white student in one of my classes in the late 1980s who argued that African Canadians and First Nations Peoples did not deserve education and employment equity because they have not contributed anything to Canada. But Blacks have contributed to Canadian society through their labour (e.g., as slaves, domestics and professionals) and their struggles (Calliste 1994, 1995; Walker 1981). They also have contributed to science, education and the arts and they have organized self-help associations (such as the Black Youth Organization, the Black Education Project [BEP] and the Black Heritage Association in Toronto in the early 1970s) and developed programs which worked for economic and cultural self-sufficiency (see for example, *Contrast*, July 19, 1971; D'Oyley 1994; Haber 1970). However, African Canadians' contributions, educational initiatives, and struggles have been largely ignored in social science research (See Bruner 1979; Davis and Krauter 1971; Winks 1971). For example, African Canadians' contributions to the initiation of the Transition(al) Year Program at the University of Toronto and Dalhousie University have not been recognised.

This chapter analyzes African Canadians' anti-racist education struggles between the late 1960s and the mid-1990s from a social movement perspective. It examines the conditions under which anti-racist struggles materialized, the constraints placed upon them and the effects of these struggles. The late 1960s demarcates the politicization of Black consciousness in Canada with the influence of the civil rights and Black Power Movements in the United States and the decolonization of African and Caribbean states. In Canada, several politically-conscious organizations — such as the BEP and the Black Students Union of Ontario and the Afro-Canadian Liberation Movement in Halifax — were formed to eliminate all forms of anti-Black racism (Calliste 1995). Special attention was given to racism in the educational system because of the crucial role education plays in preparing individuals for the labour market. The 1990s is characterized by the demand for Afrocentric and anti-racist education (Asante 1990; Black Learners Advisory Committee [BLAC] 1994; Dei 1995a, 1995b; James 1995; Lee 1985). This paper draws on new social movement theory because it helps to explain African Canadians' anti-racist educational struggles between the 1960s–1990s.

Anti-Racism Organizing and New Social Movements

Social movements are a heterogenous array of socio-political forms of activism against different oppressions such as racism, sexism and militarism (Cohen 1983; Epstein 1990; Laclau and Mouffe 1985; Urry 1981). In contrast to orthodox Marxist theory, some writers on new social movements (Laclau and Mouffe 1985; Melucci 1980) argue that the transformation of advanced

capitalist societies in more democratic and egalitarian directions is likely to emerge from a plurality of social struggles,
with no central role relegated to the working class. They see
movements as networks composed of fragmented groups based
less on material interests and more on cultural transformation.
Their focus on identity politics (for example, the positive re-
articulation of social difference and collective subjectivity), distinguishes new social movements from pre-World War II social
movements. New social movements theory also shifts the focus
of struggle toward civil society. It argues that social power is
not centrally located in the state or the economy but is exercised and resisted at every level of society.

Some new social movement writers (Mooers and Sears
1992; Omi and Winant 1983; Wood 1986) disagree with the
view that the working class is not central to the struggles. They
argue that new social movements theory ignores the relation
between political economy and political praxis or between
structure and culture. As Barbara Epstein points out, while it is
true that new social movements have been based mainly in
middle-class constituencies, on demographic grounds alone it
is unlikely that significant social change could occur without
substantial working-class involvement. Moreover, movements
of people of colour consist largely of working-class people.
Similarly, in emphasizing the particularistic, fragmentary character of many contemporary movements and their wariness to
unify or to even construct a shared agenda, many new social
movement theorists have tended to underestimate the extent to
which these movements might share a universal vision organized around such themes as social justice and human rights
(Epstein 1990:47–48; Offe 1985:841–842). Kauffman
(1990:78) argues that the emphasis on identity politics with its
attention to lifestyle and lack of collective organization could
lead to an anti-politics of identity mirroring the ideology of the
market place. She advocates an approach that balances 'concerns with identity with an emphasis on solidarity' and 'other
key categories like interests and needs' (79).

In relation to these divergent perspectives — the 'class perspective' and the 'social movement' perspective — this chapter
argues that both are relevant to African Canadians' struggle for

education equity. African Canadians' anti-racist education struggles have not been solely an expression of working class struggle in the sense of labour's resistance to capital. Instead, they have been carried out mainly by community-development, parents,' students' and professional organizations. Moreover, in the 1960s and 1970s, some African Canadian organizations (such as the National Black Coalition of Canada) comprehended the struggle mainly in terms of racism rather than classism. More militant African Canadian organizations (example, the Afro-Canadian Liberation Movement in Halifax) analyzed the problem as the intersection of racism and classism in education (Arnold 1978; Douglas in Tullock 1975; O'Malley 1972). The current movement takes an integrative anti-racist perspective by examining structural inequalities and barriers based on race, class, gender and other forms of social difference which influence educational outcomes (Dei 1995b; James 1995).

The coexistence of legal, distributive and cultural elements in African Canadians' struggles for educational equity is evident. They aim at eliminating structural inequalities in education (e.g., streaming and barriers to post-secondary education), which has been relegating many African Canadian students to economic and political oblivion. They also focus on identity politics and representation (e.g., African-centred pedagogy, Black-focus schools and Black Studies courses in universities) to address anti-Black racism, promote Black pride and increase educational equity. Since the Black Power and anti-racist education movements also aimed at institutional transformation and power sharing (Dei 1994b) — African Canadians' organizing for educational change in the period from 1968 to 1995 has been largely a counter-hegemonic struggle.

Organizing for Educational Change in the Post World-War II Period

African Canadians have been struggling for educational equity for over 100 years (Calliste 1994; Pachai 1990). They have been more politically focussed since 1968, with the influence of the Black Power Movement in the United States and the decolonization of African and Caribbean states. Before the late 1960s, African Canadian community-development organizations sought reforms to improve their economic and social conditions, including demands for inclusive curriculum in the schools which would represent the lived experiences and contributions of people of African descent, and access to nursing schools. In the 1940s, the Halifax Colored Citizens Improvement League put pressure on nursing schools to accept Black students, a battle later taken up by Pearleen Oliver, founding member of the Nova Scotia Association for the Advancement of Colored People (NSAACP). As a result, the Children's Hospital in Halifax accepted two Black students who graduated in 1948 (Congress of Black Women of Canada 1991, Pachai 1990). The NSAACP also worked with the Nova Scotia Department of Education to establish both adult education classes and self-help projects in African-Nova Scotian communities as well as a Black Incentive Education Fund to increase retention in secondary school and to facilitate access to post-secondary education (BLAC 1994; Pachai 1990).

In Toronto, the Negro Veterans' Association led by Wilson Brooks presented a brief to the Ontario Minister of Health in 1947, asking for the cancellation of government grants to provincial hospitals which discriminated on the basis of colour. The brief resulted from the Owen Sound Hospital's refusal to admit Marisse Scott to its nurses' training school and "the general policy of discrimination against Blacks in hospitals" (*Campus*, October 10, 1947). This challenge also was supported by the trade union congresses of Canada and by the Catholic church. Ms. Scott was finally admitted to the St. Joseph's Hospital school of nursing in Guelph (Canada, House of Commons 1953).

In the 1940s and 1950s, African Canadians in Nova Scotia and Toronto protested the schools' use of derogatory materials which were insulting to people of African descent and sought to get Black history and literature included in the school curriculum. For example, the Halifax Colored Citizens Improvement League asked the provincial state in 1944 to withdraw *Little Black Sambo* from the schools because it denigrated people of African descent. They argued that the state should promote better race relations by including materials in the curriculum which represented an accurate history of Africans, including their contributions to society (Pachai 1990). Similarly, in 1954–56, a coalition of Black parents led by Danny Brathwaite, the Universal African Improvement Association (UAIA) and other interest groups successfully pressured the Toronto Board of Education to withdraw *Little Black Sambo* from the classrooms[2] (*Contrast*, December 19, 1969; Ontario Multicultural History Society 1991).

But despite these moderate successes, most African Canadians, particularly in Nova Scotia, remained marginalized in the educational system. Sealey estimated that in 1969, for example, only 3 per cent of Black students in Nova Scotia graduated from high school and only 1 per cent of the graduates would attend university (Pratt 1972:80). Before 1968, Blacks' activism tended to be non-political. Its attacked specific instances of discrimination and prejudice, rather than general attitudes (Walker 1981) and institutional practices. In the late 1960s, African Canadians realised that more militant organizing and broader strategies were needed to transform Canadian society and the educational system.

African Canadians' Organizing and Struggle for Educational Equity, 1968–1970s

The Black Power movement had a tremendous impact on the ideological mobilization of African-Canadians, increasing their militancy, political consciousness and identity. In 1968, two conferences in Montreal, the Conference of Caribbean and other Black Organizations and the Black Writers' Congress, as well as a visit to Halifax by Stokely Carmichael and a delegation of the Black Panther Party mobilized African Canadians towards a more sensitive and acute awareness of their oppression. The conferences called for power-sharing, education and employment equity and a commitment to the anti-racist struggle (Clairmont and Magill 1970; Forsythe 1971).

The influx of Black immigrants to Canada, particularly Toronto and Montreal, after the liberalization of Canada's immigration policy in 1967, was an important factor in transforming the politics of the Black community. For example, in the period 1963–67, 23,316 Caribbean immigrants entered Canada compared to 86,981 in 1968–73,[3] including many who were skilled and professional (The Green Paper on Immigration and Population 1974; see also Anderson 1993). This significantly increased and diversified the leadership and membership base for political organizing and made more prominent the designation of racism as a collective Black problem.[4]

The Conference on Caribbean and Black Organizations led to the founding of the National Black Coalition of Canada (NBCC), which included 28 organizations by 1969. The objectives of NBCC included ensuring structural integration of Blacks in Canada, eradicating all forms of discrimination in Canadian society, and developing self-identification through the inclusion of Black Studies in educational curricula. The Black Writers' Conference was the radicalizing agent for the Black population in Montreal and Toronto, particularly for students.

One of the effects of the Black Writers' Conference was a students' illegal sit-in at the computer centre of Sir George Williams University in February 1969 to protest a long-smouldering case of alleged racism by a white professor. Subsequent confrontation between the students and an armed Montreal riot squad resulted in the arrest of 96 students, 45 of whom were Black. Three of the Black students were sentenced to prison terms, and one was also ordered deported (Eber 1969; Forsythe 1971). The 'destroyed' computers subsequently were sold to a company in the United States (M. Gittens, personal communications, June 19, 1993). This situation increased student militancy and heightened social awareness and sensitivity in the Black community.

Black students and youths following the Black Power ideology of Black self-determination (Ture and Hamilton 1992), organized self-help associations (e.g., BEP) and adopted a policy of striving to be self-supporting and not applying for government funding (*Contrast*, May 27, 1972). The BEP and the Black Heritage Association were the two organizations in Toronto that were most active in the area of education in the early 1970s. Their key concerns included the streaming of Black students into vocational and remedial classes which were relegating them to economic and political oblivion; poor placement of Black children, particularly Caribbeans in the school system, Eurocentric curricula; and the quality of social relations within the school as well as between the school and the community (Brathwaite 1977; *Contrast*, April 4, 1970, April 17, 1970, September 16,

1970). The Black Heritage Program[5] was established in Thorncliffe Park, Toronto in 1970 as an independent Saturday school, to teach Black Studies designed "to offset the disadvantages of the complete absence of representative Black culture" in Ontario's school curricula (Contrast, June 1, 1970). The BEP, with the support of other organizations (e.g., the Home Services Association and the UAIA, focused on teaching Black cultural heritage, including Afrocentric values (such as co-operation and contributing one's skills to the community) to Black children and youth and provided them with tutorial assistance in regular academic subjects. BEP, adopting the Cuban motto, "If you don't know, LEARN; if you know, TEACH," also organized literacy and adult upgrading classes. Its office served as an information centre for African Canadians on the educational system, and the BEP Co-ordinator also worked in the field, visiting parents and schools (BEP, n.d.; *Contrast*, November 1, 1970).

The BEP and the Black Liaison Committee with the Toronto Board of Education also helped to pressure the school board to investigate racism and the quality of education offered to minority children in the 1970s. Partly because of the assiduous, sustained work by racial and ethnic minority communities, (e.g., Black, South Asian and Portuguese organizations) in putting forward the concerns of minority parents and youth, and the Toronto Board's concern with the growing number of sometimes violent racial incidents occurring in schools, the Board established a Subcommittee on Race Relations. The Board established the committee not because of good will, but because of pressure. The Liaison Committee was instrumental in ensuring that racial minority communities were represented on the Race Relations Committee (Brathwaite 1977).

The Board's 1979 Final Report made 119 recommendations for combatting racism in education (Toronto Board of Education 1979). However, a 1983 review found most of the recommendations were not implemented (Consultative Committee on the Education of Black Students in Toronto Schools [Consultative Committee] 1988; James and Papp 1988). Moreover, race relations policies with emphasis on multiculturalism, intercultural understanding and changing attitudes could not transform the school board to an anti-racist institution. Black youth are

still grossly over-represented in remedial and vocational courses; their retention rate in high school is extremely low and they
are severely under-represented in universities. The 1991 Every
Student Survey for the Toronto Board of Education indicates
that Black high school students are five times as likely to be in
basic and general level programs than to be in advanced level
programs. By contrast, the distribution of white students is relatively equal across all three programs (Yau, Cheng and Ziegler
1993; see Consultative Committee 1988; Dei 1994a). Effective
anti-racism policies include power-sharing, participation,
responsibility and accountability (Dei 1994b)

The Black Liaison Committee, a community generated,
autonomous body, was formed in 1974 after a meeting of the
Education Advisory Committee of the Brotherhood Community Centre Project[6] and the Toronto Board of Education to discuss the community's concerns about the quality of education
which Black students were receiving. One of the Liaison Committee's initiatives was the introduction of Black Heritage Programs under the Heritage Languages Program in some of
Toronto's Schools in 1979. Although the Heritage Languages
Program, instituted in 1976–77, was designed to accommodate
"the cultural and linguistic heritage of ethnic groups" other than
English and French, Black students were excluded. In 1977 the
Black Liaison Committee and other members of the community
made a strong case to the school board and the Minister of Education for the inclusion of Black Heritage under the Heritage
Languages policy. The battle to retain Black Heritage in Toronto's schools and to integrate it in the regular school day where
numbers justified the move was taken up in the early 1980s by
the Organization of Parents of Black Children (Brathwaite
1977; *Caribbean Focus* 1982).

African Canadians in Montreal, Halifax and Toronto also
took initiatives in the late 1960s and early 1970s to facilitate
access of Black students to universities and colleges. The idea
of the Transitional Year Program (TYP) at the University of
Toronto was conceived by Horace Campbell while still a student at York University. In 1969, he approached officials at
York University about establishing a Black Studies course and
launching a program to assist more Blacks, particularly indige-

nous African Canadians, to enter universities. The plan failed initially. In June of the same year, he met Burnley 'Rocky' Jones, then a graduate student at Dalhousie, at the Learneds Conference who shared the same concern. After some discussion, Jones suggested Campbell speak with Praxis Corporation, a group of University of Toronto faculty members who were interested in getting the university involved in the community (*Contrast*, October 1969 and August 16, 1971). Campbell presented a brief to Praxis on 'The Need for Higher Education and the Black Community.' Praxis supported the proposal. In summer 1969, the first seven participants of the project were trained intensively in the humanities, social sciences and mathematics by Black volunteer teachers.

Another contributor to the TYP is Keren Brathwaite who designed curriculum, taught and counseled in the two summer programmes in the Black community. As faculty member, she has assisted the development of TYP at the University of Toronto from 1970 to the present time. Elaine Maxwell, a student in the 1969 programme, was instrumental in recruiting many other students to TYP and has offered invaluable support to the programme since. Of the seven students in the 1969 summer programme, five successfully completed the course. Campbell proposed to the University of Toronto that the graduates be admitted on a full-time basis. However, the university accepted one of them and only because she qualified as a mature student. The other four students were accepted by York University on an experimental basis. A similar program was also held in 1970, which served a larger group of students, including Blacks and Native students. The success of the five students in university prompted a University of Toronto professor, Charles Hanley, to recommend to the Governing council of his university that it accept the proposal of making the program part of the university community. Thus, TYP was established in 1970 at Innis College, University of Toronto. The program was expanded to increase access to Blacks, First Nations Peoples and low-income students, including whites. TYP became a model for other transition programs in Canada and has helped Black students to access the University of Toronto in more significant numbers than they did in 1970.

(Brathwaite 1995; Campbell 1970; *Contrast* August 16, 1971).

The BEP with the support of other Black organizations (such as the NBCC, Ontario region), individuals and the George Brown College of Applied Arts and Technology in Toronto, launched a pilot project in 1970 to put Blacks through college. Applicants were tested and interviewed. Of the initial 21 applicants, 12 were very keen and also successful in the examination. The program began with six out of a proposed nine students attending George Brown College. Some of the students were upgrading their academic qualifications and skills while others did commercial subjects, nursing assistant, nursing aide and homemaker courses (*Contrast*, December 18, 1970).

The Transition Year Program at Dalhousie University which provides some access to African Nova Scotians and Mi'kmaqs originated from the proposal of a planning group drawn from Dalhousie Association of Graduate Students (DAGS) and members of the Afro-Canadian Liberation Movement in 1969 whose initial focus was to develop Black Studies. The planning group concluded from its preliminary investigations on the intensity of the need for higher education among African Nova Scotians that the problem warranted immediate attention (Moreau 1982; Pachai 1990; Task Force on Access to Black and Native People 1989). For example, William R. Oliver estimated that in 1969 there were only 35 African Nova Scotian university graduates (The Black Man in Nova Scotia Teach-In Report 1969).

DAGS, in consultation with the African Nova Scotian and Mi'kmaq communities, proposed the establishment of a TYP to the three Halifax universities. Dalhousie instituted the TYP in 1970 to reverse social injustices by providing African Nova Scotian and Mi'kmaq students with the academic background and financial assistance necessary to prepare them for university. However, the university's commitment to the program was questionable. Before 1990, TYP suffered from chronic lack of funding and human resources because it never received the support of senior university administrators. TYP also has been stigmatized (e.g., some of its students complained that they have been under-rated while some Black students in regular degree programs are perceived as TYP students). Despite these problems, TYP has achieved some success. In the period 1970–1980, of the approximate 140 students (probably two-thirds of whom were Black) who went through the program, 50 obtained undergraduate degrees; and 5 obtained masters degrees (BLAC 1994, 12, 128; Task Force on Access for Black and Native People 1989). It may be argued, however, that some of these graduates were qualified to enter university through the regular route, but they opted for TYP because of the financial incentive[7] attached to it. One may also question TYP's effectiveness in redressing educational inequities, given that it has been used as a band-aid policy and, until July 1995, an excuse for the province's resistance to educational change (BLAC 1994; Calliste 1994; Nova Scotia Department of Education and Culture 1995).

The Montreal's Board of Black Educators (now the Quebec Board of Black Educators), with funding from McGill University, organized the DaCosta Hall summer project to assist students to attain college- and university-entrance levels through remedial work in various matriculation subjects. The program used culturally relevant curriculum materials (such as African Canadian History and Black Writers) to enhance self-conception and promote retention and graduation. In 1970, between 60 and 70 students were expected to attend the program and places were guaranteed for successful graduates of the program by several colleges, Sir George Williams and McGill Universities (*Contrast*, August 1–15, 1970:15 and November 1, 1970:3). The DaCosta Hall project was continued for many years.

In sum, in the period 1968–1970s, African Canadians organized self-help associations and took initiatives to help to counteract the miseducation of Black children (Woodson 1933) through remedial programs, teaching Black history and culture, facilitating Black students' access to post-secondary education, as well as educating Black parents and the community about the school system and the politics of schooling (see, for example, the report on the 1971 Black People's Conference in Toronto) (*Contrast*, March 6, 1971). African Canadians also put pressure on the educational system to change (Calliste 1994). However, the forces for the status quo resisted African Canadians' demand for institutional transformation at the height of Black protests. The state co-opted and regulated the Black Power movement in several ways, for example, through an appeasement policy of multiculturalism and by funding some African Canadian organizations. These state initiatives militated against the continuation of self-supporting militant African Canadian organizations by sidetracking their energies and stifling protest (Loney 1977, Peter 1981, Stasuilis 1982). Dependence on state funding led to the demise of some militant organizations (such as BEP in 1978–9) when the federal government reduced spending on social and community-oriented projects during economic recession.

Communal Strategies and Institutional Effects, 1980–1995

By 1980, African Canadians in Toronto realised that multiculturalism and race relations policies were ineffective in combatting racism and that the educational outcomes for many African Canadian students remained unacceptable. Thus, some parents and educators organized themselves (e.g., the North York Black Educators Society, the Canadian Alliance of Black Educators, and the Organization of Parents of Black Children [OPBC]) to struggle for educational equity. OPBC, formed in 1980, with Keren Brathwaite as Chair, acts as a voice for Black parents by representing them at the level of Boards of Education (for example Toronto) and the Ministry of Education, presenting briefs (for instance, to the Royal Commission on Learning) and advising parents on how to deal with the school system. OPBC offers a monthly programme of education for parents, with focus on strengthening their skills to aid their children's education and providing them information about new policies, practices, etc. in the system (K. Brathwaite 1995). The organization also acts as an intermediary or buffer between parents and the school (OPBC, n.d.). It fights expressions of institutional racism by supporting parents in cases of racism against their own children. In this way, the parent is given the opportunity to lift the issue of a racist incident to do with his or her child from the personal to the community level, thereby broadening the base for struggle and increasing the chance of a successful outcome to action taken.

The OPBC also educates teachers and students by visiting schools to teach about aspects of the Black community, such as Black History (M. Clarke, personal communications, May 30, 1995; G. Dei, personal communications, July 9, 1995). The organization pressured the school board in 1981–82 to retain the Black Heritage Program and to integrate the classes into the schedule of the regular school day where numbers justified the move (*Caribbean Focus* 1982). OPBC also proposed to the Toronto Board of Education in 1986 that its director establish a consultative committee on the education of Black students in Toronto schools to examine the organization's concerns (such as high 'drop out' rate and over-representation of Black students in non-academic schools) and to recommend appropriate action. The committee's 1988 *Final Report* made 58 recommendations to address parents' concerns (Consultative Committee 1988; OPBC 1992). However, most of the recommendations have not been implemented. OPBC met with the Director of the school board in June 1992 to express its impatience with the board's resistance to change and called for urgent action from the board on some critical areas: accountability and implementation (e.g., making its equity and anti-racism policies a living part of the classroom), inclusive curriculum, employment equity, parental involvement in education, and Black students and the police and the justice system (OPBC 1992; see Lewis 1992). At the African Studies Association conference in Toronto in November 1994, some Blacks suggested that the community take a class action suit against the Minister of Education and school boards for miseducating Black children. This suggestion is not unique in Canada. In the 1970s, two African Nova Scotian communities took successful class action suits against their school boards for unequal access to education (Calliste 1994a).

Since the early 1980s, several Black parents' associations have been organized in metropolitan Toronto and other African Canadian communities to pressure their school boards and provinces for educational equity. In Nova Scotia, for example, after racial fights at the Cole Harbour District High School in 1989, parents and students in North Preston organized the Parent-Student Association of Preston (PSAP) to combat racism in the educational system, including a call for a public inquiry. Though the state did not institute a public inquiry, pressure from the PSAP, other African Nova Scotian organizations and individuals influenced school boards to adopt anti-racist/race relations policies. Similar pressures caused the state to appoint a Black Learners Advisory Committee [BLAC] to conduct research and an assessment of the educational realities and learning needs of African Nova Scotian communities across the province and to evaluate policies and programs which impact on Black learners (BLAC 1994; Calliste 1994a). BLAC helped to organize community-based Education Committees across the province to encourage parents to become advocates in the schools and at the school board level, and to work to improve community-school relations (BLAC 1994).

African Canadian students also have continued to organize for quality education. In Halifax, students at the Queen Elizabeth High School, dissatisfied with the Eurocentric curriculum, organized their own after-school Black History classes in the 1980s to learn about their heritage and to develop and promote Black identity and pride. Another African Nova Scotian initiative was the establishment of the Cultural Awareness Youth Group (CAYG) in 1983 to foster the educational and cultural development of Black youth in the metropolitan Halifax-Dartmouth area by focusing on Black culture and heritage. Based in high schools, CAYG chapters are youth-led with membership open to all students. CAYG educational and cultural programs (e.g., topical debates, plays based on historical and contemporary themes)successfully generate widespread interest throughout the school and the community (Mannette 1987; National Film Board 1993). Some African Canadian students at the university-level, with support from a few faculty members, have organized anti-racist education groups. The Anti-Racist Teaching Network in Halifax universities and the Ethnic Minorities and Multicultural Association (EMMA) at St. Francis Xavier University serve as illustrations. The Anti-Racist Teaching Network was organized in 1991 predominantly by Black students and two faculty members: Harvey Millar, an African Canadian, and Jo-Anne Fiske, after an African student complained that a professor showed a racist film on

Africa without counteracting or addressing the racism. The Network has organized anti-racist teaching workshops and published a guide which was widely circulated in Nova Scotia universities (Millar and Reviere 1993; H. Millar, personal communications, January 1991). The EMMA was organized in 1987 by Black and Native students with the support of their Liaison Officer to develop and promote Black and Native identity and pride through history and culture, to provide a support network for members, to facilitate access to Black and Native students, and to combat racism. In addition to annual anti-racism forums and workshops, EMMA has a Mentor Program for Black and Native high school students in Antigonish to encourage them to complete their high school education and to help to prepare them for post-secondary education (Dickson 1994; EMMA 1994; D. Anderson, personal communications, October 12, 1995).

Another African Canadian communal strategy was the organization of provincial Black educators' associations and the National Council of Black Educators of Canada (NCBEC) to work for educational equity for students, and employment equity for teachers, particularly Blacks. The associations advocate institutional changes, provide remedial education to Black students and professional development to teachers and educate the community about the school system (Canadian Alliance of Black Educators, n.d.; D'Oyley 1994; Hurshman 1978; Perry 1994). The Black Educators Association in Nova Scotia (BEA), the oldest organization,[8] serves as an illustration. Since 1991, BEA, in collaboration with the Mathematics Department, Dalhousie University, has been organizing a week-long residential university Summer Math Camp for "bright and capable" Black students in mathematics in junior high schools to help to begin to redress the severe under-representation of African Nova Scotians in mathematics, science and technology. In 1992, thirteen boys and twenty-three girls participated in the Camp (Clarke 1994: 61). The BEA also convinced the Nova Scotia Department of Education in 1991 to make the Black Incentive Fund a real incentive with emphasis on high academic performance and access to higher education by awarding it only at the post-secondary level instead of giving it at the high school level on the basis of attendance.

Thus, in 1991–94, 77 students received university entrance scholarships of $4,500 and 295 second-year students received post-secondary promotions awards of $1,000–2,000 (BLAC 1994: 107). The Black community recommended to the Department to extend the Incentive Fund from two years to four years and to cover all Black students in post-secondary institutions with an increase in the amount provided (BLAC 1994; Inter-University Committee on Access for Under-represented Populations 1992).

The provincial governments and school boards' response to community campaigns for anti-racist education following the Cole Harbour racial conflict in 1989, the Halifax and Toronto 'mini-riots' in 1991–92 (Calliste 1994a, 1994b; Lewis 1992; Working Group 1992) indicate that they tend to respond to extreme pressure. These disturbances focused attention on Black youths' frustrations regarding the impact of racism which included long-standing grievances in such areas as education, employment and police-community relations (Lee 1991; Nicoll 1991; Nova Scotia Advisory Group on Race Relations 1991). In addition to advocating for anti-racism policies and practices, Blacks in Nova Scotia and metropolitan Toronto recommended Afrocentric education (Asante 1980, 1987) as a partial solution to Black youths' disengagement from school. In Toronto a multilevel government task force, the African Canadian Community Working Group (1992), proposed that one Black-focused junior high school as an alternative school should be set up in each municipality. Such a school would teach Black history and culture and would have proportionately more Black teachers and administrators on staff than in most 'mainstream' public schools; thus Black students could develop their sense of identity and belonging to a school. The Ontario Royal Commission on Learning (1994:78) also recommended the establishment of demonstration schools. However, the political forces for the status quo have resisted the request for Black-focused schools. The Toronto Board of Education tried to appease Blacks by approving the Nighana project, "an alternative education program of black studies" for some students who 'dropped out' of high school (Lewington 1995:A4). Some Blacks argue that the project, which began in Fall 1995 with 25 students, was set up to fail. It is located in a church and it is severely under-staffed — with a part-time teacher — and grossly under-funded (G. Dei, personal communications, October 21, 1995). Moreover, given fiscal restraints and the Ontario government's regressive policies (such as cancellation of the Employment Equity legislation and the Anti-Racism Secretariat), it is highly unlikely that school boards would institute Black-focused schools or other Afrocentric programs, and implement anti-racism and education equity policies. The Black community would have to raise funds to finance Black-focussed schools.

The Nova Scotia government announced in July 1995 that it would spend $1 million this year developing an Afrocentric curriculum, including courses on Black history, traditions and culture (Lewington 1995). It accepted BLAC's recommendations (1994) to create an Afrocentric Learning Institute to assist in curriculum development and teaching modules and conduct ongoing research on issues impacting on Black learners; to provide scholarships for Blacks to enter professional programs (such as medicine) from which they have been traditionally excluded, as well as for teacher training; and to incorporate anti-racism training in teacher education programs. Instead of establishing an African Canadian Education Branch in the Department as BLAC recommended, the government created an African Canadian Services Division responsible for coordinating public school programs and services for African Nova Scotians (Nova Scotia Department of Education and Culture 1995). Some African Nova Scotians are cautiously optimistic. Given the history of containing African-Canadians' struggle for equity, we have to be vigilant in monitoring the implementation of BLAC's recommendations and in countering resistance to institutional transformation.

Conclusion

This study on African Canadians organizing for educational change between the late 1960s–1990s has for the most part supported new social movement theory. Some Blacks organized and mobilized their economic and political power resources to challenge the role of the educational system in legitimizing

Euro-Canadian hegemonic ideas and practices, which reinforce racial, class, gender inequalities and other forms of social difference in society. Blacks are demanding an educational system that is more inclusive, one which centres all students and validates their lived experiences. Given that the dominant society resists this kind of change, Blacks need to be better organized to achieve more economic and political power as well as form coalitions with other groups in the struggle for equity.

ACKNOWLEDGEMENT
The author would like to thank Muriel Clarke, past-president of OPBC, for sharing some information with her, and Debbie Murphy for typing this manuscript.

NOTES

1 The terms 'African Canadians' and 'Blacks' are interchangeable in this paper. For the purpose of this study, I define community organizing as a dynamic process in which individuals with some common identity (e.g., ancestry, gender, national origin, and political ideology) and/or interests and needs unite to provide services and educational activities for themselves, and to fight for their individual and collective rights (Lamoureux, Mayer and Panet-Raymond 1989).

2 In the 1970s and 1980s, some African Canadians in New Brunswick, Ontario and Winnipeg pressured their respective school boards to remove *Huckleberry Finn* from the classroom. Though some African Canadians, like civil liberties groups, argue that teachers should counteract racism in texts rather remove them from the classroom, some African Canadians contend that they cannot rely on the school to counteract racist curricula.

3 The data on Caribbean immigrants are under-estimated because they do not include those who came to Canada from England. Although all Caribbeans are not Black, a large proportion are Black.

4 Given the diversity of the African Canadian community in terms of national and ethnic origins, social class, language, and religion, and given that individuals have multiple identities, one would expect some disunity in the Black movement. Disunity based on social class, age and ideological differences was evident in the movement. However, movement leaders emphasized the importance of Black unity irrespective of national origin and encouraged all Blacks to develop a pan-Africanist attitude (*Contrast*, March 6, 1971; *Chronicle Herald*, December 6, 1968, Douglas in Tullock 1975).

5 The original idea for the Black Heritage Program stemmed from a conference on the Black child in the Ontario educational system sponsored by the

Black People's Movement of York University. The conference called for a committee to be set up for the purpose of developing a viable continuing education program for Black children and adults which might operate independently of the public school system and be administered by the Black community.

6 The Brotherhood Community Centre Project was a liaison and co-ordinating group consisting of 38 Black organizations in Toronto (Brathwaite 1977).

7 Unlike the TYP students at the University of Toronto, those at Dalhousie University receive free tuition, room and board (Pachai 1990; Task Force on Access to Black and Native People 1989).

8 BEA was organized in 1969 (Pachai 1990).

Chapter Six

KEEPING WATCH OVER OUR CHILDREN
THE ROLE OF AFRICAN CANADIAN PARENTS ON THE EDUCATION TEAM

KEREN BRATHWAITE

Whenever African Canadian[1] parents speak, in public forums or in personal conversations, one major topic that engages us is the education of African Canadian students. This topic is discussed beyond the parameters of personal interest in the accomplishments of one's own children; focus is more often on the performance of the African Canadian student collectivity — a group which has developed the profile of academic under-achievement in school systems which generally do not support their psychological well being nor their aspirations.

The various studies and research documents on African Canadian students, as well as their lived experiences in the classrooms of the nation, confirm that the education system is a problem for our students. Time and time again, Black parents have been publicly voicing their dissatisfaction with the outcomes of their children's schooling, most recently to Ontario's

Royal Commission on Learning (1994) and to George Dei in his research study of drop-outs (October 1995). It is reasonable to assume, therefore, that African Canadian parents would wish to be involved in their children's education, and many have done so in a variety of formal and informal ways for a very long time.

That the value of parent involvement in education is now gaining more recognition among parents, educators and governments in Canada is significant,[2] but for African Canadian parents and community, educational involvement has now assumed the status of an imperative which we must obey if we hope to improve our students' school experiences and counter the trend of poor performance among them. If the drop-out rate from school of African Canadian students is to decline and their achievement levels increase, if the practice of streaming them (by whatever name) into dead-end programmes and futures is to be arrested, if we believe that their potential is unlimited (which we do believe), then African Canadian parents must become active, serious and recognised participants in their education. African Canadian parents must be a welcome partner on the education team and must continue to push for deep systemic change in education. The experience of many parents, however, is that schools are unwelcoming and problematic institutions which tend to keep parents at a distance rather than include them as partners, in spite of the current rhetoric of parent involvement. Many parents have penetrated the pretences of the system, uncovering what has historically been beneath it: unequal education and unequal results for African Canadian students.

I will argue in this chapter that for the majority of African Canadian students to achieve success in the schools (and also in the colleges and universities), their parents, families and community will have to provide a strong support system for them. They will have to advocate on their behalf on the education team and at a political level for an education that is of good quality, relevant, inclusive of our local and global reality and anti-racist. Many parents and organizations in the Black community have already been deeply involved in providing this support to our students, but our role has not been fully appreciated by education institutions and professional educators, nor has it produced the results our students need. It is important therefore that the African Canadian presence is felt on the education team. We need to serve as "guardian angels" for our children and to keep watch over them. Who is better placed than parents (in a moral sense) to assume this role?

Two stories which stand out among the many I have heard or witnessed will help to advance my argument of the importance of parent involvement in education as it relates to African Canadians.

A teacher in 1983 recounted to me her experience with a Black student and her mother from the Caribbean. The teacher assessed the student in her Grade 5 class as unable to read and reported this perceived deficiency to the mother of the student. The mother was astounded at the teacher's assessment. How could this be so ? The girl read fluently at home and the mother would prove this to the teacher. So she brought a Bible to the school, and to the amazement of the teacher, the student read fluently from it. The teacher recalled later that she learned a very important lesson that day about the role of parents in education. She told me that parent and teacher often see students from different perspectives, and I confided to her that with Black children in Canada there was often a gap (and sometimes a chasm) between the teacher's and the parent's perception and understanding of them.

The second story I heard on the CBC Metro Morning on October 18, 1995 when Andy Berry, host of this radio show, played a recorded message of a woman's reaction to the Million Man March on Washington on October 16, 1995. On tape this parent spoke about her experience on a school trip with her child's class to Pioneer Village, Ontario. When she commented to the teacher that "it was a shame no Black pioneers were included," the teacher responded, "Why the hell should there be? There were no Black pioneers."

The parent held her ground, arguing that "Blacks had made a contribution to Canada but this is not taught in schools." The teacher retorted that "what Blacks did was so minimal it was not worth mentioning." The parent ended her taped message with the words: "It is ignorant teachers like this who are teaching our children." The host of CBC Metro Morning expressed shock at the behaviour and views of this teacher and advised him to take a journey into areas of Black history.

These two stories among the many that Black parents tell indicate a problem in the education of African Canadian students which has been long studied and discussed in the Black community and among educators and institutions.[3] However, the amelioration of this critical condition has been moving at a slow pace, to the extent that many students and members of the Black community have been losing their patience with the status quo. The public institutions in which our students study in preparation for their future have not up to this time made the significant changes which are necessary for nurturing their success. Numerous recommendations have been made to educational institutions in Ontario over many years but they have not borne much fruit in the daily experiences of Black students. It is mainly in community programmes (Saturday schools, parent organisations, tutoring programmes, Black Heritage classes, etc.) that there is direct intervention/action aimed at improving the quality of Black students' educational experiences and their academic performance as well.

As Ron Edmonds has said, "We know more than we need to know" about Black students.[4] This educator was commenting on Black students in the United States, where the National Association of Black School Educators (NABSE) has pronounced that this body of students is in a state of danger from which they need to be saved. Ron Edmonds' words are true for Canada as well. However, knowledge has not provided the necessary cure for what ails Black students—and also their parents and community. And one needs to emphasise that the malady is in the system rather than in the students who have to develop a variety of techniques for survival[5] (Patrick Solomon, panel discussion with high school students and Carl James, African Studies Association Conference, Toronto, November, 1994).

The above stories (among the many Black parents tell and live) are at the heart of my argument. They underline the urgent need for a defined place for African Canadian parents on the education team — *a vantage point from which we can keep watch over our children* and fill in the blanks and correct the distortions resulting from bias, racial prejudice and stereotyping which are often present on the institutional education team. African Canadian parents need to become vocal members of their children's education team to help neutralise the low expectations and negative stereotypes which some educators hold of Black students and to help place on the agenda of the schools an appreciation of the history, culture, experience and complex global reality of Black people.

In *keeping watch over our children*, the *voice* of African Canadian parents *must* be listened to and we must be recognised as advocates of Black students and their need of a good education built on foundations of anti-racism and justice. And, most importantly, there must be a full acknowledgement by professional educators that parents are the *first educators* of their children. This is not an empty cliché. As parents, we teach our children in the home and community before they enter formal schooling. Several Black parents I know taught their children to read before they registered them in school. For some of these children, their progress in reading was arrested on their entry to a Canadian Kindergarten. Further, parents continue to be *co-educators* of their children, and in this area, many Black parents are making a creditable but often unacknowledged contribution.

The education team might therefore be viewed as having both a formal and an informal component. On the informal level, parents in general and Black parents in particular, assume their role by nurturing, guiding and teaching their children. However, on the formal side of education Black parents as well as other parents also need to assume a stronger role as acknowledged, respected and consulted partners. For Black parents, this presence is critical due to the documented common problems many Black students face in the school system. In another article I have referred to these problems as a "Canadian dilemma,"[6] and George Dei has used the word "crisis" for this phenomenon.[7]

On the formal team, therefore, Black parents should be considered *advocates* for their children, but for effective advocacy, training and support are essential. Some of this necessary training has been provided in the Black community in many forums and workshops which are sponsored by groups such as the Canadian Alliance of Black Educators (CABE), the Black

Secretariat, the African Heritage Educators' Network (AHEN), the Organisation of Parents of Black Children (OPBC) and others. OPBC, for example, runs workshops on various aspects of parent education, including developing skills to assist children in the home and preparation for successful parent-teacher interviews. Its monthly programmes since 1980 have provided parents with information and advice on new policies and directions in education. In October 1995, to give an example, the topic of discussion was A Curriculum for All Students and reporting to parents.

Our Presence On The Education Team: Personal Reflections

The role African Canadian parents ought to assume in education has engaged my attention for many years — ever since I enrolled my two children in Kindergarten in Toronto in the mid-1970s. This experience has taught me more than academic research could that our involvement as parents is essential to our students' *success* in Canadian schools, by whatever yardstick *success* is measured. For me, success would include the students' academic achievement, preparation for their future careers, participation in various aspects of the life of the school and also participation in their community, assumption of leadership in the student body, retention of pride in their racial and cultural identity, development of confidence and a healthy self concept, nurturing their aspirations for the future with the expectation of reaching their goals, and most importantly, inculcating in them a sense of hope and belonging.

These ingredients of success will have to be pursued in another context, but it is necessary to mention them here as one parent/ educator's measures of success which needed to be expressed to those who had the institutional responsibility for educating her children. In general, "success" for an African Canadian parent would require an anti-racist, inclusive curriculum, a teacher with high and non-stereotypical expectations of a Black student, and a willingness to communicate with the student and the home in a manner that would inspire trust and confidence and help motivate the student to perform to the unlimited level of his/her potential. This notion of success would assume that the education system cares about educating all of the students entrusted to its care, including Black students.

Our presence on the education team is therefore a requisite for raising such issues and expectations concerning our students. Furthermore, since the student is central to the education process and the reason for its existence, our discussions should also include the student as an active participant. Lamentably, African Canadian students as a group, have been pushed in large numbers to the sidelines of education, as they themselves complained to Stephen Lewis in 1992 and to the Consultative Committee on the Education of Black Students in 1988. They have also expressed this in the various Black Students' Conferences in the Toronto Board of Education from 1989–1995. The "sidelining" has been confirmed by Carl James' (1990) research and most recently in George Dei's (1995) study: *Drop Out or Push Out? The Dynamics of Black Students' Disengagement From School*. Dei shows that African Canadian students are well represented in the drop-out statistics of schools. Their disproportionate number is a troubling reminder of how education institutions have failed our people and confirms the necessity that we constantly monitor them in the interest of the group of children for whom we are personally, collectively and morally responsible.

My experience of guiding my children through Ontario's education system (which I once described as a *maze*) demonstrated to me how powerless parents are generally made to feel in their relationship with the schools. I am a witness to the confusion the system generates about the parents' role. This confusion has been experienced by most parents (of different races and social classes) with whom I have interacted over many years of working in local school PTAs, Area Parent Councils, Heritage Programmes, Parent Liaison Committees, Parent Conference Planning Committees, School Staffing Committees, Principal Hiring Committees and in the Organisation of Parents of Black Children which we established in May 1980 in the Black community to be an advocacy group for Black parents and our students.

My experience has been that when parents organize to change the power relations between the educators and institutions versus the parents and community, there is more often than not much tension generated between the home and school. Dehli in her study on *Parent Activism and School Reform in Toronto* (1994) examines some of the challenges of school — community relations with "attention to the politics of parental participation in schools."[8] The causes of the tension, however, have not been sufficiently studied to date, probably because its impact has not been fully appreciated in the troubling relations between school and home/parents/community. Further investigation is needed in this area.

The power dynamics of parent/community-school relations is strongly felt but its impact has not to date been fully assessed in the schooling experiences of African Canadian students. In many workshops over the years, Black parents have spoken of some attitudes and practices in the schools which tend to limit their involvement: unwelcoming attitudes among some personnel, as well as patronising or condescending ways. Some Black parents have decided not to become members of their local school P.T.A.'s, since they feel their presence and their concerns are not sufficiently recognised by not only the school administration but also by other parents who may consider themselves to be in a position of privilege. Many Black parents, however, have sustained interest in their local groups for the good of their own children. Others involve themselves in organisations like Organisation of Parents of Black Children (OPBC) which they feel provide a more comfortable environment in which to discuss troubling education issues. My experience, however, is that parents across class and racial lines generally experience some difficulty when they question the system about policy and practices. Some of these frustrations Dehli (1994) analyses in her work.

African Canadian Parents' Brand of Educational Engagement: Historical and Contemporary

African Canadian parents and community have been addressing the theme of this chapter for many decades, dating back to the nineteenth century and earlier. Historically, we have not been silent spectators to the drama of Black students' education which has invariably been a challenge to mainstream institutions in Canada, as well as in England and the United States.[9]

Before Confederation in Canada, Black people had good reason to be concerned about racist practices in education. The Confederation in 1867 changed nothing in this respect. Education has continued to be a dilemma for us as a people. There is now a significant body of research documents and other writings about the schooling experiences of Black students, which indicate much agreement between researcher and researcher, study and study, between what Black parents and students tell in the many education forums inside and outside the Black community in Toronto and other urban centres. There is a disturbing similar resonance in the voices of Black parents, students, and community in Cole Harbour, Nova Scotia, and the voices of Black parents, students and community in Scarborough, Ontario and Côte des Neiges, Quebec. The resonance is also similar in Hamilton, Ontario, and in the voices of past generations and the present generation of Black parents, a few of whom now mistakenly believe that their complaints and their fears are new.

I have observed over 15 years in the Organisation of Parents of Black Children (OPBC) that some African Canadian parents who at one time were embarrassed to disclose their or their children's difficulties in the system became more comfortable in the company of other parents in voicing their displeasure with the school system. Some parents have confessed that until they had the good sense to communicate with others and join an organisation working for educational improvements for Black students, they were isolated in their local school, believing that it was only their child who was experiencing racial discrimination; it was only they who had a *problem*. Little wonder that in Black community organising, focus on education is a centre piece and has been so for a long time. In the Black community, there are more work-shops, conferences, forums, discussions of education than any other topic, including the justice system and Black youth which is another subject of much concern; this pre-occupation with education has remained with us as a people for a very long time.

Ever since I have been involved in education in Canada, as a parent and as an educator for more than two decades, the

Black community and parents have been vocal critics of the formal education system represented by various boards of education, separate and public, and by the Ministry of Education and the schools under their jurisdiction. The universities and colleges have also come under our scrutiny, and have been found deficient, but more research into the inequities affecting our students at this level needs to be carried out.

It must be noted, however, that we have been much more than critics of the system. The documentation referred to earlier demonstrates that the Black community, Black parents, students and educators included, has made a major contribution to critical pedagogy and other education themes over many years: anti-racism and equity in education, streaming and de-streaming, inclusive curriculum, the Heritage/International Languages Programme, teacher education, development of anti-violence policies by the Ministry of Education and school boards, Black-focused schools, and, very importantly, the role of parents and community in education.

Black people have worked not only in their own community for educational change, but have also worked in collaboration with educational institutions, governments and other groups of parents, hoping to realise benefits for our collective group of students. The Black Educators' Working Group in Ontario, chaired by Councillor Bev Salmon, is an example of a lobby group of educators which is currently doing collaborative work with the Ministry of Education and Training while being at the same time critical of the system's delivery of education to Black students. This group contains parent/educator/community membership.

The Black Liaison Committee also worked in collaboration with the Toronto Board in the 1970s with the goal of improving Black students' schooling; their work maintained a critical approach to the system. The Black Education Project of the late 1960s and 70s, however, took a more distant approach to the system, administering its own programmes of education in tutoring and counselling to supplement that of the school. These are examples of different approaches to working for needed change in the lives and schooling of Black students, but they attest to my conclusion that the Black community, including parents, has been one of the communities most vigorously engaged in education activism — and for good reason.[10] Since the level of our students' alienation is very intense — from Kindergarten to Graduate School — then keeping watch over them is one way of protecting them from perils to which many of them will fall victim.

The foregoing considerations lead to the questions: What have been the results of Black parents and community long-standing engagement in education? And why is there a myth that Black parents are not involved in education still circulating among some teachers and school administrators, and disturbingly among some Black educators as well (as I have heard some express in Black forums)? And who has benefitted from our work in education? The answer to the last question is critical, for we need to know why Black students' school experiences and academic performance have not improved significantly over many years to reflect the great mass of time, energy and ideas their parents and community have given to the formal education system.

If we cannot achieve the *change* for which we have struggled and worked, lobbied and generated new ideas, then we need to re-evaluate our past approaches to education institutions. It would seem to me that it is time to reflect again on the role African Canadian parents (and community) should assume in education. What is our place? What is our role? And with due consideration to the fact that education is both formal and informal, community based as well as school based, and that the formal system is the one which is wreaking havoc in our students' lives, then it would seem that we need a new definition of the place African Canadian parents ought to occupy on the school's education team.

This chapter proposes, in the light of all we know and agonise about in Black students' education, that we as *Black parents will need to keep watch over our children* from the close range of the education team, on which our presence is essential for protecting them from the malady that is troubling the group: the fall-out from racism and racist foundations of education. Since the education system has thus far proved itself (as a system) as incapable of knowing, nurturing and instructing our collectivity of students, we have to make new demands. We should insist on

117

having input on the school's *formal team*, making it a precondition for our participation in the system. By *participation* I mean our continuing to register our own children in the public school system. We should participate under the terms of a *partner*, not as a *customer*, the term Ontario's new Minister of Education and Training, Mr. Snobelen, recently assigned to parents (*The Toronto Star*, Sept. 13, 1995). The terms of our involvement should be drawn up by us, with the proviso that we will withdraw if our students' needs are not met within the system.

Too long have we operated under terms we knew would be obstacles to our children's success. It is time we propose to design a partnership which will either truly draw us in, or allow us the choice to develop schools that will embrace our students' total being — their total complexity within a rational context that makes good sense to us. The development of such schools is under much discussion in the Black community at the present time, and is supported by George Dei (1995), Vernon Farrell (1994) and other educators who view the "African-centred" alternative as one which should yield good benefits for many of our students.

The active participation of African Canadians in education, to which I have been alluding, is strongly supported by Agnes Calliste's research as presented in her chapter in this book, "African Canadians organising for Educational Change" (1995). Enid Lee, myself and others who presented on education in the Association of African Studies Conference in Toronto, November, 1994 focused on this community connection as a cornerstone in Black students' development. The community forums on education at this conference, organised by George Dei and others, were considered by many as the *soul* of the conference. Lee's paper "On Any Given Saturday" analysed the active work of the Black community, including parents, in programmes to support Black students: tutoring, counselling and teaching material which was not part of the regular school curriculum, etc. She made reference to CABE's (Canadian Alliance of Black Educators) Saturday Tutorial Programme, the African Heritage Educators' Network (North York) Saturday Classes, the programme of OPBC and the Scarborough Black Education Committee, etc. The Black Education Project of the 1960s and

70s as well as the work of the Black Secretariat were part of the discussion of these workshops. The model of *Black Focused Schools* surfaced in many deliberations at that conference. In addition, it was the topic of one of the community workshops where the meaning and relevance of these schools and the fears they generate were aired with the passion this topic invariably stirs up among Black people.

The work of the Organisation of Parents of Black Children (OPBC) and the Black Secretariat received much attention in these workshops. If we focus on the life of OPBC since its inception in 1980, those of us who are founding members of this organisation and have been active in it since, are witness to the persistence of Black parents' disenchantment with the education system. It was our disillusionment which made necessary the formation of this organisation in the first place, and it is our critical voices which continue to enliven it and sustain it as the group struggles for real change in education. (OPBC Tenth Anniversary document, June 9, 1990).

The work of OPBC can serve to illustrate the timbre of the voice of parents advocating on behalf of their children. A review of the various submissions by this organisation to the Toronto Board of Education, 1979–1995, Ontario Ministry of Education and the recent Royal Commission on Learning, 1994, should help us locate the persistent themes in Black parents' discussion of the education system and our children's place in it. Many of these themes have become identified with the voice of Black parents and community advocates for change. To reiterate, Black parents and community have been engaged in a struggle for educational change since the nineteenth century and earlier, but the struggle though of long duration has not produced results which we anticipated. However, the point cannot be over-emphasized that we have been active participants. Let us consider two of the submissions from OPBC as examples of the critical work of Black parents: one to the Toronto Board of Education in November, 1985, and the second to the Royal Commission on Learning June, 1994.

On November 28, 1985, a group of parents from the OPBC met with the Associate Director of Programs of Toronto Board of Education to discuss our continuing concerns about the education our children receive. This discussion later became part of an internal report which the Board reviewed on March 6, 1986. OPBC's statement of complaints included the following:

- the high drop-out rate [among Black students]
- lack of Black teachers as role models in the system
- the persistent 'invisibility' of Black Studies and Black History within the curriculum
- the present ignorance of teachers about Black culture and the history of Blacks in Canada
- the over-representation of Black students in non-academic schools
- the low level of teacher expectations of Black student achievement
- the crucial question of curriculum implementation
- *the incomprehensible school system* [Italics mine][11]

The Board Minutes in which the above statement was reported continued: "these wide-ranging concerns indicate the need for a review of the current policy and practice as they affect the education of Black children, in order that the Director of Education and the Board take effective action to deal with these concerns"[12]

It is important to note that this Toronto Board internal report for discussion at a meeting of the elected trustees of the Board was precipitated by a *motion* placed by a member of OPBC, Keren Brathwaite, the writer of this chapter, before the Board's Heritage Languages and Concurrent Programmes Consultative Committee (HELACON). The motion stated:

That the Director of Education establish a consultative committee on the education of Black students in Toronto schools with the following terms of reference:

(1) To examine, in the light of current Board policy and practice, the concerns expressed by HELACON and the Organisation of Parents of Black Children about the education of Black students in Toronto schools.

(2) To recommend to the Director and to the Board appropriate action.[13]

The above is one of many of our proposals to a Board of Education, but it is significant that this proposal to the Toronto Board to establish a consultative committee bore fruit in the *Report on the Education of Black Students in Toronto Schools*, 1988, a study which contains 58 recommendations aimed at improving education experiences and outcomes for our students. However, from 1988 to 1995 not enough measurable improvement has taken place among our students as a group.[14] It is apparent from the research that the collective condition of our students has deteriorated rather than improved in recent years, though individual Black students have excelled beyond expectations, as is often reported in our community newspapers. Individual successes of our students are laudable, but when the group continues to lag behind, we believe it is a sign of deep systemic problems which have been troubling both the parents and the students. Many parents have been at the centre of questioning and challenging the education system over these systemic conditions which have a negative influence on Black students' schooling. Often parents whose children are performing well in school who express their views in OPBC meetings, will almost apologise out of empathy with the many who expose their children's education scars. "But for the grace of God, there go I" is a sentiment not restricted to the Church.

It is important to stress that the critical themes which Black parents frequently discuss in groups such as OPBC, the Scarborough Black Education Organisation, in community forums and in one-on-one conversations I have been party to, have remained virtually the same for the past 15 years and also bear much resemblance to many of the concerns of Black people in Upper Canada (Ontario) more than a century ago.[15] The concerns about racism, equity, drop-outs, representation in curriculum and staffing, teacher expectations, setting up our own institutions and the role of parents and community in education remain persistent. OPBC's oral and written submissions to the Royal Commission on Learning (Ontario, 1994) is another echo of the concerns which parents presented nearly a decade earlier to the Toronto Board of Education.

In its June 6, 1994 written submission, OPBC drew the attention of the Royal Commission on Learning (1994) to the following:

> The school system is a reflection of the larger society in which we live with persistent problems of racism, stereotyping and the lack of equity in all areas. These problems have been discussed and documented over the past several years. It must therefore be emphasised that racism is endemic within the system of education and for us it is the major obstacle. Thus new reports, however well-meaning, will not bring about change without firm and decisive action.[16]

Here OPBC was focusing the attention of the Commission on the impact of race on the schooling of African Canadian students and pleading for *action* rather than recommendations to arrest the situation that was well known and well studied.

OPBC's written submission was preceded by an oral presentation given by 5 members representing the organisation which was invited to meet with the Commission on October 13, 1993. It is noteworthy that there was much harmony between OPBC's presentation and those of the Black Educators' Working Group, the Canadian Alliance of Black Educators and the Jamaican Canadian Association which also made their submissions on the same evening. The verbal response which was reported to me as coming from a member of the Commission was a comment on the *passion* of the parents. But *passion* indeed there should be when one's children — (one's future) have been habitually floundering in the school system, many dropping out of it or barely surviving in it. *Passion* pushes the African Canadian community to action vis a vis the school system, which this chapter has shown to be a hostile, unwelcoming place for many Black parents and our students. *Passion* sustains our struggle, which for some parents is carried out with almost religious fervour as we confront the burden of failure weighing down the group of children we are parenting. Which other group in Canada would have accepted the unjust conditions that have been impacting on our children's future for so long?

The reference to *new reports* in OPBC's submission is a reminder of the numerous documents, reports and recommendations which have resulted from the study of Black students' alienation at all levels of the education system that have remained ignored and unimplemented — "gathering dust on shelves," as the expression goes in the Black community. The reference to new reports alludes to what the system has failed to deliver to our students. *Implementation* is a word which often punctuates our discussion of education. *Implementation* and *accountability* we use as measures for the *progress* some educators and boards have attempted to lure us into believing has taken place — because some *words/recommendations* are written on paper about our cause.

The 22 pages of submission from OPBC comments on areas which are troubling in Black students' education:

- Effects of racism, labelling and stereotyping
- Curriculum Concerns
- Parent Involvement in Education
- Education Governance-Accountability
- Our Vision and Conclusion.

Our discussion is followed by 34 recommendations, 9 of which deal with School/Parent/Community Partnerships. They are:

- Schools should hold regular open forums for students to discuss their problems with school staff and parent groups.

- *Schools must include and involve parents in meaningful ways. Parents must be involved in the decision-making processes at the local school level, the Board of Education level and the Ministry of Education.*

- One member of the teaching staff in every school should be appointed as a community liaison person.

- *Parents must be involved in the evaluation of what is good quality education in the schools.*

- *Clearly defined school procedures should be instituted to allow parents and students input in the evaluation of teachers/administrators.*[17] [Italics mine].

The place for parents which our recommendations delineated gained some profile in the Report of the Royal Commission (1994) where the role of the community and parents as partners in education is seen as an essential alliance referred to as the first engine "to drive the momentum of large-scale reform."[18] The Commission went on to recommend the formation of School Community Councils, which would include parent participation, "responsible for bringing appropriate resources into the school to assume some of the obligations teachers now bear alone."[19] Recommendations 108–111 formulate the function and design of the Councils which would assume an administration function in the school.

For African Canadian parents and educators, there is now much concern over the formation of these Councils, (by whatever name). The concept has been discussed by some parents and educators in our community who see accountability in education and lack of implementation of equity policies as a major hurdle to achieving our goals. Who will sit on these Councils? How will they be selected? How representative will these Councils be of the student body, parents and community of the school? What powers will they have to influence the direction of the schools: What is taught? What are the priorities? These questions some of us have been discussing with the lone African Canadian representative on Ontario's Parent Council who conveyed our concern about representation to those charged with drawing up the guide-lines for the operation of School-community Councils which should have a role in the schools from 1996.

These questions could lead to critical examination of the design and mandate of the council. The legislation of Ontario's first Parent Council in September 1993 was considered a bold, political act by some, but for many of us who had been involved in the vibrant parent movement of the 1980s, it seemed a measure long overdue, that had already been pre-empted by the Toronto Board, for example, whose Parent Council was established earlier in 1992.

What Ought We to do Now, After the Dialogue and the Struggle?

This chapter has cited and commented on examples of African Canadian parents' engagement with the school system, as well as their central place in the historical struggle that Black people in Canada have carried out in the name of education reform for the *saving* of African Canadian students. Ours has been a righteous cause fired by our indignation over a condition which has festered for an unacceptable length of time. When our offsprings do not receive their nurturing in public institutions which we support with our dollars, then if we do not cry out, the stones will.

I have established that as a people we have not been idle, but have expended much energy and hard work on improving the academic performance of African Canadian students. Parents have put commendable effort in the pursuit of our goal of just and equitable treatment for our students. Many Black parents have participated in their children's formal education, even when schools are unwelcoming of our presence (which many are); even when Parent Teacher Associations (PTA's), Area Education Councils and Parent Involvement Committees disregard our agenda items (as many Black parents have complained over the years), or placed our concerns on the low priority list. And if some Black parents stay away from the schools, then so do many other parents from different racial, ethnic and socio-economic groups, yet the results of their general student population are far stronger than our students as the Grade Nine Student Surveys (Toronto Board) have shown over many years.[20]

Yet despite the barriers and the disappointments, the African Canadian community has made and continues to make a remarkable contribution to educational thought and critical pedagogy in Canada, probably because our concerns and fears about education have been so strong that we constantly raise the issues, ask the questions, and make suggestions to institutions in Ontario, Nova Scotia, Quebec and other provinces for arresting a condition that has produced in us a group head-ache.

Our work has been in the form of projects, interventions, innovations, proposals to education institutions, and much research. We have established independent or co-sponsored tutorial programmes, Saturday schools, parent education seminars, mentoring programmes, Black Education Projects, Each One Teach One support groups, etc., and in our community, some independent private schools have been attracting parents who can afford to pay for a service or who make the necessary sacrifice for what they hope will be academic success for their own children. Private institutions such as Higher Marks, Centre for Achievement, C.A.R.E., and the counselling provided by Goodall's Counselling Service and others have also been well utilised in our community's goal of higher educational attainment for our children. These have been used by many parents to fill the gaps in the offerings of the schools. *Innovations in Black Education* (1994) has analysed the purposes and results of some of the community efforts as well as the institutional initiatives which were designed to enhance Black students' success. Further work is needed on the variety of these programmes and their impact on our students of African heritage. Many believe that our community projects have served as a life-line for many Black youth *disengaged* from school — to use George Dei's term.

What has been our aim in this work which some have pursued with missionary zeal? What has motivated us to remain engaged? Our aim has been to bring about a *change* in formal education systems so that principles like *equity* and *justice* and *anti-racism* in which we believe will be put into practice; that our students' alienation will be lessened and their sense of belonging will be strengthened. We have been pursuing a *change* that we hoped would accomplish for our students more satisfaction than they have had up to this point in their schooling. However, this *change* requires a change in the manner in which the system views our children, how it relates to them and how much it is really interested in educating them. I have been part of this movement for change for over 20 years and the movement is now reflecting on *where we need to go and what we need to do at this time*. What is the next move we should make? Should we be tentative and careful now, or is this perhaps the time to try some bold measures to arrest a chronic condition? We need to ponder seriously these questions and seek answers to them, for the *change* we have been pursuing with much intensity has been eluding us — like a firefly whose glimmer we sometimes see, but it soon disappears.

One of the reasons why the theme of African Canadian parent education engagement has been so important to me is that I have over the years become a constant listener to narratives of frustration, disappointment or despair with the public system which is charged with educating our children. Very few Black parents are satisfied — at least among the many with whom I have been communicating over the years. Few of us are able to share narratives of *success* of our own children, not even among friends and colleagues from the professional class who expected their children to exceed their accomplishments. Some parents I know are so disappointed in their own children's performance that they are embarrassed to disclose what their true situation is. Several educators have confided to me their regret that they did not school their children outside of Canada. In an age when many parents across race, class, language and gender are experiencing various levels of disenchantment with education, the voices of Black people can be distinguished from many other voices in the clarity of our conviction of what is wrong in the system for our students.

To the African Canadian parent who made an appointment with the principal of his son's Grade Six class to complain about the unruly atmosphere in his classroom and his son's need for more challenging work, the principal's response was: "If you don't like things here, why don't you return to Barbados?" Return to *Barbados*, when the majority of these youth were born in Canada! Another parent experienced the humiliation so many have experienced when her son's principal stifled her complaints with his words, "This is my school and I run it the way I like," words with which many of us are familiar, even when they are unspoken.

Such episodes, which are myriad, confirm there is a need for improvement in the school's manner of relating to and communicating with parents in general, and very importantly with African Canadian parents. What are we to do now?

I submit that it is time for us to seriously invoke some alternative ways of educating our children, so that they will be filled not only with knowledge, some of which means miseducation, but that they will truly be *filled*. As parents, it is our duty to help our children remain whole and integrated persons, just as they were when we lovingly held their hands and walked with them to Kindergarten on the first day of school.

If we are not allowed a space on their formal education team from which space we can participate as respected and consulted partners, *then we need to pursue some alternative models of education, including the model of African-centred schools*[21] *in our community* — at least for a time — until the education system demonstrates its capability of dealing justly with our collectivity of African Canadian students. Thus far, our research studies prove that the current system does not know how to educate a significant number of our students — and for these students we are also morally responsible, as I stated earlier. Either we remain on the fringes of the traditional education team with little power to effect change or we locate ourselves where we can make a difference. Either we have a substantial role on the team in the formal education system, or we concentrate more on using the resources in our various communities to help ·educate those who need a more wholesome, nurturing environment for survival.

It is obvious to me that we now need some Marva Collins Schools[22] and more African-centred pedagogy as Abena Walker[23] employs in Washington, D.C. to help arrest the conditions I have critiqued in this paper. We need to transform some of our *Saturday Schools* into *All Week Schools* and our church basements into *African Canadian Centres of Learning*, for herein might lie some of our children's educational salvation.

DEDICATION
I dedicate this chapter to the memory of the late Lilly Snider, friend and former teacher at McMurrich Public School, with whom in the 1970's and early 80's, I often discussed the education of African Canadian students.

NOTES
1. The terms "African Canadians" and "Blacks" are interchangeable in this chapter.

2. See Toronto Board *Final Report of the Work Group on Parental Involvement*. November 1991; Report of the Royal Commission on Learning. *For the Love of Learning*, 1994; *Rethinking Schools*, Spring 1993. Vol. 7, No. 3; The Ontario Parent Council Application Statement, Ontario Ministry of Education, 1993.

3. See A. Calliste "Blacks' Struggle for Education Equity in Nova Scotia." In V. D'Oyley (ed.) *Innovations in Black Education in Canada*. Toronto: Umbrella Press, 1994; W. W. Anderson and R. W. Grant *The New Newcomers*. Toronto: Canadian Scholars Press, 1987. First published 1975; G.

Dei *Drop Out or Push Out? The Dynamics of Black Students Disengagement from School.* Final report to the Ministry of Education, Toronto, 1995; Toronto Board. *Education of Black Students in Toronto Schools,* 1988; BLAC Report on Education. *Redressing Inequity – Empowering Black Learners,* December 1994. C. E. James "I Don't Want to Talk About It." *Orbit 25*(2). 1994. pp. 26–29.

4. The Ronald Edmonds Summer Academy Document, 1995.

5. P. Solomon *Black Resistance in High School.* New York: State University of New York Press, 1992; Panel discussion with Carl James and Black students at African Studies Association Conference, Toronto, November 1994.

6. K. Brathwaite "The Black Student and the School: A Canadian Dilemma." In S. W. Chilungu and S. Niang (eds.). *African Continuities/L'Heritage Africain.* Toronto: Terebi 1989, pp. 195–216.

7. G. Dei. Presentation to OPBC on his research on African Canadian Students, May 1995.

8. K. Dehli with Ilda Januario. *Parent Activism and School Reform in Toronto.* October 1994. p. 4.

9. See A. Calliste. "Blacks' Struggle for Education Equity in Nova Scotia." In V. D'Oyley (ed.). *Innovations in Black Education in Canada.* Toronto: Umbrella Press, 1994; F. Case *Racism and National Consciousness.* Toronto: Plowshare Press, 1977; A. Cooper – Presentation to OPBC on The African Canadian Historical Struggles in Education, Feb. 1994; R. W. Winks *The Blacks in Canada: A History.* Yale University Press, 1971; OPBC Papers 1980–1995.

10. See K. Dehli and Ilda Januario *Parent Activisim and School Reform in Toronto* 1994; A Cooper's presentation to OPBC, Feb. 1994 also discussed the Black community's education activism.

11. Toronto Board. *Education of Black Students in Toronto Schools* 1988, pp. 6–7.

12. ——— p. 7

13. ——— p. 5

14. See Toronto Board of Education *The 1991 Every Student Survey*, Parts 1, 2, 3. Research Services; also Stephen Lewis *Letter to the Premier*, Toronto, 1992; Complaints brought to the Consultative Committee on the Education of Black Students. Toronto Board, 1988–1995.

15. See K. Brathwaite, A. Calliste, R. Winks.

16. OPBC Submission to the Royal Commission on Learning. Toronto, June 6, 1994. p. 3.

17. ——— p. 19–20.

18. Report of the Royal Commission on Learning 1994. A Short Version. p. 10.

19. ——— p. 11.

20. See Toronto Board of Education. *Every Student Survey*, Parts 1, 2, 3. Research Services. 1991.

21. In my view of African-centred education, I place emphasis on the African Canadian student being the centre of the education process and I believe their education must include them, motivate them and develop in them a variety of skills and knowledge. African-centred pedagogy must also utilize the complex global context in which Black people operate and interact with others, and should not be defined so narrowly that the fuller picture is missing. It should engage students in a range of challenging courses, including Language, Mathematics, Science, Culture, History and Philosophy, the Arts, Business, Physical Education, Design and Information Technology. See also George Dei "Rethinking 'African-Centred Schools' in Euro-Canadian Contexts" (1995), in this book.

22. Marva Collins' Schools in Chicago have been documented as being successful in educating African-American students who were failing in the regular system.

23. Abena Walker is an African-American educator who runs an African-centred school in Washington, D.C., supported by the State.

Chapter Seven

TEACHERS AND PARENTS
CO-EDUCATORS FOR THE SUCCESSFUL EDUCATION OF BLACK STUDENTS

VENETTA E. GOODALL

A school system is a primary component of its society. Therefore, the manner is which the society perceives such factors as race, colour, ethnicity, gender, and uses these to determine the capabilities and opportunities of its adult citizens would be similar to how its educators perceive the student population. If teachers and parents of Black students are prepared to accept this as a fact of life, they will be sending and confirming a message of hopelessness to their students, irrespective of the students' abilities, efforts and ambitions. Many Black students with whom I have had discussions have expressed a fatalistic view of their lives, based on the manner in which the school perceives them and treats them.

However, teachers and parents can be instrumental in making sure that the school experiences of Black students will not give rise to such a bleak view. In today's society teachers alone cannot educate Black children as effectively as they would like to and neither can the parents by themselves. Educators need new, meaningful and consistent approaches to educating Black students, so that their academic achievement will reflect their potential. The primary focus of this chapter is to discuss and illustrate one such approach based on the notion of *Parents as Co-educators*. This approach can make a significant and positive difference in the quality of Black students' education. But first I will offer a few observations about today's Black children and youth.

Parents and teachers must keep in mind that the Black youths of today are different from those of past generations in many ways. For this reason their parents and teachers need new attitudes and strategies in educating them both at home and at school. They must make sure that they are not pouring "New wine into old wineskins, or else the wineskins break, the wine is spilled, and the wineskins are ruined. But … put new wine into new wineskins, and both are preserved."[1] The minds, attitudes and expectations of today's youth are greatly influenced by the social and technological evolutions which bring a world of "teachers" to their fingertips outside of school and they are also influenced by their society which claims to embrace the right of every individual to be educated to their potential, irrespective of her or his race, colour or creed. Today's Black youths are more knowledgeable about their world, and more perceptive and critical of the behaviour of those who influence their lives at home, at school and in the larger society.

Black youth pose new challenges in guidance and education to their parents and teachers who might have experienced a different world as youths. Yet, they are charged with the responsibility of enabling these students to fulfil their dreams and aspirations, and to become productive and successful human beings. They need to be nurtured and guided well at home to build their confidence and their sense of self. "But confidence and self-esteem … also come from getting things done in school."[2] And, these "things" need to reflect who they are as individuals, as "products" of a new era, as Black students with a cultural heritage, whose people have made, and and continue to make, significant contributions to the world.

One of the most effective ways to really educate Black students is to have teachers and parents pooling their resources.

Black parents have a body of cultural knowledge and information about their children which is essential to their success in the formal system and to their teachers' understanding of them. Even the most brilliant and well-intentioned teacher cannot glean this information by working independently in a classroom, while getting on with the job of teaching, evaluating etc. They and the parents should be regularly engaged in sharing information and discoveries about the children. Parents also have ideas and professional skills and knowledge which can make meaningful contributions to the students' programmes. In addition, parents can be realistic role models for students. As Radwanski affirms:

> Parents have essential roles to play beyond watching from the sidelines and complaining about the quality of education.... It is important for teachers and school administrators to recognize that they do not have the monopoly on academic wisdom and insights."[3]

The above discussion suggests that teachers and parents need to become co-educators in order to educate Black students successfully. This team approach is essential, and should embrace all children's learning: "Children who are well behaved and working at grade level need this support just as much as those with learning difficulties, those who are unmotivated, or those who lack self-discipline."[4]

Many Black parents may initially think this form of participation is too demanding and time consuming, and some teachers may perceive it as intimidating or intrusive. However, it is a fact that "Children are best educated in an atmosphere of close co-operation between their parents and their school."[5]

The following are three examples of the design and implementation of my programme to involve parents as co-educators during my tenure as a teacher in Toronto. Parent involvement was part of my style of teaching, rather than a project to be formally evaluated. I utilized informal evaluation which relied largely on observation and discussion to assess the impacts of my teaching method on students' learning.

These three programmes took place in: a grade four class (Shirley Street Junior Public School), in a Special Education Programme — Senior, and in a grade eight class (Winona Drive senior Public School). The parents with whom I worked came from a variety of ethnic, racial and socio-economic backgrounds, and they had diverse jobs and careers.

My primary aim for each class was to identify a need which was common to all of the students and which their parents could help me to meet. I then dialogued with the parents as a group to ascertain how they could work with me and the children in meeting these needs. I also wanted to have at least one monthly discussion with them about the students' general progress and development.

Grade Four Programme of Parent Involvement

In the grade four class I taught, the children needed practical experiences in at least the basic subjects — reading, language and mathematics. My objective was to get the parents involved in providing this practical experience. After meeting and discussing the children's curriculum with the parents, they decided to work with the children and produce a Spring Carnival which would help the students gain the practical experience. They also decided to take up my proposal of monthly parents' meetings.

At these meetings we focussed on the general progress of the class and I dealt with specific children privately. The parents felt comfortable about talking about their children: their improvement in school, their behaviour at home etc. With their help, I got to know the children very well. At the official reporting sessions, the parents came well informed, which made the sessions meaningful, relaxed and pleasant. At the meetings we also made plans for the Carnival. The parents decided that the children should raise money for it, and they did. The parents provided the other necessary items.

The children wrote and sent letters and invitations to teachers, relatives and friends. They created posters and other forms of advertisements which they displayed in the school and the community. They composed a carnival song which inspired the composition of a class song. They were responsible for the entertainment which was comprised of songs, skits, dances etc.... They made and bought games of chance and operated the stalls with their parents.

With the proceeds from the Carnival the class opened an account at a neighbourhood bank. This was the occasion of a field trip. The manager of the bank welcomed the class and spent time with the children sharing his knowledge of banking and answering their questions. The children donated one hundred dollars to the Hospital For Sick Children to help in research in Multiple Sclerosis. This gave occasion for another field trip which parents also attended. The proceeds also financed a visit to the African Lion Safari. The balance went towards purchasing gifts for the children's end-of-year awards.

Impacts of the Parents As Co-Educators

The parents' participation in this programme had an impact on the programme, the children, the parents themselves and the teacher.

The Programme

It was evident that the parents' involvement provided a variety of practical experiences for every area of the programme — mathematics, reading, oral and written language, music, drama, art, enrichment. The music consultant used the children's music compositions in workshops in the music programme and the children were elated and felt very special as a class.

The Children

The children became a very happy and relaxed group: they displayed an eagerness, not anxiety, to do well academically. Problems of discipline were eliminated. They became more responsible, co-operative and caring; "gangs" or "clubs" were reunited, and even family "impasses" got resolved! Attendance and oral communication improved considerably: the children were in school more and so had more need and opportunities to communicate with one another and their teachers. It was also evident that they became more aware of the fact that their parents can play a role in their schooling. One could see and "hear" their pride. Their increasing confidence and self-esteem were evident in every aspect of their academic performance.

The Parents

The parents became more communicative with both the teacher and the school. They shared their children's out-of-school difficulties more comfortably and freely with the teacher and they realized that teachers are interested in the total development of the child and not only in her/his academic progress. They became more interested in the education of the class: it became not only, " How is my child doing?" but "How's the class doing?" Some parents wanted to know if other classes in the school were having similar parent support. They later expressed their desire to their children's teacher in the following year to continue this interaction as a support group.

The Teacher

As a teacher, I became more knowledgeable about the children. Their parents' input into my programme helped to make the job of teaching easier and more enjoyable. There were no behaviourial problems; the children became very co-operative, got their work done and reporting was much less strenuous. I had a better understanding of how to handle the "inappropriate" behaviour of some parents. I recall the case of a girl who was away frequently on Mondays. The notes which gave the reasons always came on Tuesday mornings. After a while, I thought the pattern of absenteeism was too consistent and this warranted a discussion with her parent(s). Her mother subsequently confided that she worked late each evening during the week and on Saturday. On Sunday she had many chores but was "free" on Monday and it was the only day she could make the time to love and nurture her daughter and to make her feel very special. After that I did not need a letter of explanation when that student was away on a Monday.

The Special Education Class — Senior

Involving the Parents

In the Special Education class my objective in working with the parents was twofold — to help the students to perform better academically and to improve their confidence and self-esteem. After sharing these aims with them, they agreed to: 1)

Attend the monthly parent-teacher meetings; 2) Monitor their children's academic work at home and every two weeks indicate their opinions on forms which I would provide; 3) Try to criticize their children positively, rather than negatively.

The parents were consistent in following this plan of action and this helped me in realizing my teaching objectives, as the following observations by the parents, the students and the teacher indicate.

Parents' Observations

The parents said that they became more aware of their children's programme and that they saw a steady progress in their academic performance, their confidence and their self-esteem. They felt the children were showing more interest in, and had better attitudes towards, going to school and doing their school work. They also observed that at home the children's discipline had shown marked improvement and that communication between them and their children had improved significantly. They felt more involved in their children's formal education and experienced a more meaningful participation in the school.

Students' Participation

The following is a summary of the students' responses to the question, "What do you think are the results of your parents' involvement in your eduction?" They felt their parents' participation helped to make them feel "good" and confident. It also made them try harder to improve the quality of their work and behaviour. In their opinions, their parents had a better understanding of what they were doing in school and that helped "to keep us on our toes," and they communicated better with their parents. In their view, the monitoring of their work by their parents "is a pretty good operation that has worked for us." They had more respect for their parents' opinions also.

Teacher's Observations

I observed that the students developed a better feeling of self-worth following the inclusion of their parents in the programme: they demonstrated more confidence in expressing themselves without seeming inferior or aggressive. They were eager to raise the standard of their academic work and one student went from grade 1.0 to grade 3.6 in reading in the first term. Four students eventually had half or full-time integration into the regular grade eight class and went on to general level programmes in secondary schools. The students did their home work consistently and the standard improved significantly.

Those who had disciplinary problems showed remarkable improvement in self-control: one student who came from a behavioural class had no unusual difficulty in abiding by the expectations of the class and the school. In the classroom they became much more congenial towards one another. Their regular attendance was a contributing factor to all of the above.

Grade Eight Programme:
Interactions with Parents

After a discussion with the grade eight class about their educational aspirations, I realized that they needed exposure to a wider variety of career options and real role models. Providing this exposure became one of my aims as I included their parents as co-educators in this area. I invited the parents to a meeting, and after a discussion, they demonstrated a willingness to participate in their children's formal education. I gave them the grade eight curriculum and invited them to think of areas in which they could lend their professional knowledge and skills. A number of parents volunteered to do so and they all agreed to attend the monthly parent-teacher meetings.

At the meetings, we discussed the general progress of the students and the parents looked over the children's work for the month and discussed their impressions of their children at home.

Several parents held workshops with the students in different subjects. For example, one parent, the director of Leukemia Research at the Toronto Western Hospital, had the students in his laboratory for a day and exposed them to every facet of his work which allowed the students to expand their knowledge of science and technology, and also to learn more about the careers which were involved.

A poet held several sessions in poetry and a journalist conducted workshops on different forms of writing, etc.

At the end of the school year, the parents and the students organized a banquet to which they invited Toronto Board trustees, senior administrators and teachers. The students decided on a formal dress-code for that event.

Outcomes

The students' academic performance improved dramatically. Their growth in self-esteem, confidence, responsible behaviour and independence was noticed by other teachers in the school. Students noted that they became more aware of career choices because of the parents who participated in the programme. One female student commented, "Now I know that I don't have to be a doctor or a nurse in order to work in a hospital." The parents and the students observed that they understood each other better and that their shared experiences and communication were the main reasons for this.

Conclusion

It was obvious to me that all the goals I had for the students' improvement were overwhelmingly realized primarily because of their parents' input as co-educators. The knowledge which the parents shared with me about their children on an ongoing basis was invaluable and contributed to how I listened to students, interpreted their behaviour, perceived and handled their personal needs, interacted with them, programmed for them, and guided them in their education during the year.

The parents' participation also influenced the children's perception of themselves and their parents in very positive ways: their academic success, social growth and changes of attitude attested to this.

It is also clear that their parents' involvement provided a level of enrichment for their classroom programmes through projects which the parents worked on with the class. This is a bonus which meaningful and planned use of parents as co-educators can contribute to children's education.

Evidently, all the students in these classes benefited from their parents being co-educators with their teacher. I would like to share a few observations about the Black students in these classes. They, *almost suddenly*, exhibited a pronounced improvement in their school performance, in their general attitude and particularly in their sense of optimism about their abilities. Was this attributable to the fact that their teacher was Black? Neither the parents nor the students openly noted this link during our discussions. It probably was a contributing factor in the sense that I was a role model. However, their distinct changes really became obvious to me when their parents became involved in their schooling. They expressed this in our discussions and so did the parents: one mother remarked that she could not believe the sudden positive change in her son. It was evident that their teacher being Black was not the primary reason for their very noticeable progress because, logically speaking, the Caucasian students should not have done as well as they did because their teacher was not of their race or ethnic origin. I am convinced that the following variables, in order of significance, were the major reasons for the extra-ordinary progress the Black students made in those classes.

1. Their parents were their co-educators and were respected as such by their teacher.

2. The exchange of information between their teacher and their parents about the students was invaluable in understanding, planning, guiding and supporting them at school and at home.

3. The curriculum acknowledged that their own people (Black people) were among the contributing people in their society and the world: their programmes also reflected their heritage, and Black parents were among those who shared their professional skills with the classes.

4. Their teacher expected them, as well as the other students, to achieve success consistently and gave them the necessary support to do so.

5. Their teacher, being Black, was a role model.

Conclusion

The reality of our society is that Black students are being taught by teachers of all races and ethnic backgrounds. So,

how can this generation of Black youths, who are so knowledgeable of their world and aware of the rights and privileges
their society should afford them, be educated well? My suggestion is that their teachers and parents become co-educators
and work together in the best interest of Black students.

Governments' educational policies and financial restraints
will come and go, but the need for Black students' education
to be solid and meaningful remains constant. Their education
must give them a sense of worthiness, confidence, the opportunities to achieve academic and economic success, and hope for
a meaningful future. The teachers and parents of Black students, working as co-educators, hold the key to their proper
education.

NOTES

1 Robert H. Schuller, *Possibility Thinkers Bible*, Matthew chapter 9 verse
17.

2 Marjorie R. Simic, Melinda McClain, Micheal Shermis, *The Confident
Learner,* pp. 4–5.

3 George Radwanski, *Ontario Study of the Relevance of Education, and the
Issue of Dropouts*, p. 182.

4 Marjorie R. Simic, Melinda McClain, Micheal Shermis, *The Confident
Learner*, pp. 120–121.

5 George Radwanski, *Ontario Study of the Relevance of Education, and the
Issue of Dropouts*, pp. 182.

Note

DEAR PRINCIPAL

I would like to introduce myself to you as the mother of a Grade Six student who recently enrolled in your school. I believe in good communication between the home and the school, and hope that you and my child's teacher will communicate with me as I will try to work with you in the interest of my child.

As a parent, I take my role seriously and consider myself as an important partner in the education of my child. I have learned through experience that Black parents have to be very vigilant when we enroll our children in school due to low expectations and negative attitudes some teachers have of Black students. I have already experienced some of this in my child's previous schooling, for even though she performed well, she sometimes felt excluded and passed over in the class-room. Like other parents, I wish that my child will feel part of the school, that she will see herself reflected in the curriculum and in the composition of the teaching body. I do not want school to be an alienating experience for her, as it has been for so many of our students over the years.

I would also like to share with you some of my observations about the education of Black students. My involvement in the black community in Toronto and in the Organisation of Parents of Black Children (OPBC) has exposed to me the depth of the problems Black students generally face in schools due to racism, exclusion, steretyping and low expectations of many teachers. I have listened to parents discuss their children's difficulties in school, and have tried to counsel and support some who felt intimidated by the system. Because of my knowledge of the research on Black students as well as the discussions in the conferences and workshops in which I have participated, I am very fearful about my child's education and future. I do not want her to become a high school dropout statistic nor do I want her to be streamed and be limited in any way. I have expectations of her completing her education and allowing herself options in terms of future studies and careers. So please, allow me to be involved in her education so that I can work with the school to help her accomplish her goals.

In my child's previous schools, even though I tried to be part of the school activities and attended all the meetings, I still felt a sense of unease. I felt that the schools are not sufficiently welcoming of us as parents in general, and especially of Black parents. Many of us feel that the atmosphere in the school does not include us. This exclusion of our African heritage must impact negatively on our children's self-esteem, and must affect their academic performance, I believe. Let us be fair to the students. It is important that the school reflects all of them, including my child and other Black sudents. Her connection to her studies is very important to my daughter, as well as to me.

Just as I encourage my child to do her best in school, so I am asking the school to provide the best support for her in every area: the curriculum, the activities, the attitudes and expectations of the teacher, and involvement of parents. The kind of support she needs can be provided only in an anti-racist, inclusive environment in which she can grow and blossom.

I hope that my daughter will enjoy attending your school and will achieve good academic success as I know she is capable of. I hope that she will be taught by caring teachers who will appreciate her heritage and support her aspirations.

Let us work together for the good of my child.

Sincerely,
Muriel Clarke,
Parent

PART THREE

DO THEY MAKE A DIFFERENCE?
DIFFERENCE?
EXAMINING CURRICULAR
PROGRAMMES

Chapter Eight

To: Denny
"Enjoy the reading"
Andrew Allen
may 8, 1996

"I DON'T WANT TO READ THIS"
STUDENTS' RESPONSES TO ILLUSTRATIONS OF BLACK CHARACTERS IN CHILDREN'S PICTURE BOOKS

ANDREW M.A. ALLEN

Introduction

In recent years, there has been an increase in the number of multicultural children's picture books available that depict characters of various racial and ethnic backgrounds. Some of these books eventually become very popular and find their way into most libraries and classrooms. As an elementary school teacher, I was very excited about introducing my students to the rich variety of multicultural literature that was available. I was eager to establish a literature-based reading program in my class that presented the images and experiences that I believed were reflective of all my students and their backgrounds.

Hence, I purchased several multicultural picture books that I believed featured images of people that looked like the various groups of children in the class. I selected several other multicultural picture books from both our local and school libraries as additional reading material for the classroom to introduce the images and experiences of other cultures not represented in my class. I displayed them all around the classroom and in our classroom library or book corner. At that time, I was convinced that this would enhance my reading program by helping to stimulate students' interest and attract them to books, affirm individual self-worth, develop and promote respect and understanding between groups of students from different backgrounds, and enrich the overall classroom learning environment.

My Grade 2 class consisted primarily of students of immigrant and/or working-class backgrounds, whose parents originated from the Caribbean, East Africa, and South and East Asia. I noticed that they seemed uninterested in reading most of the multicultural picture books I had brought to the class. Most of the multicultural literature, and even the more "popular" and award winning picture books, went almost untouched the whole year. I also noticed that my Black students, in particular, became quiet and withdrawn during story time when I read particular picture books depicting Black characters. At times, they even became disruptive and had some difficulty sitting still through some stories.

I became even more interested when I observed that only the Black students continued to resist interacting with the literature with Black characters even after I tried to encourage them to select these books to read. When given a choice, they selected books with traditional European characters and avoided the books with Black characters. They did not seem to share my interest or excitement in the multicultural books. Why was this so? What were their perceptions of the images in the literature? How did this affect their literacy development and my attempts at teaching them to read?

As a way of further exploring my initial observations of the students in my classroom, I arranged to have a number of informal reading lessons with several groups of first and second grade Black students from other classes at my school. I wanted to investigate how these Black students from an urban working-class community respond to picture books depicting Blacks as the main characters. My investigation sought to answer the following questions:

1. How do Black children select or choose picture books to read in their classrooms?

2. How do they perceive Black characters or illustrations portraying the Black experience in books for children?

3. What are the effects of using multicultural literacy materials in literacy programs for Black students?

4. What are the implications of my findings for the education of Black children of working-class backgrounds?

The Argument

The success or failure of Black working-class students in high school is likely to be related to some of their early experiences in school, as well as to the cumulative effect of the entire schooling process. The kinds of attitudes towards books and reading skills they develop in the primary grades might be dependent on a number of factors inherent in the school curriculum and these factors have impact on their educational outcomes. Children's literature, including multicultural picture books, may be the children's first contact with literature, reading and literacy learning (Kiefer, 1983). Thus they are an important starting point for examining the experiences of the students; understanding students' reactions to multicultural picture books would help me, I assumed, to learn more about their literacy development and develop proactive measures to help address the needs of my students.

This chapter attempts to examine Black children's particular reactions and responses to images in children's picture books and interprets those, making assumptions with respect to their experiences as Black children of working-class backgrounds. The students in my school live in a culturally, ethnically and racially diverse urban community with high population density and significant economic disparities. The community has a high immigration and migration rate as well as a high unemployment and under-employment rate and a large amount of government subsidized housing. I will begin by examining the research that outlines the experiences, needs and problems of Black students in the public school system in Ontario.

The Black Experience in Ontario Schools

A review of the academic achievement and retention rates of Black students in the Ontario public school system reveals that these students do not receive the same quality of education as other groups of students, and that they face many barriers to academic success. A number of recent reports, including the *Report of The Royal Commission on Learning* (1994), the Toronto Board of Education *Every Student Survey* (1993), the Stephen Lewis Report (1992) and the *Report of the Four level Government and African Canadian Community Working Group* (1992), all concluded that Black high school students typically had low academic achievement and retention rates, and high truancy and failure rates and were most frequently streamed into low academic tracks. The studies concluded that the policies and actual practices of schools, as well as the curriculum and learning materials, were limiting the opportunities for academic advancement and achievement of Black students. The schools failed to respond effectively to the educational needs of Black students (Dei, 1993; Solomon, 1992 Curtis, Livingstone & Smaller, 1992; James, 1990;).

Black students of working-class families in particular, were most likely to be affected by the "barriers" imposed by academic and social structures, and by ideologies, policies and practices that serve to maintain hegemonic domination of the educational system and the larger social order. For working-class Black students, race and class both affect their school experiences and impact on their educational success. Schools help to reproduce class distinctions, because most working-class children, as a result of their educational and social experiences, tend to remain in their class of origin (Curtis et al. 1992).

Some of the problems of Black students can be attributed to their early schooling experiences, particularly with early classroom reading instruction and materials. Examining multicultural literature portraying Black characters and contexts and the ways Black children interpret them lead to an understanding of some of these experiences. The following sections examine the importance of illustrations and stories in children's literature; particularly the apparently implicit, yet powerful, information and social messages contained in the authors' or illustrators' words and images and their effects on the readers.

The Importance of Illustrations

Children's picture books are a major part of literacy programs. They are designed to be attractive and colourful to motivate children to want to read. Ralston (1990) describes children's literature as an essential teaching tool, a main focus and a springboard to creative activity in whole-language classrooms. Picture books enhance cognitive development; they help readers to form mental images of the information, decode words and comprehend sentences better; they are designed to increase vocabulary levels, and offer opportunities to acquire and practice reading skills, spark imagination and lead to the creation of writing or art; and they also highlight social and moral concerns (Harris, 1990; Elster & Simons, 1985; Schallert, 1980).

Blacks in Children's Picture Books

Traditional representations of Blacks in children's literature and educational media have been characterized by omission or exaggeration. This pattern of selective tradition of domination and subordination of Blacks in children's literature favours the perspectives and world views of the dominant social group, and tends to focus on the exotic, sensational or negative representations, based on the persistent and pervasive use of over generalizations, distortions, misconceptions, misrepresentations, stereotypes and demeaning views of Blacks. Most books are written primarily by and for a middle class audience and they are increasingly alienated from and irrelevant to the realities, concerns and problems of the urban working-class Black children (Taxel, 1993; Harris, 1993; Sims, 1993; Walker & Rasamimanana, 1993; Pierterse, 1992; Harris, 1990; MacCann & Woodard, 1985; Broderick, 1973).

In a recent study examining the historical development of literature written for African American children, Harris (1990) described the depiction of Blacks in children's literature as "essentially stereotyped, pejorative, and unauthentic." She argues that illustrations in children's literature typically show Black people as grotesque caricatures of their race's physical features, simian-like or with protruding eyes and large red lips, and extremely dark skin. She says Black children are portrayed as "pickaninnies": dark skinned, plain, mischievous, comical and poor. She believes the literature reflects the values, knowledge and interpretations of whites, particularly Anglo-Saxons. Harris (1990) also argues that children's literature is potentially a valuable and valued cultural commodity. It mediates between children, cultural knowledge, and socialization by adults and it shapes children's perceptions of the world and their roles in it.

The illustrations also reflect the ideologies, experience and background of the illustrators. Images tell more about the feelings and ideas of the artist or illustrator than about the lives or perspectives of the subject they represent. A racist, sexist and elitist society tends to reproduce race, class and gender biases and the literature it produces tends to mirror the societal attitudes towards particular racial and ethnic groups (Delpit, 1988; Taxel, 1993; Sims, 1993).

The values, principles and assumptions affirmed in children's books are internalized by their readers to such an extent that they become a part of the way they learn to construct the social conventions of their social reality (Taxel, 1993; Sims, 1983). Children also learn not to question the established social order which supports poverty, social class and the different values placed on various groups in society. When poverty and social class are apparent in the images and text, but the literature fails to define it and explain the reason for the disparity, the literature serves to socialize the children to maintain the "status quo" of passivity and conformity. The lack of discussion and explanation further perpetuates the "myth of a classless society" (Ramsay, 1993; Langston, 1988).

The Effects on the Learner

James (1994) points out that when learning materials do not reflect the interests, needs and life experiences of Black and other racial minority students, the information presented to them can serve to marginalize and disengage them from learning and participating in the classroom. When children perceive images as negative, and in conflict with their reality, or as denigrating their self-image and the world they experience, then the effect of the images is oppressive and damaging. James argues that low self-esteem may develop when a child's racial group is constantly portrayed through stereotypes, as low achievers, primitive, or slum dwellers, particularly if there are no discussions which address the issues of bias around these images. He says that without discussion, the Black children may feel their voices are not valued or accepted, and as a result they may be silenced and rendered powerless and invisible in the classroom.

When Black students do not see positive reflections of themselves or positive affirmation of their heritage, they sometimes respond or react in negative ways; it is quite likely that they will not read or value schooling as much, and many of these students may respond by choosing not to learn (James, 1994; Delpit, 1995; Asante, 1991; Harris, 1990). The ways the behaviours of working-class Black students are perceived by the school system affect their educational success in school. Positive responses, attentiveness or conformity and compliance are usually interpreted as reading readiness, or academic ability and they maximize students' literacy success and academic achievement. Negative responses, social resistance or lack of interest are interpreted as deficiency or deviance and impede their success in school (Gilmore, 1992; Solomon 1992).

The students' disproportionately lower reading scores and reading levels may well be the result of their reactions to the curriculum and to instructional strategies. They may also reflect the way school personnel understand these students and respond to their behaviours. Since children's literature is such a powerful part of the schools' socialization and educational processes, it is necessary to interrogate the images we present in relation to the experiences of the readers. How are working-class Black children experiencing the books we use to teach them to read? How are their perceptions of the images in the literature informed by the experiences of their daily lives? Does the representation of Blacks in multicultural picture books reflect the reality of working-class Black children? The following section gives an account of my observations of the responses and reactions of a focus group of first and second grade Black students of working-class backgrounds to a collection of multicultural picture books with Blacks as the main characters.

Black Students' Responses and Reactions

Looking at Illustrations

I presented a collection of multicultural picture books depicting mostly Black characters, attractively displayed on a table in my classroom as part of a reading lesson. The selection consisted mostly of Black or "multicultural" literature from the students' classrooms. The children were invited to freely examine the books. I asked them to pick the stories they wanted to read or wanted me to read to them. I asked the students why they chose particular book(s) or type of books to read. I also asked why they did not choose other books. I probed their responses to find out more about their reactions to the books, particularly their decisions to read or not to read particular books. I wanted to find out what it was about certain books that would make them avoid or refuse to read them.

Some of the children were eager to examine the books. Others, reluctant at first, began looking at the pictures after prompting from their more excited peers. All searched first for books they were familiar with. They looked at the covers, focusing for a longer time on some, and then leafed randomly through the pages, skipping several pages at a time. They continued to pay more attention to the pictures than to the text. They were eager to discuss what they remembered from the illustrations and passed some books on to one another; they scanned the covers of others.

The students were first attracted to, and looked for books or illustrations in books that were familiar to them. These were books they had seen or read before or ones the teacher had read. For example, the book *Daniel's Dog* (Bogart, 1990) was a favourite with many of the children.

Mike: I know this book. Our teacher read this to us. I'm reading this. It is the best. I read it at school before, because he has a friend, he laughs and he has a dog.

Kimberly: It is such exciting. It is about a dog and it is about a baby sister. I like the pictures and I like the story. Because it is such lots of fun and you can learn new words in them. Some pages are very fun. It is a clean book.

The main character of the book, *Daniel's Dog*, is a Black boy who has an imaginary dog. The realistic images portray a range of expressions of the characters, from excitement to sadness. The pictures were brightly coloured and the background was filled with objects that reflected an environment familiar to those living in an urban setting.

Familiar or recognizable objects in the pictures, and the background or setting of the pictures, including the context or environment as perceived by the students, were also other factors that prompted children to read certain books. These books included familiar situations or points of reference for children and related to their reality. For instance, the book *Jonathan and his Mommy*, (Smalls, 1992), elicited these responses from the students:

> **Trini**: Oh! I like this book. Because I just read it. They are walking down the street and stuff. And these kids are colouring with a chalk. She likes walking and talking with her mom and she likes skipping and all those stuff and she likes walking with her son.

> **Kimberly**: This one. Because it is interesting. I like this book. Because it has a lot of words to read and her little boy learns how to do good stuff. The pictures look very interesting. I enjoyed this one.

There were two main Black characters on the cover of the book *Jonathan and His Mommy*: a mother and her son strolling and playing in an outdoor urban environment. The features on the characters were realistically drawn to near photographic likeness. These images were familiar and recognizable to these children and reflected their own urban environment.

The students were attracted to images of characters that were recognizable or tended to closely resemble someone they knew. For instance, Billy was convinced that the character on the cover of the book *Jonathan and His Mommy*, (Smalls, 1992) was that of their gym teacher.

> **Billy**: Mrs. Huxstable! That looks like Mrs. Huxstable. Mrs. Huxstable our teacher.

The children's appraisal of the illustrations was an important criteria for selecting books to read. They tended to prefer more realistic drawings in which the characters' features are clear and recognizable. They were able to identify these books as distinct from those using sketches and simpler portrayal of Black characters. For example, Freddie selected three particular Black picture books he wanted to read because of the style of illustration: *Jamal's Busy Day*, (Hudson, 1991), *Daniel's Dog*, (Bogart, 1990) and *Jonathan and His Mommy*, (Smalls, 1992). These three Black picture books contain realistic representation of the characters and their urban settings.

> **Freddie**: This one is about a busy day. It has good drawings. Good colour. It looks nice. This and this and this is drawing. [points to the three books he selected] This is drawing and this is painting. But these, they're not good enough, because they are painting. [referring to other Black picture books]

Like the other two books Freddie selected, *Jamal's Busy Day* focusses on the experiences of a Black boy in a generic urban environment. The character is shown eagerly going to school to do work, to help the teacher and solve problems.

What Freddie has indicated here is consistent with some of the research on children's preference for artistic styles in illustrations in children's literature. That is, children preferred picture books with detailed realistic or representational styles of drawing (Smerdon, 1976; Keifer, 1983; Harris, 1990). On the other hand, the students tended to ignore and refuse to read most of the other picture books with Blacks as the main character; typically they rejected books that portrayed the Black characters in a simplistic style. For example, the students were particularly opposed to the illustrations in *Galimoto*, (Williams, 1990) and *Hi, Cat!*, (Keats, 1970). Both these books showed simple colour sketches of Black characters.

> **Kimberly**: I don't like this one either. Because it doesn't look that nice. I don't like the way they write the pictures. (*Galimoto*)

> **Freddie**: I don't want to read this, because the pictures are ugly. They look funny. Because the guy's hair look funny and the cat's whiskers are bend-ed. (*Hi, Cat!*)

Inherent in the illustrations of these books, are the hardships, and deprivation associated with poverty. The characters live in two very harsh environments. *Hi, Cat!* portrays Black characters living in a ghetto environment. *Galimoto* depicts a Black boy on the cover in an empty outdoor swampy grassland environment. He is shown wearing no shoes, very little clothing and he has to rummage through garbage to make his own toy.

When the students were asked to elaborate on their initial responses, they indicated that they preferred lighter or more colourful pictures. For example, Freddie had this to say about several of the books on the table:

Freddie: No! I don't want to read these. They are a little dark. The colours [on this one (*Galimoto*)] are a little more light but they could be light light. This and this is dark [pointing to the character's face, arms and legs].

The students rejected those Black picture books which used very dark colours in the illustrations. For instance, regarding the covers of *The Orphan Boy*, (Mollel, 1990) and *The Black Snowman*, (Mendez, 1989) which are mostly coloured in dark shades of brown and blue, and black, the students observed:

Freddie: They are not light. I don't want to read this one because it is dark colours. Look for a good colour, look for something that's good. The pictures, the cover and everything. Just look for ones with bright colours.

Kimberly: It doesn't look interesting to me. It doesn't have that much colours that I like.

Tommy: It doesn't have too much bright colours. That's why I don't like that one.

Jason: Because it doesn't have the right colour. I don't like that colour.

The Orphan Boy is based on a Maasai folktale and the illustrations portray the characters in a harsh, dry, primitive environment. *The Black Snowman* portrays both urban and rural environments with Black characters. The expressions and gestures of the characters are intensely emotional. The characters are mainly seen as angry, sad or pensive. The illustrator used predominantly dark colours or a nighttime setting to depict the story.

When I asked the children why they did not like dark colours, they said they didn't like stories set in darkness or stories about nighttime. They wanted to read stories with familiar daytime settings and they wanted bright colours.

In some of these books, the ways the dark colours, shadows or shading were used tended to set a grim or depressing mood, exaggerating the skin tone of the characters or blocking out some of their features. For example, the children did not like, the shaded-in features of the characters on the cover of *Stevie* (Steptoe, 1969).

> **Leo**: My head (face) is not like that. I don't have any thing black here.

> **Raph**: That looks like a moustache.... No, that doesn't look like me, I'm brown black, he's [Don] light black and that's [the character] dark black.

> **Mike**: Because I don't like his face. It is his head, it's covering here ... on his moustache.

> **Theodore**: The face doesn't show good.

> **Maggie**: I can't see the eyes.

The story in the book *Stevie* is set in an urban environment, but like *The Black Snowman*, the images look depressing and the illustrations exaggerate the shading and dark colours used for the characters' features. The faces on the cover did not have any discernible eyes, nostrils or mouth. Dark shaded areas appeared in the places where these features are supposed to be. The illustrations are so ambiguous in this book that the children confused the character's lips for his moustache. They each said they didn't want to read this book.

With reference to illustrations with bright colourful pictures, the children expressed acceptance for most of the brightly coloured books. For example, they liked the colours in the picture book *Wait and See*, (Munsch, 1993).

> **Simon**: This is my favourite book. I like the colour. This one! My favourite colour and I like the colours. This one is pretty. Woah! It got colours in it. Ooh! This is pretty. Woow! Cool!

> **Jason**: I like colours like this.

Minnie: Because the drawer who made them made it pretty, over here and over here. Pretty colours. Because he made the party hats look pretty and the candle and the cake.

This brightly coloured picture book featured a family of Black characters in a residential suburban environment and included objects familiar to the children. The illustrations depicted familiar children's situations of a birthday party. The children accepted the simple sketches in the illustrations.

On the other hand, the children rejected books they thought exaggerated or overemphasized certain features of the Black characters. For example, the children pointed out that the size of one of one character's head was grossly exaggerated on the cover of *Galimoto* (Williams, 1990). The children interpreted these exaggerated features as meaning that the story related to a specific social or cultural setting that would not be pleasing or interesting to them.

Don: These books are funny. He has a big head.

Leo: Yes, that looks like an African guy that fights. He fights because some people who have heads like that and live in Africa and they fight.

They also rejected illustrations with images depicting situations of poverty; especially where the characters are wearing little or no clothing, or no shoes. Two other students had this to say about the book *Galimoto*.

Raph: There is going to be a slave about this one. There is going to be slaving. I don't want to read about slaving. I just don't!

Mike: I don't want to read it because it is ugly. He's from [Africa], I know, I just look at his face. And his shirt is rip-ted…. It is not interesting because his feet, he's step-ted on mud. I don't want this book.

The book *Galimoto* shows a Black child in an empty open area with no familiar urban reference in the picture showing things like houses, streets or trees. This book failed to motivate the children to want to learn to read it. The children perceived the image on the cover as an indication that the book would be about slavery, war or poverty. Their responses clearly indicated that they didn't want to read about these issues. Consequently, these books did not make them interested in reading.

In another instance, the children pointed and laughed at the illustration of a Black girl in *The River That Gave Gifts: An Afro-American Story* (Humphrey, 1978). Her lips were portrayed red and pink; she also wore ragged clothes, and was barefooted. The illustrator used brightly coloured pictures and simple sketches to portray the Black characters. The features seemed distorted or exaggerated to the children.

> **Leo**: She looks funny. These are funny (pointing to the illustrations on the covers).

The River That Gave Gifts: An Afro-American Story, is also an African-American folktale. The moral of the story centres around teaching the readers to respect the elderly and valuing their own personal gifts and achievements.

The students seemed to take into consideration a number of inter-related factors when looking at illustrations. The common thread through all these factors is familiarity based on their own frames of reference. The children preferred illustrations which depicted Black characters situated in familiar locations, with familiar objects, represented in familiar styles of clothing and involved in familiar activities.

Looking at the Text

Some students read the author's name, or looked at the inside cover or back cover, to find a picture of the author when they were choosing books to read. They were also attracted to books with familiar authors. Some students read aloud the title and the author's name on the cover.

> **Jason**: Fox in Sox by Dr. Seuss. This is Dr. Seuss. It is going to be a tongue twister.

> **Ariel**: Wait and See by Robert Munsch. This is a book I would read. I like Robert Munsch. Because my sister brought one book home with Robert Munsch and I read it and it was fun.

Ariel had read another book before by the author Robert Munsch and had liked the story. She was willing to read this book even though she had never read it before or she had never seen the cover or the pictures before. She was attracted to and chose to read this book mostly because of the familiar author. They also chose other books like *Fox in Sox* Seuss (1965), that featured songs, chants, rhymes or other participatory activities which serve to entertain or involve the students.

The names of characters were also important. Two of the students selected books because the names of the characters in the books, in the title or on the cover were familiar or had some relevance to their lives. An example was, *Where Are You going Emma?*, (Titherington, 1988). One student said she liked the book and had this to say about it:

> **Jasmine**: Because it has a lot of my mom's name. Her name is Emma and it has Emma.

Another student was very excited about seeing his name in the title on one of the book covers, feeling the story might relate to him or someone like himself. He said he liked the book, "Because it has my name on it." He proceeded to show the cover and some of the pictures inside to everyone at the table. When the names used for characters in children's books relate to familiar ethnic or culturally specific names of various groups of students the books become more appealing. Familiarity is important as it helps to attract the children to the books.

Some of the students were attracted to books that seemed to have a small amount of text on the pages. They associated smaller text with easier readability. They also wanted to read simple word books, alphabet books and books at a lower reading level with simpler words. They were able to read some of these books because the text was easier to decode. When asked why they chose certain books, they indicated that the books contained easy or familiar "short" words.

Some of the multicultural books had large amounts of text informing the children about a particular aspect of Black or African heritage. The quantity of text per page was a deterrent to the children. They perceived that less text made a book easier to read.

Discussion

A close examination of the books used in this study produces

161

some interesting generalizations. The illustrations in some of these picture books depict Blacks with exaggerated features, or features obscured by shadows and shading, wearing pauper clothing, and represented by sketches instead of detailed realistic drawing. Many Black characters tend to be portrayed looking unhappy, depressed, upset or as having silly (mischievous or comical) grins. They were rarely portrayed as happy, contented or enthusiastic.

In many of the books examined, there was a large amount of text and the context of the story was unfamiliar to the children at this age. The picture books often exaggerated poverty and the Black characters depicted were usually situated in an environment filled with adversity and ladened with traditional stereotypes. The backgrounds in most of the books were dark and gloomy or portrayed a stereotypical urban ghetto, or jungle, or harsh dry barren flatland with grass huts and meagre starving animals, or conditions of enslavement, or hardships after emancipation.

The children perceived these scenes as unfamiliar or uninteresting. There were few familiar objects and no exciting children's objects in the background of these pictures. The illustrations did not seem to capture or reflect the children's interests and the images were harsh and unpleasing to them. The illustrations presented scenarios, images and situations that were very different from the children's realities and perceptions. Most of the books examined by the students failed to motivate them to want to read.

Therefore, familiarity with the images and story content is very important when children are learning to read. The students are less likely to select any material they perceive as unfamiliar or outside their reality or world of interest. The appeal of story content and the illustrations and text are based on their background knowledge and experiences, and their social and developmental constructions of reality as six and seven year old children.

Since these students reacted negatively to the multicultural literature I was using in my classroom, I assumed it had some negative effect on them. The ways that Black characters, in particular, were depicted in the picture books failed to attract my Black students to the books and so discouraged them from reading them. Their attitude towards reading in general, their engagement with reading materials and consequently their reading and literacy development suffered as a result.

It seems that the use of Black or multicultural picture books and the ways in which I have been using them in my classroom posed a barrier to the literacy development of my Black students. The children acted out by becoming disruptive or silent, uninterested or inattentive. Sometimes they refused to participate in storytime or silent reading, or generally tried to avoid interacting with the literature. For instance, during one of the reading lessons, Leo asked to be dismissed to go to the washroom when I started reading *Hi Cat!* (Keats, 1970). The others all started asking to go at the same time. They appeared uninterested and they fidgeted constantly in their seats. I reflected on the number of times this may have happened in my classroom and concluded that before we blame children for inattention, we must learn to read their signs of resistance to the literature we offer them.

Conclusion

I have learned a great deal from my observations of the students, from their responses, and from reading the research literature on related issues. As an elementary teacher working with a diverse group of students in a working-class community, using multicultural literature, I needed to take into account my students' racial and social class backgrounds and how it contrasted, or even conflicted, with my own. I needed first to recognize and interrogate my own biases as they relate to the learning materials I use, my instructional strategies and my reading program.

I have come to realize that I had hardly ever asked my students about their perceptions of the material I brought to the classroom for them to read. I needed to give up my traditional role as a teacher and consult with my students. I had also neglected to engage the students in any critical discussions of the multicultural children's literature that I used. As a teacher, I needed to seek out all the perspectives of my students, and particularly those that would likely differ most from my own, and I needed to learn to understand my own power in the classroom as a teacher. Most of all, I needed to listen and be willing to hear those voices silenced in the discussions regarding issues of power and pedagogy (see Delpit, 1988).

I needed to admit my cultural and class bound perceptions of my students, especially when these students do not respond to schooling in ways that I have come to expect. I needed to understand the cultural, economic, and social lives of students to appreciate how they interpret their school experience. Well-intentioned teachers may actually serve to reinforce and produce traditional socialization of students to social roles differentiated by social class, race, and gender because they cannot understand their students' perspectives (Van Galen, 1993; Delpit 1988).

My initial reaction at the beginning of my observations was to remove all those picture books that the students avoided or refused to read. I now realize that I can retain the current popular multicultural picture books and materials being used and use them to teach the children to examine the literature critically. As a teacher, I can help students to point out the negative stereotypes and exaggerated features used in the picture books. Shannon (1992) argues that these books can serve to teach students to detect bias as they read. Students and teachers can discuss the reasons they think the literature might want to portray them in this way. They can discuss strategies to deal with the material and come up with their own strategies for change.

Some Strategies

Both reading materials and teaching techniques used need to address the problem working-class Black emergent readers face when they select books to read. The following is a summary of the instructional strategies I would recommend for using multicultural literature in the primary grades:

- involve students in selecting, reviewing and critiquing of books,
- teach students to detect bias in materials they read,
- help students develop critical thinking skills so that they learn to evaluate how genre, era, plot, setting and images of characters might better represent various groups in the literature,

- examine your own position or frames of reference with respect to your power, social class, access, privilege and perpetuating the status quo,
- become aware of students' location or frames of reference and how it is implicated in reading materials,
- be more careful when you introduce new materials and be particularly aware of how books are introduced and taken-up in class,
- select books featuring possible familiar frames of reference for your students, using books that connect with the community in which the school is located. Books that have familiar scenes and familiar names to the students and involve familiar children's objects and situations (including imaginative play) are especially important,
- slowly introduce and expose students to new or unfamiliar situations in books, discussing any issues that arise in the class,
- try to select even more multicultural picture books designed primarily to entertain. These may include poetry, rhymes, songs and rhythmic play,
- name and locate social class, poverty and racial and other institutional forms of oppression displayed in the literature.

The following is a summary of the recommended strategies for evaluating multicultural literature in the primary grades;

- take into account the perspectives and interpretations of the author and illustrator,
- examine the type of images and illustrations to detect race, class and gender biases and stereotyping,
- examine the story context, backgrounds, situations, characters' clothing and points of reference to detect bias and stereotyping,
- examine the amount of text used in the book and plan a strategy for introducing books with a larger amount of text,
- examine the quality of the text as it relates to the story

plot, its relations to children's experiences and interests,

- examine the social messages in the books being used in the classroom to ensure a balance between books that promote social or cultural information and books designed to entertain,
- be attentive to the students' reactions and seek out their opinions and perspectives.

More Research Needed

There is a need for research into the effects of various multicultural classroom materials on students' academic performance. Studies should also be conducted on the texts of these multicultural books and how children respond to the story content as well as the illustrations in the books. Multicultural picture books need to be analyzed for the richness of the language and the various styles of writing that appeal to children. Such studies could determine whether a text is appropriate for beginning readers and whether it enhances children's literacy development.

Children's Books Cited

Bogart, J. (1990). *Daniel's Dog*. Toronto: Scholastic Inc.

Humphrey, M. (1978). *The River that Gave Gifts: An Afro American Story*. San Francisco: Children's Book Press.

Hudson, W. (1991). *Jamal's Busy Day*. Orange NJ: Just Us Books.

Keats, E. J. (1970). *Hi, Cat!*. New York: Aladdin Books.

Mendez, P. (1989). *The Black Snowman*. Toronto: Scholastic Inc.

Mollel, T. M. (1990). *The Orphan Boy*. Toronto: Oxford University Press.

Munsch, R. (1993). *Wait and See*. Toronto: Annick Press Ltd.

Seuss, Dr. (1965). *Fox in Socks*. New York: Beginner Books.

Smalls, I. (1992). *Jonathan and His Mommy*. Toronto: Little, Brown & Company (Canada) Limited.

Steptoe, J. (1969). *Stevie*. New York: Harper & Row Publishers.

Titherington, J. (1988). *Where Are You Going, Emma?* New York: Greenwillow Books.

Williams, K. L. (1990). *Galimoto*. New York: Lothrop, Lee & Shepard Books.

Chapter Nine

BLACK HISTORY MONTH
A MULTICULTURAL MYTH OR "HAVE-BLACK-HISTORY-MONTH-KIT-WILL-TRAVEL"

ALTHEA PRINCE

Many self-respecting African-Canadian educators, artists, parents — children, many of US — have participated in it: The 'Great Canadian Multicultural Myth' called "Black History Week"; then later, "Black History Month." We do it in the name of community and history, for our children, for ourselves, for our society. We want to see our faces, hear our voices, read our words, speak them. We want our children to do those things too.

We seize opportunities to share who we are, explore where we came from, discuss where we are going. Black History Week was such a time when such a space would be opened. Black History Month showed progress, some people thought: twenty-eight whole days (and twenty-nine in each leap year), even though it is the coldest and shortest month of the year.

So, during this shortest, coldest month of the year, many of us educators and artists traverse the land bringing "Black History Month" to schools, libraries, community centres, churches, universities — anywhere and everywhere.

How do we transport Black history with such agility? It's sort of "Have-Black-History-Month-Kit-Will-Travel"; and travel we do. One February, I wore out a whole pair of boots and a whole pair of running shoes. But we press on, because it's all we've got; and didn't our parents teach us not to fly in the face of our good?

What's in a Black History Month Kit? "Everything!" the customers think. Once, it was suggested that instead of reading from my children's book, that I read a story from a collection of Anansi stories collected in Haiti(!) by someone with an eastern-European-sort-of-name. The woman (librarian) who thrust the book at me, mumbled something about none of the children being Black and that all children were able to understand Anansi.[1] She also mumbled that they were going to have "difficulty" with my children's book.

I did not reach out my hand for the questionable Anansi collection. I had been brought to the school as a children's author and was ready to read from one of my books, which was set in nineteenth century Antigua. As had been pre-arranged with the principal, the children had already read the book. From somewhere in the depths of my soul, I found my mother's Bolans-Village-Antigua-power. I opened my briefcase, took out my own books and asked politely, "Where shall I sit for the story-telling session?"

I won the unspoken battle. I list it in my personal struggle for a more inclusive cultural vision. I should add that the story-telling session went extremely well. Not only did the children have no trouble with the book, they asked if I could tell them another story. Their teachers also invited me to come back for the next year's Black-History-Month. I agreed, smiling. Inside, my weary heart thought, "When will it end?"

I tell this little tale to dramatise the point that the Black-History-Month-Kit demands great flexibility. Given the oppurtunity, teachers and librarians can, at will, dictate their own vision of Black History Month.

Clearly, the history of African-Canadian peoples needs to be dealt with within the schools. A month is not the way. An inclusive curriculum is not only desirable, but clamours to be developed. It feels sometimes as if we are in a bind. For if we continue to enable the ghettoised version of our history as a people, allowing it to be relegated to one month, then we are complicit in the perpetuation of a hegemony that denies our existence. Yet if we do not take this Black History Month crumb that is offered, we may find that our children, and all children, for that matter, have no access to even this ghettoised version of the history of African peoples.

Antonio Gramsci (1971), an Italian political activist and theorist, writing of Italy while in prison between 1929 and 1935, used the term *egemonia* (hegemony) to describe the pervasive cultural domination exerted by a ruling power bloc. In Gramsci's view, domination is exercised through popular consensus building as well as by physical coersion (or threat of it), especially in advanced capitalist countries where education, the media, law, mass culture etc. take on this role. Gramsci also argued that in order to challenge existing power relations, oppressed groups need to struggle on the cultural level as well as on the economic and political level. The dominant "consensus" needs to be challenged by the building of an inclusive counter-hegemonic ideology, which reflects more honestly the experiences of the majority. African-Canadians' historical reality then would surface and would be included in the overall hegemony that determines the history curriculum.

The fact that the history of African peoples is not included in the school's curriculum is an example of how cultural hegemony operates in the Canadian school system. I say these things in as bold a way as I can, for I observe that to be heard we sometimes have to be blunt, and sometimes we have to be bold, as if these things about which we speak are *a given*.

I would like to illustrate the notion of cultural hegemony by using the metaphor of a giant umbrella which reaches over us (refer to fig. 1 on the following page). We languish under the guise of this "multicultural" umbrella and actually, we suffer. For multiculturalism suggests equality in the plurality of cultures that exist in Canada and thus serves as the mechanism

Figure 1 Hegemony in Canada as a Giant Umbrella

under which some groups in the society are denied access to real power. In this case, we are looking at the unequal distribution of power as it manifests in that most important social institution: The School. The umbrella, disguised as shelter, is actually a control mechanism. Nothing is exempt. All the way through the school system, up to and including O.A.C., our children do not find themselves and their people in the curriculum.

The weave of the umbrella clearly displays that the fabric does not contain representation of certain racial and ethnic groups. Yet all groups are made to stand under the umbrella. When it rains, it is the position of the umbrella that determines where all groups may seek shelter. Any attempt to deviate from the weave of the fabric of the umbrella creates quite a stir in the hands that control the umbrella. Groups desperately seeking shelter under this kind of oppressive umbrella, soon find that there is no shelter. What is to be had under the seeming 'shelter' of the umbrella, is in fact, oppressive cultural hegemony. History = *their* history; that is, the historical interpretation of the dominant group. In the context of our discussion, Black history = Have-Black-History-Month-Kits-Will-Travel.

If we accept Gramsci's notion of 'hegemony' we recognise that there is a meaningful distinction to be made between 'hegemony' and 'direct domination.' Subordinate groups can be oppressed through cultural policies and practices just as effectively as by such coersive state mechanisms as the police and the army. To challenge the domimant order, oppressed groups need to come to an understanding of themselves, their past and their social and political rights. They need to do this by creating an inclusive, counter-hegemonic culture. In other words, a struggle has to be waged in the cultural arena as well as in the political arena.

In my view, the Gramscian concept of hegemony is useful for us African people living in Canada. I want to suggest that we challenge the hegemonic "umbrella" by constructing a counter-hegemonic culture in The School. We can do this, in part, through insisting on the creation and utilisation of an inclusive curriculum which enables US to read about US, speak about US, hear our own words in what is taught to children; not just *our* children, but all children. Again, here is a point made by Gramsci about the emergence of a new transformative cultural vision, a new potential "hegemony"created from below, which is useful for our discussion. He writes:

> ... it must be stressed that the political development of the concept of hegemony represents a great philosophical advance as well as a politico-practical one. For it necessarily supposes an intellectual unity and an ethic in conformity with a conception of reality that has gone beyond common sense and has become, if only within narrow limits, a critical conception. (Gramsci: 1971:334)

I am, of course, suggesting a marriage between theory and praxis: a step taken theoretically that has a matching step made in the practical realm of 'the real,' in this case, The School. We understand, theoretically and philosophically, the need to have wholeness in The School's curriculum. It is not only African-Canadian children who get cheated by a curriculum in which they are not included. All children suffer from this distorted interpretation of history. Clearly, a curriculum which adequately includes African peoples would enhance the intellectual understanding of all children who participate in the educational process. This is simple common sense, requiring no large-scale treatise. However, with the umbrella principle in full operation, it is necessary for us, as African-Canadian intellectuals, to spell out the problems for our children and for all children that are created by a one-dimensional curriculum. I am speaking here of history, but there is a need to look at the entire school curriculum with this eye.

Children are in the process of 'becoming.' If we accept this, we understand that to facilitate that process, education and educators have a responsibility to provide whole concepts and not partial concepts, whole 'stories' and not one-dimensional 'stories,' whole history and not partial history. Again, I refer to Gramsci:

> ... man's nature is 'history' (and in this sense, history equals spirit, the nature of man is the spirit), if history is given the meaning of 'becoming' in a *concordia discors* which does not destroy unity but contains within itself grounds for a possible unity . Therefore 'human nature' is not to be found in any one particular man but in the whole history of mankind (and the fact that we naturally use the word 'kind' is significant), while in each single individual are found characteristics made distinct through their difference from the characteristics of other individuals. The concept of 'spirit' in traditional philosophy and the concept of 'human nature' in biology also, should be defined as scientific utopias which are substitutes for the greater utopia 'human nature' sought for in God (and in man, the son of God), and which indicate the travail of history, rational and emotional hopes, etc. It is true, of course, that the religions which preached the equality of men as the sons of God, as well as those philosophies which affirmed man's equality on the basis of his reasoning faculty, were the expressions of complex revolutionary movements (the transformation of the classical world, the transformation of the medieval world), and that these forged the strongest links in the chain of historical development. (Gramsci:1987:80)

We must forgive Gramsci for his use of the words "man" and "men" to signify human beings, writing as he was, in the times that he lived. We move beyond that, however, to hear the ways in which his words resonate with the business of history and epistemology and pedagogy. The historical development of peoples of the world, their differences, their similarities, their relationships with each other over time, are important conceptual understandings to which all children need access.

To break this down into what my Antiguan language calls "common-a-garden talk": in order not to repeat historical mistakes, historical atrocities, historical oppression, historical crimes of peoples' inhumanity to other peoples, it is important for children to understand the rhythm of world historical events. It is necessary therefore, for children to understand why Europe carved up Africa. The spread and greed of European capitalism, driving Europeans to employ that inevitable tentacle: imperialism, complete with the criminal activity of annexing others' land, people and resources — all of this will be understood by children if it is taught with an enlightened, humanistic commitment to historical truth.

It is necessary also, for children to know that Africans resisted their domination, spawning several generals onto the world stage, embodied in persons like Queen Nzinga of Angola, who spearheaded her army against the invading Portuguese; the market women of Nigeria who waged 'The Women's War' against British colonial government agents(Prince and Taylor, forthcoming); and Chaka, king of the Zulu, who received the British with outrage, coupled with brilliant and effective tactics of war and resistance against his people's domination. It is similarly important for children in Canada to know that African people's resistance to their enslavement in Jamaica brought the first large numbers of Africans to Nova Scotia (James, 1996).

The list is never-ending. So much truth is clouded in the umbrella's smothering hegemonic weave, that to redefine it, to re-weave it, requires the skill and dexterity of an Antiguan patchwork-maker. I speak here, not of multi-cultural 'ethnic' demonstrations, but rather, of a conscious, conscientious inclusive curriculum. The Antiguan patchwork does not ghettoise any piece of fabric, relegating it to an obscure corner, but rather, ensures that all pieces of fabric have full display, because they are all parts of the whole design.

This kind of story-making, this kind of wholeness of history, would, in fact, be liberating for all of us in Canadian society. For we would see ourselves adequately portrayed in the fabric of society. The careful logic with which the Antiguan patchwork is created, would be represented by the epistemological underpinnings of the curriculum. The pedagogical method is the enabling mechanism, much like the thread and the border which hold the patchwork together.

Sometimes, the Black-History-Month-Kit makes me shake with 'fear and trembling,' afraid for us all as human beings. I have listened to distortions of Martin Luther King as an icon of all that we need to do, hear and say. I watch Malcolm X ignored by the status quo, because of his early rhetoric, taken out of its historical context and detached from his later and much more dangerous political theory that understood class consciousness to be an all-race issue. The "danger" in this latter theoretical position is that it has the capacity of uniting the under-classes of American (and Canadian) society. The children need to be taught about King, Malcolm, Mahatma Ghandi, Fidel Castro and Che Geuvara in the same breath, representing as they do, different responses to the same oppression. Understanding these political theorists and political actors, could have far-reaching implications for all children. The decision about what constitutes a hero or heroine and how he or she is interpreted and presented to children, is again made through the lens of the dominant group, operating out of the powerful position of having control over the fabric of the umbrella. Hence, the librarian could dare to suggest that an Anansi story would be more acceptable to the children than a story set in nineteenth century Antigua. Even Black History Month receives censorship, for its truth is not always palatable to the dominant group. Martin Luther King is presented as a hero and Malcolm X is not. Taken to its logical conclusion, this makes a parody of the whole notion of "Black History."

Under the umbrella, groups of people who get to be called "minorities" experience the 'rain' of life with damp shoulders, soaking wet feet and straw hats which leak water onto their faces. Still struggling to understand why they should open their mouths and sing "Oh Canada," members of these groups find themselves vilified for daring to say that they have difficulty singing the song.

One day, I overheard a white child sing "Oh Canada, we stand on God for thee" instead of "We stand on guard for thee." I smiled inwardly. I have never forgotten that childish voice, raised in a high-pitched treble, reaffirming what we, springing as we do, from Fanon's hordes of hungry masses, experience as reality (Fanon:1963). For to deny people their real place in historical recounting, in story-making, is indeed to "stand on God" in the name of country.

I am reminded of the child's voice, too, whenever I hear adult voices saying, "If you don't like it here, then leave." Usually, these voices are suggesting that if what people see in the weave of the umbrella is not to their liking, they ought to go back to "wherever they came from." For history = the history of the dominant group and African-Canadian people ought to be grateful for the twenty-eight day crumbs. Historical distortion and exclusion are responsible for some people thinking that "here" is their preserve. I have never heard First Nations peoples ask anyone to leave; not even their oppressors, let alone other oppressed groups in the society.

Sometimes, the "crumbs" (Black History Month activities) are so confusing that the children themselves question their authenticity. Once as I was being introduced and waited for my turn to speak, a white teacher explained that Black people were taking this time to praise their kings and queens, their heroes and heroines. "They want their children to have a sense of Black pride," she said.

One bright little, Black girl raised her hand and asked "What is Black Pride?" I was so glad that she had asked the question that I wanted to give her what Antiguans call "a big hug-up." She had given me an opening with which to dispense with my introduction without insulting the teacher. I had no intention of speaking about Black pride. In fact, I was going to tell the children an Anansi story from Bolans Village, Antigua. This particular story had been one of my early lessons in fractions, on being fair, about having integrity and a whole host of things.

None of these things were, however, about 'Black pride.' I introduced to those little children, epistemology, African cosmology — their way of seeing. But at no point and at no time did I speak of this nebulous thing called 'Black pride.'

I do not by any means, wish to deny kings and queens their place in history. We have indeed had our share of these high-ranking people. But they were unlikely to have been the source from which we all sprung. Further, what kind of class consciousness is it to teach children that to be somebody, one had to have been descended from a king and/or a queen?

These things need to be taught, not as isolated incidents in Black Heritage classes and Black History Months, distorted as icons of something called 'Black pride.' Rather, they need to be taught as parts of a whole, parts of world history. In Gramscian terms, "links in the chain of historical development." For that is what they are indeed: "links in the chain of historical development." When my daughter dared to ask for this interpretation of her people to be included for intellectual balance, her OAC history teacher referred to historians who wrote of such things as "a few quacks." The African experience as one of the "links in the chain of historical development" was not, in his view, a historical truth. This truth will never surface in ghettoised Black-History-Month-Kits, just as it will not surface in the kind of curriculum which refers to Africans in the New World simply as 'the slaves.'

This brings me to a discussion of how the teaching of distorted history, or history isolated into a series of interpreted pieces of information can effectively distort a peoples' whole existence. I refer to that notion of 'the slaves.' It is the non-inclusive curriculum which relegates African peoples in the New World to the category of 'the slaves.' Gone is their Africanness, gone is their cultural persona, gone is their rootedness in African soil and African race definition. Gone. All gone into the great void of 'the slaves.' For without a world historical perspective, the definition of these uprooted people is left to the interpreted piece of information that describes them only in terms of their relation to their oppressors. They were enslaved by the white planter class in the New World, and thus they are defined as 'the slaves.' Saying that they had been the children of kings and queens does not wipe out the words: 'the slaves.' Historical truth alone will do that. An inclusive curriculum, dedicated to exploring the broad spectrum of world events, would of necessity, continuously refer to African peoples as what and who they were and are: African peoples. It was only to their oppressors that they were 'the slaves.' To themselves, they were and are people, from whence they had come, Africa.

I refer often in my work and in my public speaking, to my Bolans-Village-Antigua-ancestry. It is my closest ancestral memory, my *particular*, although Africa is a strong part of my collective memory. I mention it now in order to enhance and enliven the discussion of this business of 'the slaves' versus African peoples. For I recall that Bolans villagers refer to their ancestors as '(their) generation' and to the period of the enslavement of African peoples as 'slavery days.' Never have I heard them speak of 'the slaves.' This is 'agency' taken to an incredible, empowering degree.

Black-History-Month-kits simply cannot redress these historical distortions in one fell swoop. Twenty-eight days is not sufficient time to rewrite history. Hence, psychological band-aids of stories of kings and queens and stories of the slaves' journey on the Underground Railroad to freedom in Canada will fail every time to empower our children. Pretending that Black History Month is able to redress historical atrocities and provide succor for the souls of African-Canadians, is an act that The School can no longer be allowed to practice. This is simply another multicultural myth which gives validity to the hegemony represented by the dominant weave of the umbrella. I am reminded always that the Act For The Preservation and Enhancement of Multiculturalism in Canada, passed in 1988 contains within it, a clause which states:

> encourage and assist the social, cultural, economic, and political institutions of Canada to be both respectful and inclusive of Canada's multicultural character.

We are not, after all, asking for anything extraordinary. It is our due. It is also common sense and wisdom.

Frantz Fanon made this point in *The Wretched of The Earth* in 1963. Like Gramsci, Fanon uses male-biased language, but his political analysis has significance for us. He reminded us that the way forward is merely a question of

> ... starting a new history of Man, a history which will have regard to the sometimes prodigious theses which Europe has put forward, but which will also not forget Europe's crimes, of which the most horrible was committed in the heart of man, and consisted of the pathological tearing apart of his functions and the crumbling away of his unity. And in the framework of the collectivity there were the differentiations, the stratification, and the bloodthirsty tensions fed by classes; and finally, on the immense scale of humanity, there were racial hatreds, slavery, exploitation, and above all the bloodless genocide which consisted in the setting aside of fifteen thousand millions of men. (Fanon:1963:313)

It is a fitting note on which to end.

NOTE

1 Anansi is a trickster spider who is the centre of stories which African people brought to the Caribbean with them from West Africa. There is much irony for me therefore, in an African person being offered a collection of Anansi stories, collected by someone who is European. The issue of appropriation of culture, coupled with the underlying insult of denying the validity of my children's books makes this incident stand out in my personal struggle for a more inclusive cultural vision.

Chapter Ten

TEACHING AFRICAN HERITAGE IN ONTARIO SCHOOLS
PROBLEMS AND PROSPECTS

BERNARD MOITT

If students are to acquire a critical knowledge of Africa, school boards in Ontario must adopt a systematic approach to the teaching of African heritage in the schools under their jurisdiction. This requires proper and systematic teacher training, the development of adequate academic resources and the implementation and monitoring of policies pertaining to the education of Blacks in the educational system.

Some boards of education in Ontario, notably the Toronto and the North York boards, have long recognized the need to diversify their curriculums to include courses on Africa and other areas which have been traditionally ignored in school texts. Until quite recently however, the teaching of African heritage took place after the normal school day, and was optional. Those who wished to acquire a detailed knowledge of the African heritage therefore had to be willing to sacrifice part of the time they would normally dedicate to after school activities (which also included academic pursuits) to learning about the continent, its peoples and culture. Changes to this situation have been painfully slow, in spite of policy changes in education, hard work and continuous effort on the part of school boards and community organizations. For the most part, Africa is still taught in the school system as an appendage of courses on world civilization and the like. Given the ethnic composition of the population in areas such as Metro Toronto, which consists of large numbers of African Canadians (as is the case in some Toronto schools as well) greater progress ought to have been made in terms of the institutionalization of African heritage courses in the school curriculum.

This chapter examines some of the problems involved in the teaching of African heritage in the Ontario school system and the prospects for its advancement in the years ahead. It does so from the point of view of a Black parent and educator who has been actively involved in the Black community in Metro Toronto for more than two decades. It concentrates mainly on the Toronto Board of Education — the board with which I am most familiar — and demonstrates that efforts have been made to promote the study of Black heritage in the schools, but they have been sporadic and have not yielded the results that many of us had hoped to see.

Black Heritage: A Background

Interest in the teaching of Black heritage is not a new phenomenon in Ontario. In 1935, Marcus Garvey opened a School of African Philosophy in Toronto. Ten students graduated from the three-week seminar course which Garvey conducted himself, but plans to expand the program of study were thwarted by his death in 1940.[1] In 1968, there was a short item in the *Toronto Star* about Gwen Lee — an African Canadian woman who used a church basement in Toronto to teach children — black and white about the African heritage. This was part of a joint project between the Ontario Insitute for Studies in Education (OISE) and the Toronto Board of Education funded by the Province of Ontario. The project revolved around a central question: To what extent can environment and inclusive history change attitudes? With the influx of large numbers of Blacks (mostly from the Caribbean) after 1960, interest in the teaching of Black heritage reached greater heights. The 1960s were a time when the Black Education Project (BEP), the Harriet Tubman Centre and United Improvement Negro Association (UNIA) served in one way or other as centres of focus for Black studies. Thus in 1979 when the Toronto Board of Education introduced the Black Cultural Heritage programmes — the first school board in Metro Toronto to do so — there were many conscientious people in the Black community who had already been sensitized to the problems Black children faced in the school system.

The Black Cultural Heritage programmes came about as a result of an Ontario Ministry of Education memorandum (#77:46), released in June, 1977. Its objective was to:

> provide for the teaching of Heritage Languages as part of the offerings of the Continuing Education Department for 2 1/2 hours per week after regular school hours, on non-school days, or, where numbers warranted, by an extension of the regular school day.[2]

The Heritage programmes were geared to the specific needs of the various ethno-cultural groups in the school system. Also, parental participation was highly encouraged in that parents of any school board in Ontario had the right to demand heritage language classes from their local administration. Moreover, each school in which there was a Heritage programme was required to set up a liaison committee composed of parents to assess the programme. Black community representatives such as Keren Brathwaite, Coleen Issaac and Irene Jordan, who were later instrumental in the formation of the Organization of Parents of Black Children in 1980, became liaison persons at various schools, including Mc Murrich, Queen Victoria and Dewson.

By this time it had become evident that Black students as a whole were not doing very well in the school system. The Toronto Board had conducted research in 1970 and 1975 on the composition of the school population which revealed that a significant part of the student body was born outside of Canada. The board's annual surveys of grade 9 students from 1980-83 showed a proportional increase in the number of Black students in the overall student population — from 3 per cent in 1970 to

7 percent in 1980. Thus there was a need to pay attention to language and other needs among the student body, and to foster a healthy multicultural setting in which all students could thrive. When the Board's "Work Group on Multiculturalism, Race Relations and Heritage Languages" submitted its Final Report in 1976, some of its key recommendations revolved around heritage and curriculum issues. In recommendation 36, the Work Group proposed that:

> A curriculum review and development project be initiated in each curriculum department in accordance with Ministry guidelines, and that the Director of Education be requested to assemble reports from each department on the feasibility of implementing this recommendation as a summer project to accomplish the following:
>
> (i) Identification of materials that reflect a positive and creative attitude toward Canadian Cultural Pluralism;
>
> (ii) Identification of culturally and racially biased content;
>
> (iii) Assembly and development of appropriate materials."[3]

These are the circumstances under which Black community representatives were brought together through the efforts of the School Community Relations office at the Toronto Board to talk about Black heritage. In the process, they realized that the problems they were dealing with were deep, much greater than they appeared on the surface, and merited appropriate action. They believed that by organizing a conference they could study the origin of the problems, give them greater exposure, and explore common experiences. The Toronto Board facilitated this conference by providing a venue and making school community workers available to help with the organization.

The conference on Education for Parents of Black Children was held on May 10, 1980 at Oakwood Collegiate and heralded the beginning of a new dimension in the struggle for the teaching of Black heritage. It was also an important demonstration of what the Toronto Board and the Black community could achieve by working together. Attended by over 500 people (mainly parents), many coming from other school boards, the Separate School System and areas beyond the boundaries of Metro

Toronto, the conference was very successful.

For the community representatives, the realization that the textbooks used in the schools contained little if any representation of Blacks was sobering. In addition, they recognised that whatever representation there was tended to be negative. Thus they viewed curriculum as a major problem area from the outset. The Heritage programmes were really language-oriented, which means that they focussed on language and culture. This posed a particular problem for Blacks in Metro Toronto who were mostly of Caribbean parentage and spoke European languages and a variety of creoles. As the creoles spoken in the Caribbean were not considered languages (no doubt because of the biases in European definition of "language") the Black Heritage programmes emphasized history and culture.

Achievements

Notable achievements in the 1980s reflected the trend towards using history and culture in promoting Black heritage. One such achievement was the publication of *Black Studies* in 1983.[4] Produced by a writing team that consisted of Rella Brathwaite, a historian, Lewis Thompson, a principal, several teachers from the public and separate school boards, as well as consultants and community workers, this was a commendable start. The writing team also benefited from the comments and suggestions provided by a number of people in the community, among them students, parents, teachers, university professors, school board personnel and librarians. It is difficult to say what role each member of this impressive advisory body played. Its members are too numerous to mention, but many have since become crucial players in the educational life of Ontario students at all levels. It is however, noteworthy that the team included the late Fran Endicott, then a student at (OISE), whose remarkable contribution as a Ward 7 school trustee of the Toronto Board of Education is a matter of public record.

The importance of history and culture is evident at the outset of *Black Studies*. The introduction begins as follows:

> This document has been developed to help teachers and local curriculum committees to integrate the Black Canadian experi-

ence and heritage into the curriculum for the Intermediate Division. It is designed to assist teachers by providing a framework within which this perspective can be applied. Because of the scarcity of information about Blacks in most textbooks and learning manuals currently in use in Ontario, the document is intended to serve as a guide to practical application.[5]

Black Studies is a clearly written and well presented work that contains valuable information about the contribution of Blacks to Canadian society. It is enriched by annotated resource lists as well as sections on suggested activities designed to aid students and teachers. Like other texts, it has shortcomings. It sought to correct the virtual exclusion of Blacks in the textbooks used in the school system by presenting a "record of Black roots and achievement" and providing "opportunities for Black students to develop a sense of identity and a positive self-concept by gaining a better understanding of their own heritage."[6] Though an admirable and well conceived approach, the authors concentrated on the Black experience in Canada, thereby leaving out the African background.

Published in 1988, *Etudes Afro-Canadiennes*[7] is a major modification of *Black Studies* designed for use in the French school system. It corrected many of the shortcomings in *Black Studies*, but both works still suffer from similar problems. A writing team headed by Professor Fred Case, Principal of New College (University of Toronto) added sections on African and Caribbean history and African music among others. It modified many sections of *Black Studies* as well. As the author of some of the units, including those on pre-colonial Africa and Haiti, I gained valuable insights into curriculum writing and development, and into the gaps which existed in the historical literature on Africa at the primary and secondary levels. There were fewer resources available to recommend in French, than in English, to students and teachers who wished to pursue Black heritage at the Intermediate Division. Both *Black Studies* and *Etudes Afro-Canadiennes* suffer from the problem of having resource lists to which students and teachers in Ontario may not find easy access. The works are generally available at university libraries and some public libraries, which means that their acquisition requires some effort on the part of students and teachers. The reality is that even in the best of circumstances most teachers are unlikely to spend time searching for texts on university bookshelves, especially those dealing with areas of study that do not constitute part of their regular course loads. Also, from the point of view of providing guidance, many of the texts can best be used by teachers who possess a supplementary knowledge of Black heritage. Even at the university level, it is still difficult to find suitable main texts to teach introductory courses in African studies. Indeed, some instructors do not use a main text at all, turning to a compilation of journal articles and chapters in books instead. To my knowledge, neither *Black Studies* nor *Etudes Afro-Canadiennes* is being used in any discernible way in the school system. All of this suggests that the academic resources needed for teaching African heritage in the schools must not only be specifically written and geared to the different levels, but must become part of the regular curriculum.

Policies, Recommendations and Action

With the foregoing in mind, it comes as no surprise that by the late 1980s, two issues assumed great importance. One was the need for the integration and teaching of material on African heritage across the curriculum. The other was the need for curriculum writing geared to the Black experience. In this regard the *Final Report of the Consultative Committee on the Education of Black Students* was crucial. This report was the culmination of a long process which began in November, 1985 when representatives of the Organization of Parents of Black Children (OPBC) met with the Associate Director of Education (Program), and identified a series of concerns including high drop-out rates among Black students, low self-esteem, the "persistent 'invisibility' of Black studies and Black history within the curriculum," the persistent ignorance of teachers about Black history and culture, and the streaming of Black students.[8]

In March, 1986 the Toronto Board adopted a recommendation from HELACON, proposed by Keren Brathwaite, which called on the Director of Education to establish a consultative committee on the education of Black students in Toronto schools. The terms of reference were as follows:

that the Director of Education establish a consultative committee on the education of Black students in Toronto schools with the following terms of reference:

(i) To examine, in light of current Board policy and practice, the concerns expressed by HELACON and the Organization of Parents of Black Children about the education of Black students in Toronto schools.

(ii) To recommend to the Director and to the Board appropriate action.

That the committee bring forward am interim report through HELACON to the Director of Education and to the Board by June 1986, and a final report in the fall of 1986, in order to ensure that the implementation of the committee's recommendation begin no later than January 1987.[9]

The concerns raised by the OPBC about the condition of Black students in the school system are reflected in the 60 recommendations in the *Final Report*. To be sure, they are an indication that the present state of African heritage in Ontario schools has not resulted from a lack of effort, hard work and specificity. Indeed, three pages of the report fall under the heading "Curriculum Issues and Black Cultural Studies." They call for annual curriculum reviews "to determine the degree to which the cultural backgrounds of the students in Toronto are integrated into the curriculum ..."[10] so that corrective measures may be taken.

The recommendations that deal with curriculum are particularly insightful. They are well worth exploring at length but two — recommendations 37 and 40 which appear below — are particularly relevant for the present chapter. Recommendation 37:

That secondary school principals and School Superintendents consider offering an optional Black Studies Credit Course, or units of study in existing courses, and involve the parents, the Ministry of Education and other resources, as well as appropriate Board staff, for example, the curriculum Advisor on Race Relations and Multiculturalism, in developing the course of study.

Recommendation 40:

That the following initiatives be undertaken:

(a) The role of Black people throughout history:

- in politics (global and national)
- in cultural activities (art, music, literature)
- in science and mathematics
- in human rights
- in economic development, and so on

be included in the appropriate curricula across all disciplines under the direction of principals and School Superintendents so that all students are exposed so this material naturally and repeatedly during their educational experience;

(b) Each of the appropriate departments of Curriculum and the Program Division (e.g. Language Study Centre, Science, Mathematics, Social Studies, Music and Visual Arts) individually and collectively develop suggestions for teachers as to how this can be done at all grade levels not only for Blacks but for other cultural groups as well; and

(c) The Associate Director of Education- Program make these materials available for use in schools beginning September, 1989.[11]

Taken as a whole, the recommendations are as relevant today as they were in 1988 when the Toronto Board released the document. While some elements of the 60 recommendations have been implemented in one way or other (there is, for example, an annual Black Student Conference as outlined in recommendation 46 of the *Final Report*) the curriculum issues have not been satisfactorily dealt with. Where are the Black Studies courses? Why does an inclusive curriculum continue to elude us? Why has there not been more change?

Those who are familiar with the way in which school boards and school systems in Ontario function know how difficult it is to bring about change, if only because of the many levels of administration and jurisdiction. These systems are not inpenetrable, but working within them can often be frustrating, even agonizing. Administratively, it is the responsibility of the Director of Education to ensure that board policies are in place and recommendations are implemented. But directors of education, like others who occupy similar positions, delegate responsibility to a host of officials within their school boards. The associate directors of education responsible for programmes and curriculum,

superintendents, the officials in charge of equity and race relations, as well as the school trustees, all have some degree of
influence, but school principals appear to be in a separate category, wielding great authority in the system. As School principals are in charge of the day-to-day running of the schools,
including the hiring of teachers, they are particularly well-placed
to effect or block change. Directors of Education obviously feel
the need to keep principals on side, but many parents and community organizations who have dealt with the system over the
years have found that principals are often a major stumbling
block to change. There are, for example, a number of highly
qualified, Black teachers who have not been able to find permanent employment with the school boards, despite the equity policies, targets and timetables in place. Aside from Westview, some
schools in Metro Toronto with significant Black student populations do not have a single Black teacher, although the boards are
cognizant of the importance of role modelling. We may therefore
have to examine closely the role of the principal to better understand how change occurs in the school system.

As an OPBC representative on the Toronto Board's Race
Relations Committee from 1986–92, and the Consultative
Committee on the Education of Black Students from 1989–92,
I felt privileged to have observed and participated in the process of change, however limited. Chaired by Dr. Ouida Wright
for the first several years, the Consultative Committee on the
Education of Black Students was an excellent vantage point
for this exercise. As its main purpose was to recommend ways
of implementing the 60 recommendations in the *Final Report*,
I gained valuable insight into the workings of the system. That
the committee consisted of school superintendents and other
board personnel, principals, teachers and community representatives made the experience all the more valuable.

Though enhanced by the integrity of Dr. Wright, the committee's work was often frought with difficulties. After making
numerous recommendations over many months, community
representatives, in particular, never ceased to ask, "What have
we achieved so far? What tangible results can we point to"?
Periodic assessment reports commissioned by Dr. Wright
revealed that different elements of the *Final Report* had been

implemented in different schools at different times. There was no consistent pattern of implementation. It became clear that much depended on the principals. Working with a modest, independent budget however, the committee itself achieved certain notable objectives.

There was a successful lecture series under which Black intellectuals such as Dr. George McKenna of the United States and Dr. Mervyn Morris of Jamaica delivered dynamic performances to capacity audiences at the Ontario Institue for Studies in Education (OISE) auditorium. The committee also approved and promoted a successful and well attended exhibit on Haiti mounted by Mr. Terry Jackson, an ardent art collector and member of OPBC, whose interest in Haitian history and culture has had a positive impact on the community. For at least two weeks in May 1992, children from Toronto Board schools visited the exhibit on McCaul Street where they learned about the struggles of the Haitian people whose ancestors-slaves from Africa-staged the only successful slave revolt leading to independence in world history.

The committee also approved curriculum projects. These were given to teachers who sometimes dedicate their summer holidays to such projects. This is not an unusual occurrence as curriculum writing is normally done by people within the system. One such project was a writing project dealing with Ancient Egypt designed for use in the school system. I do not know what the status of this project is, but good material on Ancient Egypt is sorely needed in the schools. The other project was a video production on Mr. Harry Gairy — the Grand Old Man of the Black Community — who died in 1943. Although the video suffers from technical and other problems, it has merit from the point of view of history. In the video, Jean Augustine, now Member of Parliament for Lakeshore, explained that in the early 1960s Mr. Gairy's house was a place of congregation and socialization for many Blacks, even those who did not know him. Indeed, Blacks who came to the Toronto area from the Caribbean at the time knew that they would be welcomed there. The Black community has grown extensively since, but it is important for us to look back and place our existence in Canada in proper historical context. To what extent this video is being used in the system is a valid question.

Teaching African Heritage

Some curriculum work has been done by people outside the school system as well. Akwatu Khenti has prepared African Canadian Infusion Units for grades 7 and 8 for the North York Board of Education. These units have undergone review and revision, as units of that kind should; one can only hope that they will see the light of day.

In 1992–93, Khenti, along with Abdullah Hakim Quick, an Imam and Ph.D. candidate in the Department of History at the University of Toronto, also conducted a course in African history for teachers in the Toronto Board. This was done under the auspices of the curriculum division and the Equal Opportunity Office under which the race relations portfolio falls. I did the same in summer, 1993. The ultimate objective of the board was to prepare teachers sufficiently in African Studies to allow them to teach this subject with confidence in the system. Not all of the teachers who enroled in the course may have been interested in teaching African heritage in their schools, but all had a general interest in Africa. Many among them could well be considered "committed" teachers.

My course was a ten week course, one evening, once a week for three hours. I selected a wide range of topics, just as I would in giving a general introductory course on Africa. Although I had many years of experience from teaching courses in Africa and the Caribbean at the University of Toronto, I had never taught school teachers before. It has been said repeatedly that teachers are a difficult group to teach. As it turned out, I found that there was merit to this saying. For me the experience was largely negative, as it probably was for most of the teachers.

This was a mixed group of teachers, Black and white. Most had some knowledge of Africa, a few much more so than others. My intention was to begin with geography and methodology and then proceed to critically examine aspects of African history including Ancient Egypt, state formation, the rise of kingdoms, slavery, the slave trade, religion, race and resistance and so forth. Almost from the outset, it became clear to me that the teachers did not wish to be lectured to; they wanted to be instructed in how to teach an African Studies course in the school system. This was a legitimate request, but one which, in my view, required a different process. I strongly believed that a knowledge base had to be first established before this could be done, using perhaps a smaller group of teachers.

To establish this base I began by giving a map exercise. The teachers were required to fill in a selection of countries on a blank map of Africa. This I did to determine the level of knowledge about the location of African countries. A few of the teachers did very well, but the exercise was a struggle for most. This may seem insignificant, but I believe that this is part of the knowledge base teachers ought to possess in order to teach African heritage. Methodology is crucial in the building of this knowledge base as well. Methodology is important in any branch of intellectual inquiry, but especially so in the case of African studies, I think, since so much harm has been done to the image of Africa over several centuries. For the most part, Africans recorded their history in the form of oral traditions, and did not begin to write about their societies until fairly recently. Indeed, the first novel dealing with Africa, written by an African — Chinua Achebe — was published only in 1958.[12] There were important centres of learning based on Islam and Arabic writing in Timbuktu (Mali) in the Middle Ages, but oral traditions prevailed everywhere. How much can oral traditions tell us about Africa? How accurate are they? How can they be used to write African history? These are important questions, even for beginners.

On the other hand, writing about Africa is centuries old. We must be critical about this writing. The medieval Arabic scholars from North Africa — al-Bekri (1029–1094), Ibn Battuta (1304–1369) and Ibn Khaldun (1332–1406) — were among the earliest to write about African societies, if we leave aside the ancient writers like Herodotus and Manethon. Even now, there is a heavy reliance on al-Bakri's account of life in the Medieval Kingdoms of the western Sudan. But there are difficulties in assessing the authority of the information he and others provide, as it is not always clear how it was obtained. Also, the translations from the original Arabic texts to other languages pose other problems.

The writings of Europeans from the fifteenth century have

done great harm to Africa and Africans, and those who wish to teach African heritage must understand the major currents in the literature. After all, Africans in every part of the world are faced with the fallout from these writings. Too many works in the past portrayed Africa as a continent of 'savages,' a 'dark' continent of Black peoples who were lower on the human scale than other races. Africans did not counter this image in writing and the Atlantic slave trade from the fifteenth to the nineteenth centuries, followed by European conquest and colonization in the second half of the nineteenth century, only served to reinforce European pseudoscientific racism which still haunts Africans everywhere. The negative perception of self held by many Black students and their parents can be traced back to this literature. The belief that Africa had no history and that its people had achieved nothing of substance came to be internalized by Blacks and produced disastrous results. Indeed, European writing about Africa was usually a record of European activity on the continent. Even in 1963, the renowned British historian-Professor Hugh Trevor Roper-could pronounce:

> Perhaps, in the future, there will be some African history to teach. But at present there is none: there is only the history of Europeans in Africa. The rest is darkness ... and darkness is not a subject of history.[13]

Awareness of the methodological problems and the strengths and weaknesses in the historical literature of Africa will put those interested in teaching African heritage in a strong position to be critical of books recommended to them. They should possess a general knowledge about where the most recent research on Africa can be found. They should also know what some of the major questions in African studies are. This is not too much to ask.

Since the 1960s with the independence of most of the African countries and the establishment of African studies programmes in universities in the United States, there has been more enlightened writing about Africa, both by Africans and non-Africans. There has also been an attempt to write about Africa from an African perspective. This is the manner in which African history should be written, but the question remains: how do we do that?

In the 1980s, Dr. Molefi Asante, chair of the Department of African American Studies at Temple University in Philadelphia, became the leading proponent of the concept 'Afrocentricity' which he describes as "the belief in the centrality of Africans in post modern history, our mythology, our creative motif, and our ethos exemplifying our collective will."[14] Afrocentricity is a philosophy which puts Africa at the centre in terms of viewing the world and analyzing events. Thus it goes beyond writing about Africa from an African point of view.

Adopting an Afrocentric approach to writing about Africa should be acceptable to all, but scholars should avoid the temptation of going beyond their data in order to place Africans at the centre of every invention or historical event of importance. The debate over Afrocentricity has been divisive and should be of interest to teachers of African heritage. Dr. Henry Louis Gates, Director of the Afro-American Studies Department at Harvard University, has been central in this debate in terms of opposing Afrocentricity. Gates has called for rigorous scholarship rather than "ethnic cheerleading" to separate truth from fiction. According to the *New York Times*, he contends that "some of the work being done in the more than 200 Afro-American studies programs around the country [the United States] is intellectually 'bogus' because ... they are essentially inventing an African past that never was." Gates wonders why the most important issue in Afro-American studies departments is not the causes of poverty and its remedies. Rather, the "most important issue is whether Cleopatra was Black. This is classic escapism and romanticism."[15]

Gates is correct in calling for rigorous scholarship, but he is wrong to suggest that rigorous scholarship and Afrocentricity are mutually exclusive. Can an Afrocentric scholar not be a good scholar? He simplifies the concerns of Afrocentrists as well. After all, Africans have consciously been written out of history over time and must now fight to restore their place in world civilization. In doing so, some will naturally be over enthusiastic and will tip the balance the other way from time to time. But that will pass; it is just a matter of time.

Still the debates rage on. The race of the Ancient Egyptians remains a thorny issue. The late Senegalese scholar, Cheik Anta Diop, has became fairly well known for his ideas about the Ancient Egyptians whom he argued were Black Africans. Diop first promoted his ideas in a thesis subsequently published under the title *Nations nègres et cultures*.[16] For political reasons, his work is more important in areas of the African diaspora where concerns about the contributions of Africans to world civilization are more primary than in Africa. Although some aspects of Diop's methodology need to be scrutinized, his central thesis is sound. After decades of claims and counter claims, his ideas have become more acceptable, particularly among scholars outside Africa. In his highly acclaimed video series on Africa produced just over a decade ago, for example, the British historian, Basil Davidson, endorses Diop's views about the race of the ancient Egyptians after a careful methodological analysis. But there is no end to the debate in sight. On my recent visit to France, a French anthropologist who read an article I wrote on Diop[17] gave me two of his recently published articles, both of which are critical of Diop's thesis and methodology.[18]

Issues in African studies continue to surface, some of them generated more by contemporary social realities than by gaps in African historiography. One such issue is the issue of which ethnic groups participated in the Atlantic slave trade. A few decades ago, one of the more contentious issue was the number of Africans exported from Africa during the period of the Atlantic slave trade. In 1969, Philip Curtin estimated the number to be about 10,000,000.[19] This was considered controversial, as previous studies had put the total at 15,000,000 and higher. In a well conceived recent study, Joseph Inikori, a Nigerian scholar, has indicated that the 15,000,000 figure is conservative, but should stand.[20] The demographic issue is far from dead, but ethnicity has become a lightening rod. However, the prevailing view is that a multiplicity of ethnicities participated in the slave trade. This view was clearly articulated by the American Historical Association at its 1995 annual meeting:

> Atlantic slavery was an intercontinental enterprise extending over nearly four centuries. Ethnically, the participants included Arabs, Berbers, scores of African ethnic groups, Italians, Portuguese, Spaniards, Dutch, Jews, Germans, Swedes, French,

English, Danes, white Americans, Native Americans, and even thousand of New World people of African descent who became slaveholding farmers or planters themselves.[21]

The foregoing demonstrates how important methodology and critical thinking are for teachers of African heritage. The ethnicity factor in the Atlantic slave trade is a complex one and is certain to spark new research. Hopefully, argument and evidence will prevail.

Where does all of this leave us on the question of teacher training and the development of adequate resources for teaching African heritage? Teachers are a busy lot and boards of education interested in preparing them to teach African heritage should give them the time and provide them with proper incentives. It should not be acceptable for teachers to indicate on their *curriculum vitae* that they have taken a course on African heritage. They should be required to pass the course, and be recognized for it. Many of the teachers I taught attended less than half of the ten sessions. An hour length video by Basil Davidson — "Different but Equal" — which I showed the group as a means of discussing methodology was deemed too long. They suggested the use of "video clips," but I did not find that approach appropriate. Many of their comments, which I solicited at the end of the course, were largely negative, but I was encouraged by the quality of the positive comments. The most knowledgeable student in the group — a white female teacher from the Durham Board who never missed a single session — gave me a very good, in-depth review.

There are secondary schools which are now offering African studies courses, even when they may not be referred to as such. Stephen Leacock, Westwood, Albion and Oakwood are among them. I was associated with the course at Oakwood in the 1994–95 academic session, acting as Toronto Board consultant to two white, male teachers who took the initiative to draft the course even though neither had really studied Africa. Though I was not involved from the outset, working with these teachers and their students was a very rewarding experience. Even though suitable material for the course proved to be a constant problem, the level of enthusiasm among the teachers and most of the students remained very high. I taught a few of the classes and came away with as gratified a feeling as I would after teaching any of my university courses.

The teachers selected *A Short History of Africa*[22] as the main text, but it was, in my view, too advanced for the secondary system. As they went along, they agreed. There are other works — none of them problem-free. The School Certificate *History of West Africa*[23] is more suitable, but this is a regional history, as are many of the texts produced in Africa. There are also a number of African historical biographies — in English and French — written by well known African scholars which teachers of African heritage ought to consider. In addition, there are a number of literary works written by African authors that would be excellent material on secondary course lists. Chinua Achebe deserves to be on that list, and so do Bessie Head, Miriama Ba, Ferdinand Oyono, Awi Kwei Armah and Sembène Ousmane.

Conclusion

In offering African heritage courses, boards of education need to proceed with a clear plan, all the more so since the "Report of the Royal Commission on Learning" has recommended the establishment of Black-focussed schools. Recommendation # 140 of the Royal Commission report reads:

> That in jurisdictions with large numbers of Black students, school boards, academic authorities, faculties of education, and representatives of the Black community collaborate to establish demonstration schools and innovative programs based on the best practices in bringing about academic success for Black students.[24]

Teacher training and curriculum writing should now be made a priority. As agents of education, teachers are a fundamental part of the school system that is really a reflection of the larger society with its persistent problems of racism, stereotyping and the lack of equity in all areas. By itself, a sound curriculum will achieve little. Sound teacher preparation for delivering it is also essential. Solid African heritage programmes taught by well equipped, conscientious and sensitive teachers with high levels of expectation is what our children need. Great disservice has already been done to many Black children in after school

African Heritage programmes taught by individuals (not necessarily accredited teachers) who, however well meaning, lack proper credentials. There should be coordination between the schools where African Heritage classes are being taught and an assessment process designed to ensure quality. After centuries of being subjected to a distorted history, Blacks have a right to demand fundamental change.

NOTES

1 Robin W. Winks, *The Blacks in Canada* (New Haven: Yale University Press, 1971) p. 416.

2 *Final Report of the Consultative Committee on the Education of Black Students in Toronto Schools* (Toronto: Toronto Board of Education, 1988) p. 14.

3 Minutes of the Toronto Board of Education, 1976:224, reproduced in *Final Report*, pp. 12–13.

4 Ontario Ministry of Education, *Black Studies*, 1983.

5 *Black Studies*, p. 2.

6 *Black Studies*, p. 2.

7 *Etudes Afro-Canadiennes* (Toronto: Ontario Ministry of Education, 1988).

8 Minutes of the Toronto Board of Education, 1986 (148–149) reproduced in *Final Report*, pp. 6–7.

9 Minutes of the Toronto Board of Education, March 1986 (#96 — 41), reproduced in *Final Report*, p. 5.

10 *Final Report*, pp. 57–58.

11 *Final Report*, pp. 58–59.

12 Chinua Achebe, *Things Fall Apart* (London: Heinemann, 1958).

13 Quoted in J.D. Fage, "The Development of African Historiography," in (ed.) J. Ki-Zerbo, *General History of Africa*, vol. 1 (London: Heinemann, 1981) p. 31.

14 Molefi Kete Asante, *Afrocentricity* (Trenton: Africa World Press, 1989) p. 6.

15 *The New York Times*, June 3, 1992 p. B9.

16 Cheikh Anta Diop, *Nations nègres et cultures* 2 vols. (Paris: Presènce Africaine, 1979).

17 Bernard Moitt, "Cheikh Anta Diop and the African Diaspora: Historical Continuity and Socio-Cultural symbolism," in *Presènce Africaine*, 149–150, 1–2, 1989, pp. 347–360.

18 See Alain Froment, "Origin et évolution de l'homme dans la pensée de

Cheikh Anta Diop: une analyse critique," in *Cahiers d'Etudes africaines*, 121-122, XXXI, 1–2, 1991, pp. 29–64; ____," Race et histoire: la recomposition idéologique de l'image des Egyptiens anciens," in *Journal des africainistes*, *64*(11) 1994, pp. 37– 63.

19 Philip Curtin, *The Atlantic Slave Trade: A Census* (Madison: University of Wisconsin Press, 1969), p. 268.

20 Joseph Inikori, *The Chaining of a Continent: Export Demand for Captives and the History of Africa South of the Sahara, 1450–1870* (Kingston: Institute of Social and Economic Research, 1992), pp. 2–225.

21 "AHA Council Issues Policy," p. 27.

22 Roland Oliver and J.D. Fage, *A Short History of Africa* (London: Penguin, 1990).

23 *History of West Africa* (Onitsha: Africana-FEP Publishers, 1967).

24 Ontario Government, "For the Love of Learning," Report of the Royal Commission on Learning, Vol. IV, 1994, p. 178.

Comment

REFLECTIONS ON ARTS EDUCATION AND YOUTH CULTURE
A COMMENT

WENDY BRATHWAITE

In these last years of the 20th century, it is of utmost importance that we as educators, foster a socially, economically, and culturally aware and empowered generation of future leaders. The current school curriculum reflects poorly the realities of the Black student population, and is therefore not providing us with the preparation we need for the future.

I know this because I am a product of Ontario's education system. I had nearly all of my schooling here, except for my Grade Eight year which I spent in Botswana. The opportunity I have had to work in many alternative learning environments, ranging from workshops to arts training/employment programs, has given me more valuable insights into the obstacles Black students must face in order to "succeed" academically. This work has also provided me with insights into what the schools could do to respond to Black students' needs in more effective ways.

As human beings, we learn according to our environments, the relations we are able to make with the lessons taught, and the reflections that we find that help us to connect with our teachers, texts and our school curriculum. To this day, however, African-centered content in music, art, literature, history and science is virtually ignored, or absent, or condescendingly marginalized into specialized classes. In school, my complex African heritage was allowed only a *month of recognition* or placed in after school programs which I attended from very young. The Black experience is still considered an "extra-curricular" activity in the education system. Many Black youth are finding it difficult to persevere because of the negativity that they face when they attempt to assert their *Voice* within the school. Outside forums and specialized classes have become a haven for these youth who are expected to "fit in" like I was from nine to three, decipher Shakespeare, analyze the American Civil War from an "objective" point of view, sing anglicized arrangements of "Negro Spirituals," and generally blend in and excel, or get labelled and left back.

It was through the arts, especially music and poetry, that I developed my *Voice* which I now use in my work with youth in schools and in the community. Both my personal school experience and my experience in teaching Arts in alternative programs and workshops in school, have taught me that the overall lack of anti-racist, inclusive curriculum is a key factor in Black students' schooling and leads to chronic suspensions, absenteeism and high dropout rates. Working in alternative learning environments in the school, I am consistently hearing from students phrases like, "School is boring," "They don't teach me nothing," and "I hate Mr. So and So. He's racist." Yet when these same students, who are often labelled as behavioral and problematic, are engaged in learning that involves their own culture and experience, there is a significant rise in their enthusiasm, interest and productivity. I have found that basing lesson themes on the experiences of the students produces positive outcomes that could be utilised in the main curriculum. For example, themes could center around the culture of youth, including music, movies, fashion and reading materials that reflect their interests. This offers a sense of validation and self-empowerment to students. They can then be encouraged to explore their particular existence in the context of a wider worldview — that is, learn to view their situation within a more global perspective.

I will use the example of Hip Hop and show how it can lead to a variety of lessons and explorations. In a summer employment and training program for Black youth in the arts, I based a general Music Program I designed on Hip Hop music and culture, because this is the dominant youth culture of the past ten to fifteen years. First we established that Rap music was part of a larger culture that included language, visual arts, literature, ideology, commence and industry and social attitudes. We then proceeded to explore Hip Hop culture in the context of the African experience throughout history. This was conceptualized through the considerations of the African oral tradition, the role and importance of music throughout African history and the socio-political messages in the Black Arts.

This program helped the youth become aware of how their popular culture was connected with the cultures of their past. This was accomplished by a study of musical influences, from the origins of the drum to Spirituals, Blues and Jazz, Soul and R&B. Hip Hop lyrics were analyzed, and related to the rhythmic poetry of Louise Bennett, Bob Marley and Langston Hughes. Controversial themes within Hip Hop music were compared with the lyrical themes of Blues and Reggae music, and used to explore the socio-economic and political climates and struggles that created them, whether in the Caribbean or the United States.

We also used the current music industry for further analysis, asking who makes the money, who are the decisions-makers, how are finances divvied up? This led the class to an exploration of entrepreneurship, accounting and legal matters and the designing of business plans. Within this often underestimated topic — Hip Hop music — lies the foundation of a wealth of learning experiences, in the areas of history, sociology, economics, law, creative arts, media and literature.

Beginning the lessons from the place and space of those we aim to teach encourages self-empowerment and personal growth that the enlightened and open-minded educator can guide and direct. The enthusiasm, insight and intelligence that are found within the intimacy of Black Student Clubs and conferences, community centers, Rap sessions, artistic programs and in ciphers on the corner must be seriously considered in order to get to the roots of the Black Youth psyche. We must channel their voices and experiences of today, connect them to the history of yesterday and define a representative curriculum for a vast tomorrow.

Black Youth can and do learn. Let us design programs that reward them for the wealth of knowledge that they do possess and the wide range of interests that they have.

PART FOUR

PROGRAMMES TO ENHANCE THE EDUCATIONAL ATTAINMENTS OF BLACK STUDENTS

Chapter Eleven

SCHOOL – UNIVERSITY PARTNERSHIPS
THE CHALLENGE OF COMMITMENT

FREDERICK IVOR CASE

The history of education in Ontario is an anguished story of the exclusion of African Canadian children. The 1850 Education Act should be considered as a major act of violence against African Canadians which has repercussions to this day. This Act was prepared by Egerton Ryerson — after whom Ryerson Polytechnic University is named — and it ostensibly permitted any group of 12 Protestant, Catholic or "Coloured" families to set up a school independently of the local schools administered by a board of education. In fact, the 1850 Education Act permitted taxpayers of European origin to exclude African Canadians from the better funded and equipped board schools, forcing them to establish segregated schools that were invariably minimally financed.[1]

Even in those parts of Ontario, notably Toronto and Hamilton, where schools were not traditionally segregated, African Canadian students were often relegated to the back of the class, ignored and suffered greatly from lack of self-esteem as a result of the general conditions of their education.

Historical evidence informs us that African Canadian communities fought back with the means that they had at their disposal, since they realised that education was the key to their demands for equitable treatment in all spheres of life.[2]

This tradition of resistance to the cultural determination of our children and to the psychological limits placed on their growth continued until the 1960s when African Canadian university students of York University and the University of Toronto together with other educators founded the Black Education Project and the Transitional Year Program. The vision of these university students led to the first major school-community-university partnerships that I know of.

It is important to state that even though these initiatives were undertaken by Canadians of African origin, both the Black Education Project and the Transitional Year Program at the University of Toronto concentrated their efforts on the education of any ethnic communities or social class that was systemically marginalised by the Ontario educational system. At the very origins of the Transitional Year Program, we find students who were of Aboriginal, African, Asian and southern European origins. In the 1970s, when I was directly involved with the Black Education Project, we served the needs of students of every racial and ethnic group who presented themselves, although the majority of our students were of African and Asian origins.

This type of partnership between university students, a very few faculty members and the community is an ideal formula for cooperation since "ownership" of the process belongs to the community. As social conditions evolve, the relationship between the various parties concerned is modified. This immediate reaction of each party provides the cultural and psychological flexibility that is essential in any successful educational project.

However, there are few surviving examples of community-based partnerships between schools and universities and the major part of this article will deal with institutionalised forms of collaboration which have the potential for growth and expansion into the community.

There are various types of institution centred school university partnerships that have existed for decades in Ontario. The "evidence" in this article is based on the author's personal knowledge of such partnerships and the reference to specific institutions is kept to the minimum. The purpose of the article is to illustrate the several ways in which collaboration between schools and universities can be fruitful and to highlight some of the limitations, pitfalls and triumphs of such partnerships.

In the United States of America institutionalised school university partnerships have existed for generations and are to be found in every part of that nation. The commitment of the universities and school boards concerned is often very impressive.

Based on my experience in Ontario and what I have learned in and of the US, I will categorise a certain number of possibilities of collaboration.[3]

1. In Ontario, a common form of school-university collaboration is the visit of the high school class to the local university. This often involves an individual faculty member or university department that has taken an interest in a particular high school through alumni teaching there. The school sees this as a means of encouraging its students to higher achievement whilst the university sees these visits as a means of recruiting the highest achievers and enhancing the celebrity of their academic programs. Continuation of such programs depends on the goodwill of individuals.

This type of visit is highly selective and rewarding for the participants since the primary purpose is recruitment.

2. There is another type of visit that is much more focussed and demands a great deal of reflection and organisation before it is carried out. This is the visit that aims at addressing the question of representation in the university. For example, visits are organised for female high school students to particular departments and faculties where women are under-represented. The visit of Aboriginal students to a university in order to show them the academic options that they have. The visit of students from an inner-city school to the campus to meet university students of their own background.

Visits involving specific groups of students should be prepared in very close collaboration with the students themselves, their teachers, community members and faculty members or staff who have some knowledge of the social, economic and political environment of the students. On arrival at the university, it is essential that the high school students be met by university students and faculty who are sympathetic to the aims of the program.

3. University departments and teachers sometimes organise competitions in their discipline and the annual French, Mathematics or English competition and the prize giving that accompanies it are firmly institutionalised. The ultimate stage of establishing such a connection is the participation of two or three local university departments in a given subject organising activities with a local group of subject area teachers. There are some remarkable successes in this context. A number of university departments organise annual local competitions in their domain of specialisation. For example, Erindale College (University of Toronto), holds annual essay writing competitions for high school students in English and French. The essays are marked by faculty members of Erindale College and the winners are invited to the College to receive their awards. Over the years a good working relationship has been established between the schools and the College. The commitment of the teachers and faculty is very evident but it is the College as an academic institution that sanctions the activity and produces the framework in which it continues.

4. A variation on (3) is the annual competition in French organised by the Ontario Modern Language Teachers Association. The competition is based on written tests which are held in turn at Glendon College (York University) and New, St. Michael's, University and Victoria Colleges at the University of Toronto. In this case, the driving force is the organisation of teachers since there is little direct involvement by faculty members of the University. The prizes are awarded in the college in which the competition is held. The colleges concerned provide a venue in which

the students can more readily appreciate the academic importance of what they are doing.

5. In 1991 a formal agreement was signed between the University of Toronto and Flemington Public School, North York. Already a group of professors of the Department of Mathematics had devoted much time and energy to the children of this inner-city K-5 school. They had tutored students and also encouraged and assisted them in their annual Science Share activities. The commitment of these professors and the vision of the then principal of the school acted as a stimulus to the students, their parents and the teachers.

Flemington Public School is in every way a community school in which there is a nursery, day care, the K-5 school and an ESL program housed in the same building. The racial and ethnic diversity of the students is reflected in the composition of the staff of the school.

It was the Office of Development and Community Affairs of the University of Toronto that approached me to sign the agreement on behalf of the President of the University. It was this "accident" that propelled me, as Principal of New College, into a formal partnership that I welcomed.

I soon discovered that the success of a school-university partnership depends on a certain number of precise factors:

a) trust and collaboration between a senior university administrator and a designated contact person at the school;[4]

b) the collaboration of the parents of the students;

c) direct contact between students of the school and those of the university;

d) access of both school and university contact persons to someone on staff at the university who can facilitate activities involving various faculties and colleges;[5]

e) frequent telephone calls or personal contact between the parties concerned.

The partnership between Flemington Public School and New College takes the following forms:

- visits to New College by Grade 5 students who spend an entire working day with the Principal. Two or three students come on each visit. They meet other staff and are taken on a tour of residences by students of the College. They also visit other parts of the campus in which they have expressed an interest. They are expected to make a presentation to their class on their return to school. Parents undertake to bring the children to the University and return at the end of the day to take them back to their community.

- tutoring of Flemington Public School students by New College students. Many of our students hope to enter the Faculty of Education and the supervised classroom experience they gain is useful for them. The Principal of Flemington and the Principal of New College have agreed to give each participating university student a joint letter to confirm that the tutoring has been done. New College recruits the university students who volunteer as tutors and the school holds an orientation for the tutors and fully organises their participation in the activities of the school.

- visits to Flemington Public School by the Principal of New College, students of New College and any other person requested by the school. These visits are usually initiated by the school and are planned when there is a specific occasion involving the Grade 5 class. For example, on their graduation; at the conclusion of their cultural heritage program; to mark the beginning of the academic year of collaboration between the School and the College.

- participation of Flemington students in the Mini-University programs run by the Department of Athletics and Recreation. The registration costs of these programs are beyond the means of many of the families served by Flemington Public School. Parents are expected to make a modest contribution and the Department of Athletics and Recreation and New College divide the rest of the costs. This permits the inner-city students to share in an experience that they would not normally enjoy

- invitation of Flemington students to participate in any University activity from which they can derive some further familiarity with the world of post-secondary education: U. of T. day — which is an open house event at the University; Remembrance Day ceremonies at Soldiers' Tower on the main campus.

I have always disliked the tendency of African Canadians to espouse the principle of role models. I consider it to be quite dangerous in the tendency to encourage sycophancy of the worst kind. However, particularly in my relationship with Flemington Public School, I know that the fact that I am an African Canadian male has made a great difference in the perspectives of some of the African Canadian students. Nevertheless, it is always much more important to emphasise the achievements of our university students who look young enough to be the older siblings of the elementary students. Still, at times the difficulty has been finding a number of African Canadian students who are willing to act as volunteer tutors.

Most of the Grade 5 students who leave Flemington Public School attend Lawrence Heights Middle School. Victoria College (University of Toronto) has developed a partnership with Lawrence Heights and a number of University of Toronto students tutor at the school. Victoria College holds an orientation for tutors at the beginning of the academic year and the Principal of that college as well as the Dean of Students are fully committed to the program.

New College also has a partnership with Eastdale Collegiate — an inner city high school in Toronto. This partnership grew out of a visit to the school by myself and Gordon Cressy, then Vice-president, Development and Community Affairs. During that initial visit we met with the Principal of the school, the Vice-Principal, the teacher assigned to special projects in the school and a few senior students. The composition of this group proved to be very important. The administration of the school demonstrated its commitment to some form or other of partnership; the teacher most acquainted with the wide range of issues affecting the students was present to indicate the need of such commitment and the students expressed explicitly and

211

implicitly the type of collaborative activities that were needed.

It was immediately obvious that though this high school is only a relatively short distance from the University of Toronto, the high school students had a vision of the institution and its students that was quite inaccurate.

Very soon after this initial meeting, Ms. Sally Walker, Registrar of New College accepted the responsibility of being the contact person with the school. This is a most appropriate level of cooperation since on her visits to the school she is able to give detailed information on university admission, scholarships and financial assistance for students. Ms. Walker has also established, in the college, a group for single parents. This group meets frequently during the academic year to discuss issues of common interest that the members identify. Together with her team of registrarial staff, Ms. Walker concentrates considerably on counselling of New College students concerning financial, academic and personal matters.

In meeting with the high school students, the Registrar is able to point out to them that parenthood is not a barrier to university education. Apart from the visits to the school by the Registrar, myself and some of our students, there is an organised visit to New College during which we attempt to demystify the University of Toronto.

The Registrar is arranging for the high school students to sit in on a lecture given by one of the Fellows of the College. This will be a normal first-year lecture held in a large auditorium so that the high school students can have some experience of some aspects of learning in a university.

Whenever the school calls on us we try to respond and in this way we have collaborated with the school in a very modest way through some of our students tutoring there.[6]

Inevitably New College has been approached by other schools. Most recently we have been approached by an inner city high school with many grave problems. I made an on-site visit with a community worker and met the Principal and one of the Vice-Principals. I also met informally with other members of staff and wandered around for a couple of hours to assess the climate of the school. The expressed need at this school is for our New College students, who are very diverse in racial and ethnic origins, to tutor at the school which has an equally diverse student population, many of whom are of African origin.

In one other case we have resorted to subversion. Through visits to yet another high school, I learned from refugee students from Africa that they were not informed about admission to university despite their academic achievements and their grade.

Through a sympathetic teacher we organised a visit to New College during which the Registrar explained to the students, in detail, all the steps that should be taken.

Our aim at New College is to make high school and even elementary school students aware of the fact that university is not a mysterious nor a hallowed place of which they are unworthy. We are not recruiting students. If any of these students eventually come to New College we would be delighted but I would be equally happy if they went to another college, university or to a community college. In the particular case of African Canadian students, our partnerships serve to motivate them to continue at school and to strive for the best they can achieve. Dropping out from secondary school is a far too frequent end to the academic career of our students.[7] If we have succeeded in making the students with whom we are in contact conscious of the benefits of post-secondary education, we would have succeeded in our objectives.

There is no doubt that such partnerships take time to encourage and to promote. The more individuals involved on both sides the better and the focus has to remain on the priorities that have been set. It is, however, essential to involve the university students as much as possible. During visits to high schools or elementary schools, it is very significant that our New College students attract more attention as speakers and during the general mingling and conversation than myself or the Registrar. On one occasion, the Registrar and I were accompanied to a high school by three of our students. There was no doubt that the students of the school and their parents were far more interested in the explanations and experiences of the university students than they were in listening to the two of us.

I am very aware of the fact that I have not sufficiently

involved the student organisations of the College in our partnerships. If partnerships are to continue, they must become institutionalised in the universities and in the schools with responsibilities very clearly defined. The administrative life of a Principal is very short and partnerships are far too important to be entrusted to the whim or lack of interest of individual administrators.

With each successive generation of university students, we should identify those with leadership potential who would be willing to play an active role in the organising of the partnership. There is every reason why a university student should be the contact person on campus and why he or she should be able to take initiatives to further the specific aims of the partnership.

Like all relationships, this one demands a great deal of faith and effort. Schools have to learn more about post-secondary institutions and we in turn have to learn more about the stresses of teaching in the classroom. For too long education has functioned in quite separate and remote compartments. Partnerships help us a little along the road toward a coherent and just system in which all students from K to 13 know that post-secondary education is not a privilege for a few but a right that they have, wherever they might live in Canada.

In the very specific context of the education of African Canadian students, it is essential that community-based organisations such as the Organisation of Parents of Black Children and the dozens of African and Caribbean social organisations begin to exert some influence on post-secondary institutions. There are many opportunities for community-based initiatives in school-university partnerships but this would be the subject of yet another article.

NOTES

1 For documentation on these issues see R. W. Winks, *The Blacks in Canada: A History*, Montreal, McGill-Queen's/New Haven & London, Yale University Press, 1971; F. Case, *Racism and National Consciousness*, Plowshare, 1977; C. P. Ripley (ed.) *The Black Abolitionist Papers. Vol II: Canada. 1830–1865*, Chapel Hill & London, University of North Carolina Press, 1986.

2 In particular see several of the letters and documents in Ripley (1986).

3 In this article I will not consider the visits made by university officials to graduating high school classes to make them aware of the academic opportunities available to them.

4 The first school contact person with whom I collaborated was Ms. Richards. She was succeeded by Ms. Monica Clarke. Both of these teachers are of Caribbean origin and have consistently committed time and energy to find innovative ways to keep the partnership alive. The program could not continue without their persistence and focus on the aims to be achieved.

5 M. Susan Grant formerly of the Office of Development and Community Affairs at the University of Toronto, is at the origin of most of the activities that I describe in this section. Her sensitive intervention, thoroughness, calm and sense of initiative have served the University and the community in many ways.

6 See Norma Vale, "Bringing two worlds together," in *University Affairs/ Affaires Universitaires*, November 1995. p. 11.

7 See George J. Sefa Dei et al., *Drop out or push out? The Dynamics of Black Students' disengagement from school*, Toronto, O.I.S.E., 1995.

Chapter Twelve

CREATING AN OPPORTUNITY STRUCTURE FOR BLACKS AND OTHER TEACHERS OF COLOUR

R. Patrick Solomon

Introduction

> Where are the visible minority teachers? Why are there so few role models? Why do our white guidance counsellors know so little of different cultural backgrounds? ... Why do they discourage us from University?
>
> (Stephen Lewis Report, 1992, p. 20)

These are some the ways Black/African Canadians and other students of colour have critiqued the urban, racial and ethnoculturally diverse schools in which they are being educated. An overview of the research on the education of such students in multicultural societies such as Britain (Coard, 1971; Department of Education and Science (DES), 1985; Gillborn, 1988) the United States (Ogbu, 1974; Irvine, 1990; Macleod, 1987) and Canada (Solomon, 1992; James, 1990; Dei, 1993; Toronto Board of Education, 1993) has confirmed gross inadequacy of mainstream schools in preparing students of colour equitably for life. They underachieve academically and are alienated and disaffected by the content and process of schooling. Many resist the process and end up dropping out of school before acquiring the skills, competencies and credentials for productive life in an increasingly complex work environment. Many such disaffected youth have raised compelling arguments for *their own* schools with a curriculum and teaching staff that represent their interests. Such demands are not lone voices in the wilderness; support for alternative forms of schooling such as African-centred schools has come from racial minority communities, educators and researchers (Asante, 1991; Dei, 1994; Royal Commission on Learning, 1994).

Central to the argument for a more representative curriculum, alternative teaching strategies and positive social relations in the classroom is the value conventional wisdom assigns to role modelling. Researching the limited presence of African-American teachers in U.S. schools, King (1993:120) concludes:

> ... Children of colour need role models. African-American teachers are of critical importance not just because children need to see that teachers of colour exist or that people of colour can assume leadership positions. They are needed because of their many other roles, perspectives and practices.

Other educators and researchers support King's assertion that representative role models from various racial and ethnocultural groups serve not only as examples of accomplishment and success, but as teachers who are ideally positioned to enrich the curriculum with pertinent cultural and cognitive strategies that may lead to higher functioning of students of colour (Cummins, 1986; Gill, 1989; Loehr, 1988; Foster, 1989; Henry, 1992; D'Oyley, 1994). Dominant group students also benefit from their exposure to teachers of colour as professionals and this may help to modify stereotypes and beliefs they may have of racial minorities (Alexander and Miller, 1989; Irvine, 1988).

The debate over teachers of colour as role models for students of colour is far from conclusive. Cizek's (1995) critique of the research points to the lack of empirical evidence to support the claim that the exposure of students of colour to teachers of their own racial group improves their academic achievement.

What the research has shown without any doubt, is that dominant group teachers have differential expectations of students from different race and ethnic backgrounds and such expectations often influence curriculum offering, teaching approaches and student-teacher relations in school (Ross and Jackson, 1991; Rubovitz and Maehr, 1973; James, 1990; Solomon, 1992). On the other hand, teachers of colour see themselves as having high expectations of students from their own racial group and provide the learning environment for them to achieve to the best of their potential (Henry, 1992; Ladson-Billings, 1992; Allen, 1994).

Although Allen is ambivalent about the role model functions for females and students of colour because of its linkages with the affirmative action movement in the United States, she offers a useful analysis of how role modelling may work to enhance the schooling of these groups. She argues (1994:190):

> All teachers are role models. But not every teacher is a role model in every sense. They "model" their roles as teachers. They are what I call "ethical templates," men and women whose conduct sets standards for the exercise of responsibilities. Only some teachers are role models in the stronger, equally familiar senses I will label "symbols" of special achievement and "nurturers" of students' special needs.

She concludes that by their mere presence role models can reshape conceptions of who can teach, they "inspire others to believe that they too may be capable of high accomplishments" (p. 191).

From a synthesis of the research has emerged compelling arguments for a more diversified teaching force to meet the challenges of the growing racial and ethnic diversity within schools and society at large. Demographic projections are that by the turn of the century people of colour will have grown to over forty percent of the population in urban centres such as Metropolitan Toronto (Samuel, 1992). Schools and teacher education institutions can no longer ignore this reality. A more representative teaching force must be created to provide the learning environment with diverse curricula, perspectives and practices; an environment with teachers of diverse backgrounds who have high expectations of all students; and more importantly, teachers who are committed to be role models, mentors or advocates for students of colour who are "at risk" in dominant group institutions.

How do you move from a homogeneously white teaching force to one that is more representative of the population that it serves?[1] Teacher education institutions in the United States and Canada have experimented with unconventional recruitment, admission and retention approaches (Dilworth, 1992; Garibaldi, 1989; Orlikow and Young, 1993; Hesch, 1994; Lundy and Lawrence, 1993). But untraditional approaches to the recruitment of racial minority teachers are not without tensions and controversy. For many skeptics, making post-secondary and professional education accessible to the non-traditional (usually racial minority and working class) student means "lowering admission standards" and "sacrificing program quality." For such critics access and quality are conceptualized as mutually exclusive institutional objectives (see Richardson and Skinner's, 1991:10 critique of this position).

Proponents of teaching force diversity argue that quality and diversity do not necessarily conflict if institutions "adapt their environment to accommodate greater diversity without relinquishing their commitment to high standard of achievement for all students" (Richardson and Skinner, 1991:13). Upon reviewing the findings of their large scale research on institutional adaptation to student diversity, Richardson and Skinner (p. 254) conclude:

> We have emphasized the importance of acting on a definition of quality that incorporates diversity by adapting institutional environments so that they enroll and graduate a clientele more nearly reflective of the composition of the society they serve.

This chapter describes York University's Faculty of Education initiative to promote access and equity in its teacher education program. Using the model of institutional adaptation advanced by Richardson and Skinner (1991), I will analyze York's initiative to determine the extent to which its organizational culture shift has made its learning environment more accessible and accommodative to teacher candidates of colour. This model was developed to describe and analyze the experiences of colleges and universities in the United States as they adapted to accommodate the underrepresented while maintaining program quality and integrity. The model posits the reactive, strategic and adaptive stages of transformation institutions experience when increasing diversity and achievement. Where necessary, adjusted or alternative approaches will be suggested to capture the unique features of the York initiative.

Institutional Adaptation to Student Diversity

The Reactive Stage: Outreach and Recruitment

- Special admission procedures in response to pressures for greater participation of underrepresented groups
- Increase in the expectations of previously excluded groups.

The Strategic Stage: Changing the environment

- Mentoring and advising minority students
- Transforming the social environment to accommodate racial minority students
- Increasing faculty from minority groups

The Adaptive Stage: Curriculum and Pedagogy

- Change in educational practices, curriculum content, teaching practices
- Development of sensitivity to minority experiences for all students
- Intensive faculty involvement signalling fundamental shifts in organizational culture.

Adapted from Richardson and Skinner's model (1991:12)

Equity and Inclusion: York's Initiative

In 1991 the Dean for the Faculty of Education established the Antidiscriminatory Advisory Group (ADAG) to examine how institutional structures and practices affect student diversity and professional preparation, and to recommend ways the faculty may address specific issues of access and outreach for underrepresented groups, retention and support, curriculum and pedagogy, and faculty and staff development (Shapson, 1994). ADAG was composed of representatives from the Faculty of Education staff, students and faculty, York Federation of Students, the Centre for Race and Ethnic Relations, The Office of Learning Disabilities, and other interest groups. ADAG's ongoing advice to the Dean was to a large extent informed by these university organizations, educational practitioners within schools, and advocacy groups from the local communities. These groups, initially submitted briefs to the Faculty and participated in ADAG meetings on an ongoing basis. One of the main issues expressed by these groups and supported by research findings (Found, 1992) was that despite the University's rich race and ethnocultural diversity, the Faculty of Education clientele had remained predominantly white.

The first task of the Faculty was to improve access for four groups that were traditionally underrepresented in its program: People of Colour, Aboriginal/First Nation Peoples, People of refugee background and the Differently abled.[2] Outreach to these groups included advertisements in campus and local ethnic community newspapers, scheduled large group information sessions and individual sessions with prospective applicants.

A unique requirement of the Access Initiative is for applicants to submit an autobiographical statement that discusses "the kinds of factors, which in their view, have affected their chances or limited their opportunities to become teachers" (from Faculty of Education Admissions package 1992–93). The statement guidelines also suggest that applicants describe their "involvement in activities, settings, community organizations or situations, particularly involving children or adolescents, which have influenced his or her decision to pursue a career in teaching." This autobiographical statement gave, for the first time, people of colour and other marginalized groups, the opportunity to discuss barriers they have confronted in striving to enter teacher education.

The next sections detail structural and procedural changes to the admissions process that made it more equitable for people of colour and other groups that are underrepresented in the teaching profession.

Academic Credentials

This new opportunity structure moves beyond grade point average (G.P.A.) as the first, and sometimes only screening factor for applicants to teacher education programs. The importance attached to G.P.A. called into question some institutions' preoccupation with "quantifiable indices," an overly one-dimensional concern with proven academic achievement. Although the minimum G.P.A. for consideration at York is C+, in a large, highly credentialed applicant pool only applicants with high-end G.P.A.s had a fair chance of passing the initial screening. The general belief that G.P.A. is positively related to program quality and outcome has traditionally dictated this institutional practice.

York's new access initiative now considers a broader range of post secondary schooling experiences and academic credentials as part of the admission criteria. For example, community college experience, additional university courses, honours degree, second and graduate degrees all contribute to the applicants' academic profile, restricting the screening-out potential of grade point average alone.

Such a reconceptualization of academic standing improved the admission opportunities for those applicants of colour with broad and comprehensive academic profiles. This rethinking of G.P.A. as a screening factor also recognizes the fact that some applicants' low G.P.A. may have been more a result of social, cultural and curricular factors within their learning environments than a reflection of their academic capacity or their potential to develop as professional teachers.

Accreditation of Experience

The second admission requirement is work experience with children. The experiences most highly rated by application screeners were those gained in mainstream public schools and classrooms during the regular teaching day. This tradition often eliminated many people of colour. For many, their socio-economic lives as wage earners restricted their opportunities to gain this valuable experience as volunteers during the regular school day. Those who can overcome the socio-economic obstacle face gatekeepers who control access to schools. People of colour were far more likely than their white counterparts to be refused volunteer positions within mainstream schools.[3]

The new opportunity structure now credits applicants with other relevant work experience with children and adolescents. These include early childhood education in institutional settings, heritage language programs, nursery school and day care programs, youth counselling in the community, recreation and camp counselling in summer programs and various other related experiences with children in ethno-cultural or general community agencies.

An evaluation process has been developed to assess the quality and quantity of these experiences with children. York's decision to move these experiences from the margins to the mainstream and to reward them appropriately has improved the admission chances of people of colour. It is significant that under this revised process, the category "work experience with children" is given an equally strong weighting as academic credentials. This signals a shift in emphasis to work experience as a good predictor of success in teacher education and the teaching profession. Of course, this assumption is subject to empirical research and verification.

Democratizing the Interview Process

Perhaps the most subjective and problematic admission screening process for applicants of colour was the interview protocol and the gatekeeping function of the interviewers who administered them. Content analysis conducted on the *Interview Report Form* revealed the presence of cultural, language and social class biases. The personal characteristics of applicants were judged on such factors as: sense of humour, appearance, quality of other interests, appropriate energy level and appropriate strength of personal presence. Teacher-scholar potential was evaluated on such factors as: attitudes toward the teaching process, clarity of speech, interesting/worthwhile ideas, and breadth of general knowledge. These items are value-laden and carry the potential of eliminating those applicants who do not project dominant group cultural norms.

Further, interviewers who rated applicant responses to these value-laden categories were almost exclusively dominant, white, middle class educators. Research has shown this group to be traditionally conservative with little tolerance for cultural difference (Lortie, 1975; Solomon and Levine-Rasky, 1994; Sleeter, 1992; Mock and Masemann, 1990). Ideologically, some may not embrace cultural pluralism as a fact of life in Canadian society and advocate, instead, the assimilationist ideal. Not surprisingly, some exercised very few cross-cultural skills in the interview process and were known to reject applicants because of their accents, and the usual "no Canadian experience." This face-to-face encounter made the "interviewer as gatekeeper" the final arbiter of personal suitability for teacher education and the profession at large.

York's Access Initiative has revised the content and restructured the interview process making it more equitable for applicants of colour and other underrepresented groups in teacher education. First, value-laden and culturally biased items were replaced by ones that relied less on interviewers' subjective judgements and culture bias. The *Teacher-scholar* and *Personal Characteristic* categories were replaced by a broad-based scale that focused more on experience with children, commitment to teaching and awareness of contemporary educational issues.

The interviewer pool, initially predominantly white, was reconstituted to reflect the racial and ethnocultural diversity of applicants and communities from which they come. The recruitment of new interviewers moved beyond educators to include other groups that were familiar with and had vested interest in the schooling process.

Finally, the Faculty requires all interviewers in the pool to participate in orientation sessions that, among other things, provide an introduction to cross-cultural interviewing. Here, the workshop addresses the question: "How do I avoid misunderstandings and communicate most effectively with people who are different from me?" and explores the awareness, sensitivity, knowledge, and power relationships involved in working equitably with a diverse group of applicants.[4]

This brief overview of structural and procedural changes provides insights into York's initiative to diversify its teacher candidate pool: the formation of an advisory group to the Dean, innovations in the admissions criteria such as redefining academic credentials, redefining what counts as work experience with children and adolescents, democratizing and implementing an interview process that is more equitable for all applicants, especially those from underrepresented groups. This is what Richardson and Skinner conceptualize in their model as the Reactive Stage of institutional transformation.

Some Encouraging Outcomes

The dramatic annual growth of applicants reflected in Table 1 is an indication of the Access Initiative's success in attracting and admitting people of colour and other underrepresented groups to teacher education. Such an interest in the program dispels the myth that racial minority groups are not interested in teaching as a profession (see The Canadian Education Association (1992) report: Teacher Recruitment and Retention).

Table 1

Access Initiative: Growth in Applications and Admissions

Year	No. of Applicants	No. of Admissions
1991–92	18	15
1992–93	220	65
1993–94	429	91
1994–95	529	133
1995–96	440	173

(a)   Statistics reflect applicants and admissions in both the concurrent and consecutive programs.[5]

(b)   Statistics do not include applicants of the target groups who applied and were admitted through the general admissions process.

Institutional restructuring of the admissions process and the creation of an opportunity structure that admits underrepresented groups is affirmed by comparing the responses of dominant and minority group applicants. The dominant group respondent spoke with confidence, "I felt I had a good chance at making it. I had submitted a good [application] package," and "I was not totally sure, but I knew my chances were good." Applicants of colour, on the other hand, were less confident, less optimistic. They spoke of "not being sure ... not thinking I had a shot [at gaining admission]" One confided:

> I knew you [the Faculty of Education] wanted more visible minorities in the program but I know there was subtle discrimination against the Access Initiative in the program. In the real world there is a need but I knew I would have to face subtle barriers. I was very nervous.

Candidates who gained admission through the Access Initiative describe the program as "a God-send."

The Faculty, through its Access Initiative, has demonstrated that an opportunity structure can be created to correct past discriminatory practices and to equalize admission opportunities for people of colour. However, there is a long way to go to correct the racial imbalance in teacher education programs and the savage inequalities in the teaching force at large. While the 1994-95 statistics revealed that 23.5% of the applicants of colour were admitted to the program, this group amounted to a mere 14.5% of the total Faculty intake of 768 for that year.

The long term goal of the Faculty is to revise its admission criteria and to restructure the process, thus integrating into the mainstream, successful Access Initiative interventions. Such institutional restructuring will hopefully eliminate the need for an Access Initiative that has become a controversial political issue and has gained such unpopular labels as "reverse discrimination," "reverse racism," and "affirmative action." As will be shown later, attitudes that generate these labels also have tremendous negative impact on teacher candidates of colour in a teaching environment that is not ready for change.

Creating Equitable Learning Environments

The Strategic Stage of the Richardson and Skinner model is working directly with students of colour in their new environment while transforming the environment to accommodate this group. To help achieve this objective York created a new faculty position: Access Initiative Coordinator. With the guidance and support of the Antidiscriminatory Advisory Group (ADAG) the Coordinator undertook such responsibilities as: planning and conducting orientation sessions for teacher candidates admitted through Access Initiative; conducting discussion sessions utilizing the knowledge, experience and expertise of senior teacher candidates and graduates; responding to concerns such as dissatisfaction with practicum placements, personal and family problems, racism and other forms of discrimination faced in the program and the university at large; and providing ongoing support, counselling, and mentoring for teacher candidates of colour as well as others who felt the need for these services. (see Parris, 1995, for a more comprehensive description of the Coordinator's role).

As we have seen, institutional leaders can revise admission policies and restructure processes. They can also develop and implement strategic plans for organizational change. But creating new learning environments that are responsive to the academic and social needs of teacher candidates of colour and other underrepresented groups require the genuine commitment and intervention of all staff and faculty working with these students. The provision of a learning environment that is welcoming and supportive, and a curriculum and pedagogy that is equity-conscious, requires major shifts in institutional culture. It requires educators who can adapt their environments to accommodate the learning needs, the perspectives and the experiences of racial minorities and other social groups traditionally underrepresented in teacher education. This section draws on ethnographic research to explore the experiences of teacher candidates of colour as they strive to locate themselves in the social environment of the institution, and in the curriculum and pedagogy of their educators. It concludes with suggestions for overcoming hostile environments and unyielding, conventional teacher education practices.

Living and working with social difference in the context of a teacher education program has proven to be a challenge for all engaged in the process: dominant group teacher candidates and faculty as well as teacher candidates of colour. A major contributing factor for these groups is the conflict and contradiction of being socialized into a profession that claims "race makes no difference" when in reality prior personal identity formation in a race-conscious society claims that it does. In addition, institutional and systemic factors within and outside the teacher education environment that contribute to social differentiation and racial polarization of teacher candidates are: the perception that the Faculty's Access Initiative is discriminatory and unmeritocratic, and has admitted unqualified people of colour into its programs; the perception that Boards of Education "target hiring" practices are giving preferential treatment to teachers of colour; the advocacy endeavours of teacher candidates of colour to have their interests represented in the social and academic spheres of the program are marginalizing the dominant groups; and the cliquing of teacher candidates of colour for mutual support and solidarity has resulted in racial group polarization. These factors have combined to create tensions and a "chilly climate" for teacher candidates of colour, both at the teacher education centres and on practicum sites (Solomon, Dippo, Schenke and Fullerton, 1994; Schenke, 1993; Wiggan, 1992; James, 1994).

One institutional response to such tensions and "chilliness" in the social world of teacher candidates is the development and testing of a pedagogical innovation in which dominant and racial minority groups have an opportunity to develop teaching abilities and professional relationships in a collaborative, interdependent manner.[6] This is accomplished through the creation of dyad partnerships between dominant and minority group teacher candidates in many aspects of program: planning and presenting seminars, journals sharing, field experience in the community and practicum teaching in classroom. The need for such intergroup collaboration is based on the premise that social boundaries will dissipate, cross-group misconceptions clarified, and hostilities reduced when groups are provided the environmental structure in which to share their experiences, knowledge, needs and concerns.

Of course, restructuring the social environment does not deal with the broader issues of equity and inclusion for people of colour in teacher education, the teaching force, or other Canadian institutions. These are systemic issues that must be integrated into the mainstream of teacher education scholarship. To what extent is such integration being realized?

The following excerpts of teacher candidates' voices from

the research of Solomon and Riviere (1993), Parris (1995) and Schenke (1993) capture the range of dissatisfaction with the way issues of race, racism, culture and multiculturalism are dealt with in the teacher education curriculum and the social and academic environment of learning to teach:

> Not enough time is spent on this [racial issues] and it could not be raised in this seminar. I tried, but nobody wanted to deal with it. In fact, one person said to me, "I've had enough of this defeatist attitude. I'd rather not talk about it unless it relates to math or something." (Solomon and Riviere, 1993, p. 11)

> When issues of race and ethnicity came up, I always felt that people were waiting for me to stand up and show my *Blackness*. (Parris 1995, p. 12)

> There are discriminatory tactics used, usually by white T.C.s (teacher candidates) to diffuse any critical discussion around the issues of race and culture in the seminar sessions. (Parris, 1995, p. 12)

> Questions of race were not raised to the extent that [they] should have been, I think. For example, one of the professors was talking about Inuits, and she spoke for an hour, and she kept calling this Inuit child, "Eskimo child." Someone raised their hand and said, "From what I understand, we are calling them Inuit now." And she [professor] replied, "I've always used this term." So, end of conversation. (Schenke, 1993, p. 59)

> [Multiculturalism/Native issues], were never really addressed in any long way. In our final Foundations class, we had a one-day workshop on multiculturalism with a guest speaker coming in, but it didn't get much further than now we can use different types of literature. Yet every body said multiculturalism is such an important focus for classrooms today. But never did we do anything but scrape the surface of it. (Schenke, 1993, p. 58)

> When there was racism in the classroom amongst grade 5/6 students, I think it would have really helped me to know how to handle it best, not just to handle it for the moment ... so, I think if my teacher education had provided more of that, it would have been helpful. (Schenke, 1993, p. 58)

Emerging from these excerpts are specific concerns: the marginalization of race and cultural matters in the teacher education curriculum, naive or closed-minded attitudes and assumptions about the presence of racism in the educational system, and the lack of skill development approaches for dealing with racism in the classroom. Teacher candidates who attempted to bring such issues into the mainstream of educational discourse were stigmatized as "surplus visibility," a term used by Daphne Patai (1991:52) and reported in Schenke (1993:40) to describe those who give voice to issues of racism. This labelling often has a silencing effect on students and tended to foreclose discourses that have the potential to be transformative (Schenke, 1993:41).

At the level of program design and delivery, courses such as Foundations and Models of Education that focus on the equity and inclusion of race, class and gender groups in education were critiqued as too short and offered too late in the teacher education program. Administrative response to the programming issue was prompt. The Foundations and Models of Education courses were restructured and reprogrammed to run the entire length of the one-year teacher education program, giving teacher candidates the time and opportunity to be reflective and responsive to course materials. Curriculum content and process continue to be problematic: anti-racist pedagogy and other forms of equity education remained in the domain of Foundations and Models courses; content was additive instead of integrative, and some course directors, unprepared to take leadership in this area, continued to utilize guest speakers for program delivery.

Given the nature and pace of curriculum transformation in the area of antiracist pedagogy, teacher candidates of colour must structure their own opportunities for change. First, they need to challenge the traditional, Eurocentric teacher education curriculum as unrepresentative of the diverse groups in Canadian schools and society. Second, teacher candidates of colour and other underrepresented groups should advocate for the inclusion of minority knowledge forms and experiences as legitimate curriculum content. Finally, teacher candidates of colour, and indeed, all teacher candidates, should advocate for the inclusion of antiracist curriculum and pedagogy in all aspects of their program. An improved opportunity structure for any marginalized group can only come about through their own strategic involvement in initiating the change process.

"Movement is not automatic, nor is it irreversible." Richardson and Skinner (1991:43) remind us in this quotation that institutional transformation does not materialize without committed leadership, faculty and staff support and material resources. Nor is change fast moving. They see institution's reactive, strategic and adaptive stages as "way stations along a continuum that stretches from pre-civil rights [in the U.S.] to the present" (p.13). To the contrary, York's Access and Inclusion Initiative started in 1991 has made rapid movement through the stages, often in overlapping and interloping fashion, in response to the urgent need for teachers of colour in the school system. As this study has shown, such a rapid succession of responses is not without challenges. These glitches are being experienced at the adaptive stage of change that requires fundamental shifts in the organizational culture. For example, without intensive faculty involvement in the change of educational practice, curriculum content and teaching practices, quality and diversity in teacher education will not be achieved.

Conclusion

Will African Canadian students in the school system benefit from the opportunity structure that prepares teachers of colour for the classroom? Will school administrators seize the opportunity to increase the representation of African Canadian and other teachers of colour in classrooms with substantial racial and ethnocultural diversity? Research in the United States has shown that despite the drastic increase in the diversity of its student population, teachers of colour have remained at a constant 10% of the teaching force over the years, and have even declined in some jurisdictions (Irvine, 1988; Dilworth, 1990). While there are no reliable estimates of teachers of colour in Canadian classrooms, it is quite safe to speculate that they are grossly underrepresented. Racial minority students lose culturally and cognitively from such underrepresentation. They do not benefit from the rich experiences and resources, from the role modelling and mentoring that teachers of colour could potentially contribute to the teaching-learning process. In addition, their absence from the classroom may signal to students of colour that the teaching profession is "not theirs," thus contributing to the cycle of minority underrepresentation in the teaching profession.[7]

School administrators are therefore challenged to move beyond the rhetoric of being an "equal opportunity employer" and create an opportunity structure that complements that of teacher education institutions such as York's. No longer can school agents escape accountability by employing the token African Canadian and other teachers of colour while forcing the majority into the reserve army of unemployed supply teachers.

ACKNOWLEDGEMENTS

Thanks to Carl James and Gary Bunch for their critical comments and suggestions.

NOTES

1. Toronto Board of Education (1992) data indicate that only 11–12% of its teachers are visible minorities when the student population number about 36% visible minorities (Brown et al 1992).

2. Throughout this paper People of Colour/racial minorities and underrepresented groups will be used interchangeably since the underrepresented are predominantly People of Colour. Aboriginal/First Nation Peoples, and People of Refugee background make up a very small portion of our target groups and are collapsed into the People of Colour category for the purposes of this paper. Where relevant, students in the Differently Abled category will be addressed separately.

3. Data collected from teacher candidates of colour point to racial differentiation in the volunteer selection process. Schools with predominantly white, homogeneous student populations are notorious for restricting the access of volunteers of colour. More recently, schools with race and ethnoculturally diverse student populations are more accommodative to such volunteers.

4. Audio-visuals such as the video: "Communicating Across Cultures" (Copeland Griggs Production) are a good introduction to issues that are emotionally charged, and can help reduce the tension and make cross-cultural interviews a more productive communications process.

5. In the concurrent program a B.A. or B.Sc degree is done concurrently with the B.Ed. while the consecutive program is taken by students who have already completed a Baccalaureate degree.

6. This is one of the main objectives of the pilot program: Access Plus

Teacher Education Program (Diversity Initiative), started by the Faculty of Education in 1994. The research component will analyze the extent to which this objective is realized.

7. In her recent practicum experience in the classroom, an African-Canadian teacher candidate was approached by an African-Canadian kindergarten girl who queried, "Are you a kindergarten teacher too?" An answer in the affirmative generated this response, "No, you're not, you're Black!"

Chapter Thirteen

THE TRANSITIONAL YEAR PROGRAMME AT THE UNIVERSITY OF TORONTO
A LIFE-LINE FOR BLACKS SEEKING A UNIVERSITY EDUCATION

BY KEITH A. ALLEN

Introduction

> ... until all existing but latent talents and capabilities among our young people have been freed from the chains which may be forged by environmental factors, we do not have true equality of educational opportunity or true equality of access to university[1]

University education has long been a symbol of social and educational achievement in Canadian society. The benefits of this education accrue not just to the individuals who participate in it, but also to the communities from which the students come as well as to the society as a whole. It is perhaps true to say that the extent to which the members of particular ethnospecific groups are represented in the university system is one important index of the degree to which that group can be said to be participating successfully and productively in Canadian society. But it is well known that historically, Blacks, some other visible minorities, and people from low socio-economic backgrounds generally have had very little access to university. This paper will discuss the difficulties that Blacks have experienced in gaining access to university education in Ontario through the traditional high school matriculation route. It will show that the Transitional Year Programme (TYP), at the University of Toronto, which developed out of an earlier voluntary initiative by the Black community to increase access to university for Blacks, has been a significant means of increasing access to degree programs for Blacks, and some other categories of students, who historically have been underrepresented within the university system. For many Blacks the TYP has become a virtual life-line to a university education. However, the significance of this program lies not only in the extent to which it has increased access to university for Blacks, and other groups underrepresented within the university system; it lies, too, in the positive changes that the TYP has encouraged in curricula and pedagogy and in the impact that exposure to university has had on the lives of individual students, their families, their communities and obviously on the greater society as a whole.

The 1950s and 1960s were periods of unprecedented growth in student enrollment in the university system in Ontario and elsewhere in Canada as well. In order to accommodate the bulging population of so called "baby boomers," universities expanded their existing campuses or developed satellite campuses.[2] The Ontario Government also developed several new universities.[3] Since, for many of the new university students, money was seen as the main barrier to accessibility, a new financial aid package known as the Ontario Student Assistance Program (OSAP) was also put in place. However, despite the growth in the university system, and its apparent increased accessibility, many groups that had traditionally been excluded when the university system was much smaller and more elitist, continued to be excluded. This was so for several reasons. Government, despite its rhetoric to the contrary, continued to take a gender neutral, age neutral, class neutral, and race/ethnicity neutral position on accessibility.[4] Universities, for the most part, acquiesced in this policy.[5] A second set of factors which caused the traditionally underrepresented groups to remain largely excluded from the university system relate to the admission policies of universities. They, or some of their faculties, placed unreasonably high entry requirements, measured almost entirely by high school matriculation grades. Such practices totally disregarded the fact that, for a variety of reasons — socio-economic, cultural, demographic, psychological, administrative and professional — many students who have the potential to succeed in university studies would not be able to demonstrate their potential through their performance in high school. It is well known that many students drop out of high school or underachieve in school. Nevertheless, the universities were, for the most part, tied to the notion that their mandate was to educate only those students who, at entry, possessed the requisite qualifications. They therefore continued to admit only the so-called "qualified student." By qualified students they apparently meant those who had successfully surmounted the successive academic and other hurdles that they encountered in elementary and high school, and managed to complete the Ontario Grade 13 or its equivalent,[6] with appropriate course distribution and grade point average. The schools, the universities, and the government seem to have ignored the fact that many of the hurdles which some students encounter in schools, and which contribute to their lack of academic success are the outcome of the policies and practices of the educational enterprise itself.

It is well known that the practices and policies of elementary and secondary schools, with regard to the education of students, are more conducive to the academic success of some individuals and groups of students than others. Frequently, elementary schools informally track students on the basis of perceived differences in cognitive, linguistic, and social skills. Later, the secondary schools formalize these earlier judgements through their placements into university preparatory track or non-university bound tracks. These and other seemingly innocuous school practices and policies combine with other factors, some internal others external to the schools, to unfairly contribute to a self-fulfilling prophecy of academic failure. These school practices result in the denial of opportunities to enter university to large groups of students. This is especially true in the case of Black students.

Historically, school systems have not served Black students well in those jurisdictions where Blacks are a minority or are otherwise subordinated. Apparently, educators, and the school systems generally, are more successful in educating children from the dominant socio-economic groups than they are at educating children from the lower socio-economic groups. Because of racial prejudice and discrimination, as well as other forms of oppression, Blacks are either from the lower socio-economic backgrounds, or they are so perceived.[7] The evidence from several jurisdictions has confirmed the differential effectiveness of schools for the different racial\ethnic and socio-economic groups. Whether it be the United Kingdom, South Africa, the United States or Canada, schools seem inadequate to the task of providing effective education for Blacks and other "disadvantaged" groups on a par with the education they provide for children from more privileged socio-economic backgrounds.

In the United Kingdom, several studies have reported on this apparent failure.[8] Some of these studies go back many years.[9] In South Africa, the legacy of apartheid as it relates to the education of Blacks is too well known to warrant repeating here. In the United States it is estimated that between 30% and 40% of entering freshmen need remedial instruction, and that while Blacks constitute about 9.3 percent of the students enrolled in four-year colleges, approximately 30% of them were enrolled in remedial programs.[10] The preponderance of remedial and developmental education at colleges and universities, with Blacks being disproportionately represented in these classes, and the existence of a permanent underclass made up primarily of Blacks are eloquent testimony to the failure of schools to integrate Blacks, and some other disadvantaged groups, into the American mainstream, as Bowles and Gintis have shown.[11]

Ontario schools, too, have been less effective than they could be in providing access to university for Blacks, and for some other students. An example of this failure is illustrated by data provided by the Toronto Board of Education. The Toronto

Board of Education is considered by many to be one of the most progressive boards of education in Ontario, and perhaps in all of Canada. However, even this board has admitted to its failure to adequately educate Blacks. The Board's data have consistently shown Blacks students lagging behind most other racial/ethnic groups of students in credit accumulation and in enrollment in the university preparatory track.[12] These same data show that Blacks are also far more likely to drop out of school. The persistence with which many Black parents in Ontario, and elsewhere in Canada, have been demanding accountability from the schools in the way that their children are educated are ample reminders that more must be done by the schools to effectively educate these students.[13]

Despite strenuous efforts by Black parents and their organizations over many years, there has not been any substantial improvement in the number of Black students qualifying for university through the school systems. By 1986 the underachievement of Black students in Toronto schools had become so obvious that the Toronto Board of Education, at the request of Black parents, instructed its Director to appoint a special committee to advise on the education of Black students.[14] Some have argued that many children are trapped in the poverty subculture and come to schools lacking the physical, emotional and intellectual prerequisites necessary for them to derive much benefit from the education process.[15] This argument needs to be examined; to accept this as sufficient justification for the catastrophic failure of Black children in Ontario schools would be to accept that teachers bear no professional responsibility for educating these children! In any event, the outcome is the same: vast numbers of Black children fail to achieve in schools.

Since schools are the major means by which students may gain access to university, failure on the part of the schools to adequately educate their students seriously affects some students' chances of gaining admission to university or other postsecondary institutions. This has the effect of reducing these students' opportunity for upward social mobility. This failure impacts negatively not only on the affected students, but also on the students' families, their communities and, indeed, on the entire Canadian society.

In the 1960s Black students' access to university was even more restricted than is currently the case. By 1970 the university expansion referred to earlier was largely at an end. However, there were still relatively few Black students enrolled at the University of Toronto. It was apparent that if Blacks, and other underrepresented groups, were to have a better chance at gaining admission to university, and the likelihood of succeeding there, other non-traditional admission strategies were needed.

The Black community was quick to recognize this; several Black students at University of Toronto and at York University had first hand experience of how, because of racism and other forms of oppression, the school systems had not worked for many Black students. Some of the Caribbean and African students who may not have had first hand experience of racism in schools, would nonetheless have been familiar with the oppression of social-class prejudice in their own societies and saw how it hampered the educational aspiration of many Black students. These Black university students, along with some other members of the Black community, were therefore pivotal in the development of summer upgrading programs as alternative ways of preparing deserving Black students for admission to university. This upgrading was facilitated by Horace Campbell, Keren Brethwaite, and Elaine Maxwell who was a student in the 1969 project, and other volunteers. By this means, access to university became a reality for some students who would not otherwise be able to attend university. It was out of this voluntary effort by the Black community in 1969 and 1970 that the TYP emerged.

Transitional Year Programme

The Transitional Year Programme was established at the University of Toronto to provide an opportunity for Blacks and other educationally underprepared students from "disadvantaged" backgrounds to qualify for degree studies. The Transitional Year Programme is an intensive one-year, full-time, university access program designed to prepare educationally underprepared adult students to enter degree programs, primarily in the humanities and social sciences.

History of TYP

The Programme started in September, 1970 at Innis College, University of Toronto, having emerged out of two summer programs conducted by the Black community in 1969 and 1970.[16] The first program prepared a small number of Blacks students to enter university; the second program included both Black and Aboriginal students. The majority of students from these summer programs enrolled at York University.[17] These two summer programs were part of the efforts made by the Black community in Toronto to increase the numbers of Blacks, and other visible minorities, in universities in Toronto. The organizers of the summer programs had some support from progressive members of both the University of Toronto and York University. It is however necessary to emphasize that these community outreach programs, the progenitor of the TYP, were essentially initiatives by the Black community to deal with the problem of inadequate access to university for Blacks. The conceptualization of the TYP, and its present design owes much to the Black community; the survival of the Programme is due in large part to the energetic involvement of Blacks with the TYP. They have helped over the years to maintain the Programme's place at the University against much opposition.

Non-traditional students, especially those who require substantial pre-degree academic preparation and extensive counselling — academic, personal, and financial — present both major challenges as well as major opportunities to the university in which these students are enrolled as well as the university community as a whole. Some members of the university community emphasize the challenges and ignore the opportunities that such students present. Some university teachers and administrators see the developmental and remedial work which are critical to the success of such students as trivial and peripheral to what they conceive to be the university's mission.

In 1970 the concept of access programs requiring extensive developmental and remedial work was new to the Ontario and, indeed, the Canadian university systems. This is unlike the situation in the United States where developmental studies have been present in the universities since at least 1849,[18] and where special university access programs for "disadvantaged" students have been a well recognized feature of the university system for many years. Therefore, the active support of the Black community for the TYP was particularly critical, especially in the early years when the need was especially great to convince a sceptical academic community of the academic as well as the moral and socio-economic justification for such a program within the university system.

When the TYP began operation in 1970 it was an educational innovation in the Ontario university system, and apparently had no precedent in Canada. However, a somewhat smaller program called "Transition Year Program," which is targeted to Aboriginal and Black students, started operating at Dalhousie University in Halifax, Nova Scotia that same year. The TYP at the University of Toronto, like its counterpart at Dalhousie University, provides access to university degree studies for talented and highly motivated adult students who aspire to university education, but are educationally underprepared for university studies. Blacks, and other TYP students are recruited from applicants who appear to have the potential to succeed in degree studies, but who have no other means of gaining entry to a university.

The TYP was specially designed to provide the academic preparation and the psycho-social adjustments that these non-traditional students need in order to succeed in university. Such students do not usually have a history of involvement with universities and many have had bad experience with the entire educational enterprise.

Many Black students have had negative experiences with the formal education system, and many of them perceive universities to be desirable yet strange, alien, and perhaps even hostile places with curricula and ethos dominated by white middle-class values. Such students therefore need a supportive environment while they are making the academic and psycho-social transition from their current life situation to readiness for the rigours of university life. Dr. Martha Bell, Director of SEEK Program,[19] Brooklyn College, City University of New York, uses the term "psychological security" to describe the kind of transition that such students need.[20] The TYP provides this kind educational environment for its students.

The students' special academic and socio-psychological needs are met through a specially designed curriculum, which includes extensive tutorial and counselling. In this way, TYP helps its students to dissipate their feelings of isolation and break down some of the barriers that may have seemed insurmountable. The Programme also helps students to build their self-esteem, restore their confidence, and gradually integrate them into the main stream of university life. These goals are achieved in several ways: the location of the TYP on the main St. George campus of the University; the integration of TYP students with the regularly admitted students in academic courses; the regular contacts with other students in a wide range of social, recreational, political and other activities; and the regular interactions with the TYP and other university faculty and staff.

Since 1970 when TYP was established at the University of Toronto, the Programme has served "disadvantaged" students from all racial/ethnic groups. "Disadvantaged students" is not a precise term, but at the University of Toronto it has taken on a meaning that has been used fairly consistently for the last twenty-five years. It refers to a special group of adult students who, because of socio-economic, or personal difficulty, are unable gain admission to university through conventional means. These students are primarily drop-outs from the Ontario school system or elsewhere, or persons who did not follow the university preparatory stream while in high school because of financial problems, personal or family difficulties, or other circumstances beyond their control. The TYP is the only realistic way that these students can gain admission to degree studies at the University of Toronto.

TYP students include members of the Black, Aboriginal and other minority communities, sole-support parents, people with disability, and generally people from socio-economically "disadvantaged" backgrounds.

Admission Requirements and Procedures

There is no set formal level of academic achievement that the TYP applicants need to have attained. Each applicant is considered individually and comprehensively. The prospective student needs to convince the TYP Admissions Committee that she/he has sufficient academic skills and ability to successfully complete the program of studies. Applicants must normally be Canadian citizens or permanent residents who will be at least 19 years of age by September 30 of the year of admission, and they must have been out of high school for at least one year. They must be able to demonstrate that they are unable to return to a high school to obtain the academic admission requirements or to qualify for university studies in any other way (for example, through mature student entry). They must satisfy the TYP Admissions Committee that they are highly motivated to study for a degree, and that they have the potential to succeed in such studies.

Demographic Background of the Students

The TYP registers about fifty students each year. Approximately 90% of the TYP students are from the Greater Toronto Area (GTA).[21] About 60% of the students are women, 48% of whom have dependent children. Thirty-five percent of the women are sole support parents. Students are on average just over 25 years old, have an average of 10.5 years of education, and have been away from school for an average of approximately 8 years prior to registering in the TYP.[22]

Because of the active encouragement of applications from members of the Black community, and because of the historical connection that Blacks have had with the Programme, each year a significant number of the registrants are Black. In the early years of the TYP it was estimated that as many as 50% of the students were Black. In more recent years the proportion of Blacks, although not the actual number, have declined as overall Programme registration has increased. For example, since 1989 when the TYP began systematically collecting data on the racial composition of incoming students, at least 30% of the students have annually identified themselves as members of the Black community.[23] Since the number of Black students in the University as a whole is less than 3%,[24] it is reasonable to conclude that TYP has been a major means of providing access to the University for Black students.

Curriculum

Educationally underprepared students from "disadvantaged" backgrounds present useful ways of tying academic work with social change. The traditional curricula, teaching approaches, and counselling paradigms are unlikely to be successful with these students. Therefore, more serious consideration has had to be given to curriculum development and teaching strategies including evaluation, and counselling strategies. It is clear that traditional students and the academic community generally benefit from the initiatives developed for these non-traditional students.

The TYP curriculum consists of five full-course equivalents, study skills seminars and extensive academic, personal and financial counselling. Three and one-half of the courses are specially designed, developmental, non-degree courses developed by the TYP faculty specifically for these students. The other one and one-half courses are selected from degree credit courses offered within the Faculty of Arts and Science of the University. All courses taken through the Faculty of Arts and Science may be used to fulfil degree requirements. The curriculum emphasizes humanities and social science studies, but also includes developmental work in basic mathematics and statistics as well as computer applications. Students receive extensive small group and individual tutoring in all their courses.

One of the strengths of the curriculum is that the course content is specially selected to fit with the multi-cultural orientation of the TYP and the diversity of backgrounds of the students. This helps Blacks and other students to relate to the curriculum. This is unlike the situation in many schools where the curriculum is so Eurocentric, and sometimes even racist, that it tends to render Black and other minority students "invisible."

The current curriculum appears to meet the needs of those students who have an orientation towards the humanities and/or the social sciences. However, one weakness of the curriculum is that it makes no provisions for those students who wish to pursue studies in the physical sciences, life sciences, mathematics or other disciplines requiring substantial background in mathematics. This is most unfortunate, since it prevents many Black, and other students from pursuing careers in the health sciences, and other sciences as well as careers in a wide range of areas requiring strong mathematical background. Many students as well as TYP faculty have over the years been drawing attention to this deficiency in the curriculum.

For many years, the absence of math\science access was defended on the grounds that adequate preparation in these areas could not be accomplished in a single year. However, those of us who have been advocating such access never said that it could! We have argued instead that once TYP and the University commit themselves to the inclusion of math\science access, ways could be found to effectively organize their inclusion within the curriculum.

A proposal was developed recently to include math/science access as a component of TYP. Both the TYP and the University administrations seem to have accepted the proposal in principle. Unfortunately, the financial exigencies which have now overtaken the Ontario universities and, indeed, the entire province of Ontario, make it highly unlikely that TYP will be able to include math/science access within its curriculum in the immediate future.

Evaluation

Students who achieve a passing grade in all courses and obtain an overall average of at least 60% receive a Certificate of Completion. Those who, in addition to qualifying for this certificate, achieve an average of 65% and above, including at least 60% in their Faculty of Arts and Science Elective, and have otherwise demonstrated preparedness to embark upon degree studies at the University of Toronto are recommended for admission into the Faculty of Arts and Science at the University of Toronto or at another university.

About 50% of those who register in the TYP subsequently go on to register in the Faculty of Arts and Science at the University of Toronto. Approximately 30% of these students earn undergraduate degrees from the Faculty within 5 or 6 years. A few other students transfer to other University of Toronto faculties, other universities, or community colleges. A few have dropped out of university. Most other students remain registered, and are taking a longer time to complete their degrees generally because of their need to work full-time. Some of these students will eventually earn degrees from the Faculty of Arts and Science.[25]

The TYP has to its credit a long list of Blacks and other students who have completed undergraduate degrees. Several of these students have continued their studies in graduate and professional schools, before going on to interesting jobs in the private and public sectors. Public sector careers which seem to have the greatest appeal to TYP graduates include social work, law and elementary and secondary school teaching.

Despite the impressive success in terms of degree completions, the quantitative data do not convey a sufficiently accurate picture of the impact that TYP has had on the life of individual Black students, or the full impact that TYP has had on the Black community. Many Black students who did not earn degrees, diplomas or certificates from university or colleges have nonetheless benefited from their involvement in the TYP. Some of these students who do not show up in the statistics which record degree completion, nevertheless have been able to make meaningful improvements to their lives because of their exposure to university. For example, some have become published writers, dramatists, producers and directors of theatre companies; some entrepreneurs; others have formed relationships, while on the university campus, which have significantly changed their lives for the better.

Many students have reported on other positive, although less tangible, qualitative impact that their exposure to university has had on their lives and on the lives of their families and relatives: students have spoken enthusiastically about improved attitudes that they, their children, spouses and relatives have developed towards education generally and post-secondary education specifically, as well as their own new found confidence in dealing with their personal lives; some have spoken of the new skills that they acquired in the Programme which have enabled them to become more involved in their children's education; still others have spoken of their new insights and perspectives which allow them to participate more effectively in the affairs of their community as well as their new ability to become more involved in the social and political issues of the wider community. But above all, students who have earned degrees as well as those who have not, have spoken about their improved self-esteem which they attribute to their participation in TYP and the University of Toronto.

Funding and Student Support

The TYP is funded by the province of Ontario, the University of Toronto, and student fees. Students pay the same tuition fees as full-time students taking five full-course equivalent in the Faculty of Arts and Science. However, TYP is very expensive to operate because it is a very labour intensive program requiring relatively small classes, a great deal of individual tutoring and academic, financial and personal counselling. Unfortunately, the formula that the Ontario government uses to allocate funds for the TYP is quite unrealistic since it bears little relationship to the actual cost of running the Programme.[26]

The TYP students are very needy and virtually everyone is financially supported from public funds such as OSAP, grants from the Department of Indian Affairs, provincial or municipal welfare. Despite this financial support, many students experience severe financial hardship and are therefore forced to work part-time to supplement their income. Unfortunately, most TYP students' educational deficiencies are so severe that they need to concentrate fully on their studies in order to have a reasonable chance of completing their programm successfully.

The students generally, and the Black students especially, need much more financial assistance if the dream of comprehensive access to university for Black students that the organizers of the two summer programs in 1969 and 1970 out of which TYP developed, is to be fully realized.[27]

Conclusion

The TYP has been remarkably successful in recruiting Black, and other "disadvantaged" students, and preparing them to enter degree programs at the University of Toronto. About 30% of those admitted to the Faculty of Arts and Science at the University of Toronto earn a B.A. degree in about five or six years. We know anecdotally that several other TYP graduates register at other postsecondary institutions, but have no firm data on either the exact number or their academic performance. However, the qualitative success of the students goes far beyond the earning of degrees, diplomas or certificates and can be seen also in the positive changes in the lives of many of those who did not graduate from any post secondary institution.

During the twenty-four years that the TYP has been in operation, it has demonstrated that Blacks, and other adults from "disadvantaged" backgrounds, are very capable of succeeding at university, if they are given the chance to enroll there. However, Blacks, like other students, need a learning environment which is sensitive to their backgrounds, and a faculty and staff who treat them fairly and respectfully.

Despite problems related to funding, student financial support and curriculum limitations, the TYP is now well regarded both within the University of Toronto as well as within the Ontario university community as a model access program. This program though modest in size, in comparison to most access programs in the United States, represents an excellent example of how the Black community and the University of Toronto have been able to work cooperatively to redress the problem of underrepresentation of Blacks, and some other groups at the University of Toronto and consequently, within the Ontario university system.

NOTES

1 Robert M. Pike, *Who Doesn't Get to University and Why: A Study on Accessibility to Higher Education in Canada* (Ottawa: Association of Universities and Colleges of Canada, 1970) p.7.

2 Scarborough College in Scarborough and Erindale College in Mississauga were established as constituent colleges of the University of Toronto in 1964 and 1965 respectively.

3 Lakehead University was established in 1957, York University in 1959, Laurentian University in 1960, Trent University in 1963 and Brock University in 1964.

4 Paul Anisef et al. *Accessibility to Postsecondary Education in Canada: A Review of the Literature* (Ottawa: Department of the Secretary of State, Canada, 1985)

5 See, for example, Paul Anisef et al. *The Pursuit of Equality: Evaluating and Monitoring Accessibility to Post-secondary Education in Ontario* (Ontario: Minister of Education 1982) pp.17–58.

6 Ontario Academic Credit (OAC) replaced Grade 13 during the 1980s as the normal Ontario university matriculation requirement

7 Frances Henry, *The Dynamics of Racism in Toronto* (Toronto: Department of Anthropology, York University, 1978).

8 Please see, for example, Sally Tomlinson, *Ethnic Minorities in British Schools: A Review of The Literature* (London: Heineman Educational Books 1983).

9 See, for example, Christopher Jenks et al., *Inequality: A Reassessment of the Effects of Family and Schooling in America* (New York: Basic Books, 1972).

10 Stephen Knowlton "Questions About Remedial Education in a time of Budget Cuts." *New York Times* June 7, 1995, p. B 8

11 Samuel Bowles and Herbert Gintis, *Schooling in Capitalist America* (New York: Basic Books, 1976)

12 See Maisy Cheng, Maria Yau, and Suzanne Ziegler *The 1991 Every Secondary Student Survey*, Parts 1, 2 and 3 (Toronto: Research Services, Toronto Board of Education, 1993). See also Maisy Chen et al. *Every Secondary Student Survey: Fall,1987* Toronto: Toronto Board of Education 1989).

13 After years of agitation by individual Black parents to improve the quality of education that their children were receiving in the schools in Metropolitan Toronto, the parents formed the "Organization of Parents of Black Children" in 1980 to lobby the schools and the boards of education in an effort to improve quality of their children' education.

14 See Toronto Board of Education, *Draft Report: Consultative Committee on the Education of Black Students in Toronto Schools* (Toronto: Toronto Board of Education, 1987).

15 For a popular view of this old notion of citing factors external to the educational enterprise as the major cause of the schools' failure to effectively educate some students, see Leslie Fruman's article captioned "Disadvantaged in every way" *The Toronto Star* newspaper, September 28, 1987, p.D8

16 *Transitional Year Programme, University of Toronto Calendar 1994–95.* (Toronto: Transitional Year Programme, University of Toronto 1994) p. 3

17 Information supplied by Keren Brathwaite who has been associated with the TYP from its inception, and who was a member of the group that organized the 1969 and 1970 summer programs out of which the TYP developed.

18 Graduate Programs in Developmental Education [information sheet], Reich College of Education, Appalachian State University, Boone, North Carolina, n.d.

19 SEEK stands for Search for Elevation, Education and more Knowledge. It is a special university access program which offers a broad range of educational and student services to disadvantaged students to enable them to complete degree programs at City University of New York.

20 Educational Supplement, *New York Times*, Sunday, October 21, 1988, p. 21

21 The GTA is usually thought of as comprising the area which extends east to Clarington, west to Burlington and north to Lake Simcoe

22 This information is based on unpublished data compiled by Keith Allen and A. Martin Wall from official student records.

23 This data is calculated from two sources: 1) Annual survey of TYP students, conducted since 1989, of all students who are offered admission to the TYP; 2) University of Toronto annual "Incoming Students Survey," conducted for new students. TYP students have participated in this latter survey since 1992. There are slight discrepancies between the number of Black students reported in the two sources. Because the number of missing frequencies in the second source is much greater than in the TYP survey, I regard the TYP figures as more accurate.

24 Information based on the University of Toronto annual survey of Incoming students for 1992, 1993 and 1994

25 This information is based on unpublished data compiled by Keith Allen from official student records.

26 The Ontario government funds TYP at the rate of 0.7 Basic Income Unit (BIU) per enrolled student. BIU is part of the formula used by the government to fund students at Ontario universities. BIU is deferentially weighted to represent the government's estimate of the cost of educating a student in the various undergraduate, professional and graduate programs within the Ontario university system.

27 A donor has recently made a substantial financial gift to the University of Toronto to be used to attract, retain, and encourage Black students to complete degree programs.

Comment

*The first of
many, I hope.
Keep Reading &
Writing. Marc Proudfoot*

ACCESS? SURE,
BUT INTO WHAT?
A COMMENT

MARC A. PROUDFOOT

After attending university for more than five years in a large urban centre, I never would have thought that I would hear an African Canadian student referring to the university I attended as a "Black university." This comment is based on that student's perception, which is similar to my own, that there continues to be increasing numbers of students of African descent who are now entering postsecondary institutions. In particular, the population of African Canadian students continue to swell in the undergraduate Bachelor degree programmes in the areas of law, business, the arts, and education. In addition, we can also be found hanging out in the hallways, libraries, cafeterias and social activity spots of the universities. Yet beyond our physical presence within these institutions, there is another reading, and perhaps a deeper reading, into the initial comment of the student; one which hints at a particular level of comfort or sense of belonging, in being able to declare the university — traditionally known for its class and race specific clientele — as a legitimate site for Black students seeking higher forms of education. Nevertheless, many African Canadian students continue to feel silenced and disillusioned during their university education.

There are many valid reasons for this. As we continue to participate in higher learning, we will, undoubtedly, find ourselves attending institutions in which access-oriented programmes exist — i.e. programmes which assist in lowering the systemic barriers to entrance to postsecondary institutions. The institutions must be praised for initiating these programmes, insofar as these initiatives demonstrate their recognition of the lack of representation of people of colour among university students. Some of these programmes are referred to as "access initiatives," "transitional year programmes," and "bridging programmes." From my experience, attending institutions where access programmes exist, there is a tendency for racial minority students, and African Canadians in particular, to be viewed as "access students." Does this suggest that it is impossible for African Canadians to "make it" into university on merit without the assistance of the institution? This question should be answered in conjunction with more fundamental questions. Specifically, once we are given the opportunity to enter the university, is the university ready to educate us? Will it do so in an inclusive manner by taking into consideration our interests and experiences in the content of the courses that are offered? In other words, are postsecondary institutions ready to question the content of their curriculum, which has been designed for students of European descent, and rethink the possibilities of creating a more inclusive one, one which includes us? Will the pedagogical framework and approach used by instructors and professors be reevaluated and, if need be, reconceptualized to ensure that all students are given the opportunity to voice their ideas in a classroom environment that is non-coercive and democratic? These questions alert us to the complexity of the issues associated with African Canadian students' access to, and participation in, postsecondary institutions.

Although the doors to universities appear more open than they did before, there is still no assurance that the activities beyond the door will guarantee us the quality of education that the institution proports to give to everyone. In other words, being inside the institution doesn't insure that our freedom, mobility, growth, and intellectual sustenance will be catered to in a manner that appropriately reflects our experiences as African Canadians. Access oriented programmes, the apparent beacon for those who have been historically pushed out to sea, are a start, but not enough. The problem is that postsecondary institutions seem not to look beyond the issue of entrance. What currently exists is a collection of prophetic visions of a future based on equality and fairness within a structure that has failed to recognize the inherent structural barriers which continue to prevail; consequently, the institutions continue to reproduce forms of inequity and injustice. If access programmes are to address the issues of social and systemic barriers, then they must be accompanied by penetrating structural change. Otherwise they offer only an incomplete form of participation and remain mere public relations programmes to make the institutions look good.

Given the lack of structural changes, the universities have faltered in presenting to us a model of what an inclusive form of education might look like and how it should operate. Caught up in dogmas of multicultural liberalism and equality of opportunity, postsecondary institutions fall short on examining how the ideology of white supremacy, governed by the dynamics of patriarchy, classism, and sexism, is legitimated and remains unchallenged within their structures. Consequently, the question of what would constitute an equitable education for us African Canadians is dismissed. This dismissal leads me to think that a legitimate and socially relevant form of education was not intended for us in the first place. This, in turn, situates us in a subordinate relationship within the institution. The subordinate relationship that we continue to have within the institution reflects an attitude, which has been expressed succinctly by Asa Hilliard: "[t]he person who has a vested interest in the maintenance of a system of privilege and oppression tends to have a perceptual system that denies undesirable information" (*The Maroon Within Us*. Black Classic Press, Baltimore 1995:154). This observation can be applied to educational institutions as well. The undesirable information, in this case, is the racism, classism, and sexism that exists within these institutions and are ignored by those who think that these institutions are culturally and politically neutral. This information would force a rethinking of who remains in the position of privilege within an instutition that prides itself on being democratic but has failed, nevertheless, miserably in putting this ideal into practice.

The fact that the legitimacy and merit of African Canadians' participation in university is often questioned, has profound psychological and physical effects on our educational experiences. We feel silenced and disillusioned. The silence is created and fostered when we are the recipients of such questions as: "How can you expect change overnight? Things take time, you know." Or "Why are *you* being so critical?" We become silent because of the negative responses we receive when we threaten the complacency of those who usually do not look like us. We are silenced by the contradictory messages we get, when we are told out of one side of the mouth that we belong, while the other side of the mouth tells us "to be quiet." But as Alice Walker says, "No person is your friend who demands your silence, or denies your right to grow" (In *Famous Black Quotations: And some not so famous* by Janet Cheatham Bell ed., Sabat Publications, Chicago, 1986: 10).

We become disillusioned when as African Canadian students, we decide to address the contradictory nature of this relationship. While we are perceived as privileged insiders receiving a postsecondary education, at the same time we remain outsiders, in that we are essentially excluded from course content, pedagogy and programme development — in short, from full participation in our own educational process. Despite these contradictions, and with the "working twice as hard ethos," we often persevere to prove, to both ourselves and outsiders, that we are worthy of being in the institutions. This sometimes leads to internalized frustrations or unbridled anger, and sometimes to an actual or metaphorical ulcer. Introductory handshakes ushering us into a sea of blinding whiteness is no guarantee that we will not drown.

After all is said and done — and assuming that there is a high graduation rate of African Canadian students — it would appear, on the surface, that the university has been able to cater and respond to our interests, needs and experiences. Still, the disillusionment remains after we have received the degrees or diplomas. Receiving a degree does not liberate us from the sufferings of being strangers in our own educational process. Ultimately, institutions of higher learning must undergo systemic changes in order to provide African Canadians an equitable and meaningful postsecondary education. In terms of access initiatives, it is important that supporters and "headmasters" of these programmes problematize and reconceptualize them, not just in terms of entry into the institution, but also in terms of their capacity to ensure our full participation in the whole educational process.

PART FIVE

TOWARDS THE PROVISION OF CULTURALLY APPROPRIATE EDUCATION

Chapter Fourteen

THE POSSIBILITIES OF PLAY
BLACK YOUTH, ATHLETICS AND SCHOOLING

CARL E. JAMES

Dane is a grade 6 student who identifies his favourite subjects in school as "gym and language" (in that order); and his favourite sports, the ones he plays, as "football, baseball and hockey." He also likes 'sprint (track), long jump and relays." Dane is known as a fast runnner — "the fastest in the school and the region, one who comes in first in cross country against over 300 competitors." However, this success is not reflected in Dane's recent end of year report. In fact, his classroom teacher reports that "Dane is slipping in his academic work."

While Dane's mother Brenda is pleased with his athletic accomplishments, and willingly supports him in his sports activites — by attending sports meets, and buying the necessary sports attire for him (for instance, he was wearing Ewing running shoes 33 when we met), she is concerned that Dane is putting "too much time and energy into athletics rather than his academic work." She threatens to stop him from participating in sports if he continues to do poorly in his academic work. When asked how he feels about his mother's concern, Dane replied that he knows "that academic work is important because you have to have an education to get a job." However, even with this understanding Dane still likes "sports better since it is more fun."

Brenda is fully aware of the positive effect that sports have had on Dane, but she is still concerned — concerned that Dane will not be encouraged by his teachers to realize his full academic potential and eventually aspire to university. And while Brenda agrees that it is possible for students to successfully participate in sports and do well in their academic work, she wonders whether teachers will encourage Black students to pursue academics in the same way they encourage them to pursue sports? She feels that there is a tendency to stereotype young African Canadians, particularly males, as good athletes, will result in their being "nudged" to pursue sports as a means of making it in this society. This is a problem that other students, including those from other racial minorities, do not face to to the same extent.

While many Black parents and community members share Brenda's concerns about the potential negative impact that participation in sports can have on the educational performance and achievements of African Canadians, it is important to ascertain if withdrawing their children from sports is an appropriate alternative to addressing the problem. Should Black parents discourage their children from participating in athletic activities altogether? Is this an appropriate way to ensure that youth redirect their energies into their academic work, hence addressing the problem of academic failure?

In discussing these issues, I shall argue that while there are certainly valid reasons for concern regarding the extent to which participation in athletic activities may negatively affect the academic performance of Black students, disallowing participation in sports will not necessarily help the situation. Research evidence shows that involvement in athletics has helped Black youth to build self-confidence, cultivate peer support, and connect with their school. It also shows that sports help them to cope with the alienating school environment and negotiate the structural constraints of inequality, stereotyping, racism and discrimination within the school system (James, 1995; Dei, 1994a;

1993; Yon, 1994; Solomon 1992; Mirza, 1992; Harris, 1991; MacLeod, 1987; Carrington, 1983). Therefore, what is needed is for athletic activities — physical education and extra-curricular activities — to be regarded as a necessary and integral part of the schooling process in much the same way as academic subjects.Furthermore, they have to be approached from an anti-racism perspective.

Anti-racism education is an approach which acknowledges that structural inequality based on race, class, gender, sexuality and other social identities informs the way students are differentiated, and the significance placed on such differentiation. This social differentiation is a product of power which is sustained by historical and cultural ideology (see Marqusee, 1995; McLaren, 1994; Dei, 1994a), and is responsible for the construction of Black students as more likely to succeed at athletics and white youth as more likely to succeed at academics.[1] This results in differential treatment which in turn affects students' sense of connection to, and identification with, the school, and in turn their educational outcomes. Anti-racism is one way to address the differential treatment and "the problems associated with the school as a site for reproducing societal inequalities" (Dei, 1994b). To this end, this perspective pays attention to the social realities and lived experiences of minority students by examining and supporting their struggle against the interlocking systems of racism, sexism, classism, ablism and other forms of oppression (Dei 1994b; Thomas, 1987).

In pursuing the goals and objectives of anti-racism education, educators, students, parents and others must actively engage in educational strategies which probe the 'common sense' notions that are based on racism (Thomas, 1987) and other forms of social oppression. These notions rationalize and help to perpetuate the practices and procedures which influence students' educational activities, performance and outcomes. This action-oriented strategy calls for educators to acknowledge and critique their relative power and privileged positions, the biases that inform their own and the school's philosophies, perceptions and practices. It also means that educators must critique the institutional construction of equality that is based on "the prized imperatives of a white, Anglo male heterosexual world" (McLaren, 1994:290). If all school activities are to ensure equality of educational opportunities and outcomes, they must address the inequalities that exist within the educational system and the society as a whole (James, 1994; Lee, 1994). With this consciousness, teachers and coaches will strive to engage student athletes in a critical analysis that will inform them of their relative position in society and interrogate the way in which sports is used as a form of signification of their position. As a significant part of school curricular activities, physical education and extra-curricular athletic activities must be conceptualized and practiced on the basis of equity, justice and respect for all students (Figueroa, 1993), and must serve to "empower" students so that they are able to realize their educational and career goals.

In proceeding I shall discuss: (a) the reasons for parental and community concern; (b) the relationship between athletic participation and academic success; and (c) the role that concerned parents, educators, peers and community members can play in ensuring that Black students' academic performance is not compromised because of their involvement in athletic activities.

The Concern: The Academic Success of African Canadian Students

That Black students have failed to receive the necessary school support that would lead to academic success has been well documented in many reports and studies throughout Canada. Essentially, studies show that racism, stereotyping and discrimination operate within schools, contributing to low teacher expectations which, in turn, have led to streaming of students into basic or vocational educational programs, feelings of alienation, disengagement from school programs, and high drop out rates (Dei, 1994a; 1993; Black Learners Advisory Committee (BLAC), 1994; Calliste, 1994; Cheng, Yau, Zeigler, 1993; Solomon, 1992; James, 1990; Meta, 1989).

In a major research that investigated the "past and present conditions of Black learners" in Nova Scotia, The Black Learners Advisory Committee (BLAC)[2] report that many of their respondents condemned the education system saying that

it is *"biased, insensitive and racist"*(original, 1994: vol. 1:35).
The Committee writes:

> Systemic racism was seen as manifested in student assessment
> and placement; in labelling of large numbers of Black students
> as slow learners or having behaviour problems; in streaming; in
> low teacher expectations, in denigration by and exclusion of
> Blacks from the curriculum; and in the total lack of responsive-
> ness to the needs of Black learners and concerns of the Black
> community (BLAC, 1994, vol. 1:35).

The Committee also reported that "promising Black students
were ridiculed" by their peers for, among other things, "showing an interest in academically inclined student clubs or joining
activities other than sports (Vol. 3, 1994:59). This "anti-
achievement ethic" is seen as part of how some Black youth
have come to construct what it means to be Black. According
to the Committee, it is a view which holds that formal education is useless; and social success is represented by academic
failure or mediocre grades (Vol.3, 1994: 59).

In Ontario, and Toronto in particular, a number of studies dating
as far back as the 1970s, have consistently shown that Black students share very similar experiences to those of their peers in other
provinces. As the Four-Level Government/African-Canadian
Community Working Group[3] (1992) writes: a review of a number
of reports and presentations before the Working Group clearly
indicates that, "for at least one generation, the African-Canadian
community has been crying out in anguish over the poor performance of its youth in Ontario school system. The drop out rate, the
truancy rate, the failure rate, the basic-streaming rate: all these
have pointed inexorably to the fact that, where Black kids are concerned, something is terribly wrong" (pp. 77–78). And more
recently the Royal Commission on Learning (1994), with reference to a number of studies conducted by Boards of Education
in the Toronto area, concludes that there is need for concern
with respect to school participation and achievement of Black
students.

In some situations, Black students experience marginalization
because of legal procedures. For instance, in Quebec, the situation of Black students is influenced by the French language factor. In that province, it is legislated that English mother tongue

students whose parents did not receive their primary education in English must have their schooling in French. According to Richardson (1994), in Montreal, "this has caused immense difficulties among many parents who can neither help their children nor supervise their homework because they do not speak French. Social workers have observed that children experience behavioural problems due to their inability to comprehend the language of instruction, cope with their homework, and communicate effectively in the classroom" (p. 71). Beauger, Dorsaint and Turenne (1994) also report that French-speaking immigrant students such as Haitians "experience numerous difficulties in adapting to the Quebec school system and were, therefore, always susceptible to failure" (p. 72).

Many of the studies show that Black youth are well aware that racism and its concomitant elements of stereotyping and discrimination affect their situation in school and hence their educational and occupational outcomes. Many are conscious of the need for education to effectively participate and succeed in the society and develop strategies to cope with, and negotiate the constraints of the school system in order to obtain a high school diploma (Dei et al, 1995; Dei, 1994a; 1993; Solomon, 1992; James, 1990). Some students manage to stay in school by negotiating the system through athletic activities which enable them to demonstrate their abilities and skills, build their self-esteem and confidence and enhance their academic performance (Dei et al, 1995; James, 1995; 1990; Solomon, 1994; 1992).

But as Lovell (1991) points out with reference to African Caribbean youth in Britain, sport "is a double edged sword" as it is often racism which leads Black youth into sports, and then later limits social mobility and career attainment even within the sporting power structure (p. 69). Further, Carrington (1983) argues that sport is a "convenient side-track" and "control mechanism" used by teachers who have a tendency to view Black students stereotypically, "as having skills of the body rather than skills of the mind" (p. 61). Parry and Parry (1991) state that this "coping strategy" that teachers use to deal with Black youth "who have side-tracked the academic mainstream serves to reinforce both academic failure and unacceptable behaviour" (p. 169). Schools control student athletes through the awards that are given for representing the school in sports, and when they allow athletes to leave classes early, or miss classes to participate in athletic activities (Solomon, 1992), and when teachers and coaches threaten to prevent students from participating in athletic events.

Canadian research has shown that the stereotype of the athletic Black youth has indeed influenced their educational opportunities. For instance, James (1990) found that in some cases, students gain entry into school because of the perception that they would be an asset to the school's sports team. Solomon (1992) also found that the more athletically minded students would deliberately transfer to schools where they would get the opportunity to play sports. And in a study which reports on students' experiences with discrimination in one of Toronto's boards of education, one student is quoted as saying that "the Black kids are picked to be team captain in sports and in gym, but teachers often assume their marks are bad" (Board of Education for the City of Etobicoke 1993: 53).

Gender and social class also play significant roles in determining the types of youth who tend to participate in athletic activities in school (see Shilling, 1993; Hall, Slack, Smith and Whitson, 1991; Bray, 1988). Black working class males are particularly attracted to sports (James, 1995; BLAC, 1994; Frey, 1994; Solomon, 1992; Mirza, 1992), not only because of personal interests, and their perception that they will be able to succeed through sport, but because of the acceptance and recognition they receive from school personnel (BLAC, 1994; Solomon, 1992: James, 1990). But as the Black Learners Advisory Committee (BLAC) points out, while sports affirm Black males' identity, and connection with school, there is still the need for concern, for this is "one of the damaging stereotypes of the Black male" (p. 22).

In his study of Black and white male high school basketball players in Washington D.C., Harris (1994) found that it was coaches, friends and especially teachers, and not parents, who push the youths to become involved and maintain involvement in athletics. Harris concludes with the caution that these significant others that are outside the home "may be unwittingly contributing to the unfortunate channelling of black males into an area that has few openings. In so doing, what they see as service to black males — pushing them into sport — is, in reality, a disservice to them because it fosters improbable expectations for athletics careers" (1994: 49).

The concern therefore is how to ensure the academic success of Black student athletes so that they may realize their full potential. We have seen that racism, stereotyping and discrimination inherent in the educational system have limited their educational opportunities, while involvement in sports has the potential of thwarting their academic success. However, we have also seen that there are psychological benefits to their involvement in athletic activities in that they are able to develop self-confidence and self-esteem through the recognition they receive from both peers and school staff, and that these acknowledgements in turn, often motivate them to stay in school. In light of this evidence, should we not encourage Black students to participate in the school's athletic activities? Is participation in these activities really a detriment to academic success? These questions will be explored in the following section.

Athletics and academics: Contradictory or Complementary Activities?

In addition to contributing to the health and physical fitness of students (Hall, Slack, Smith &Whitson, 1991; Crossley, 1988), participation in athletic activities helps to relieve tension, enhance cultural and gender identities, and build peer support (James 1995; Solomon, 1992; Mirza, 1992; Carrington, 1983). Athletic activities also transmit to students "the importance of hard work, character development and team work" — values which complement those necessary for success in academic life" (Harris, 1991:124). Hence, contrary to the claim that participation in athletic activities is detrimental to the attainment of academic goals, there is evidence that such participation can increase educational aspirations and academic performance (James, 1995; Fejgin, 1995; Marsh, 1993; Harris, 1991).

In a national American study, Sabo, Melnick and Vanfossen (1989) found that Black high school student athletes compared to non-athletes, tended to receive better grades, be more involved in school and community activities, be more popular among peers, aspire to community leadership positions, and in suburban areas, have lower drop out rates (pp. 4–8). The researchers speculate that lower drop out rate may be related to the fact that sport is enjoyable and fosters friendships and popularity. The authors speculate that sport may have helped Black students to develop a greater sense of allegiance to their schools or kept them on the educational track in hopes of getting a college scholarship or pro contract (Sabo, Melnick & Vanfossen, 1989).[4] In a follow-up article which examines the impact of race and gender differences on the social mobility of high school student athletes, Sabo, Melnick and Vanfossen (1993) report that overall athletic participation does not inhibit the postsecondary educational attainment or mobility aspirations of most students (p. 51).

In the already mentioned study of Black and white male high school basketball players in Washington, D.C., Harris (1991) also explored racial differences in academic performance, and the values they placed on academics and athletics. He reports that participation in sport does not negatively affect the students' performance. Specifically, it was found that while most of the student athletes felt that it was important to do well in school and sports, Blacks were more likely than whites to indicate that "doing well in school" was more important (Harris, 1991: 146). While Black basketball players do not devalue academics, basketball was shown to have "a unique centrality in their experience." This indicates that Blacks, more than whites, seem to feel that basketball can be used as a mechanism to access postsecondary institutions through athletic scholarships, and gain opportunities to compete in the professional world (Harris, 1991: 147). Harris concludes:

> Although the sport experiences of Black and white student-athletes are different, there is too little evidence to suggest Blacks are 'hooked' on sport to the exclusion of academics more than whites. Still it is apparent that Blacks suffer more scholastically from their participation in sport. However, the reasons for this are not due to emphasis on sport to the exclusion of scholastics.... The Black athletes are not poorer performers academically because of a disinterest in academics by themselves or their significant others but, rather, because they lack the

resources — good schools, good programmes, etc. — to compete with their white peers (1991:147–148).

Marsh (1993) investigated the effects of participation in sport during the last two years of high school. After controlling for race, socioeconomic status, sex, and ability level, he found that participation in sport had many positive effects on the academic self concept, educational aspiration and attainment of students. Like Sabo, Melnick and Vanfossen (1989), Marsh's results show that "participation in sport leads to an increased commitment to, involvement with, or identification with school and school values ... [and] that participation in sport apparently adds to — not detracts from — time, energy, and commitment to academic pursuits." (1993: 36). Marsh concludes by saying that schools should promote extra-curricular activities in general and sports in particular, for as his findings indicate, the "promotion of participation in sport is likely to have positive effects across a wide variety of educationally relevant outcomes for a diversity of students" (1993: 38).

In a longitudinal study of 10th graders in the United States, Fejgin (1994) found that "students who are more involved in high school competitive sports have higher grades, a higher self-concept, higher educational aspirations, a more internal locus of control, and fewer discipline problems" (p. 223). Fejgin (1995) goes on to explain:

> Participation in sports teams requires adjustment to rigid rules, regulations, and practice times, as well as to the coach's authority.... Ongoing training of individuals to comply with these rules and to endure long hours of practice, while delaying the fulfilment of other physical and social needs, teaches the importance of and the reward associated with such compliance, possibly making it easier to accept other school rules and formal authority. Furthermore, being on a school team means being recognized by the system as a "good citizen" who participates in community life beyond basic requirements. This may in turn create deeper commitment by the student, not only to the school's rules but also to the academic work that is its main mission (p. 225).[5]

Similarly, with reference to his research on the extent to which high school students' participation in school extra-curricular activities significantly affects their commitment to school, McNeal (1995) found that participation in athletics most profoundly reduces students' likelihood of dropping out of school (see also Sabo, Melnick and Vanfossen, 1989), whereas participation in fine art, academic[6] or vocational clubs has no effect. When socioeconomic and academic ability variables were controlled, it was estimated that on average, Blacks were 1.9 times less likely to drop out than whites (p. 68). McNeal notes that athletic participation reduces the probability of dropping out by about 40 percent; and the probability was greatest for Blacks, who were more likely to participate in athletics. This latter finding is consistent with a recent Toronto Board of Education study which shows that Black students, particularly those born in the Caribbean and Canada, participate in extra-curricular activities more often than the rest of the student population (Cheng, Yau & Ziegler, 1993).[7]

In studies of Caribbean students in Britain, researchers show that they are underachieving at all levels of the educational system (Mirza, 1992; Skellington and Morris, 1992; Gewirtz 1991; Carrington, 1983; Cashmore, 1982). In examining the extent to which extra-curricular sports, provides a school "with a convenient sidetrack for its disillusioned low Black achievers, for whom schooling may have little or no relevance," Carrington (1982) respondents told him, that 'playing in a school team gave them an opportunity to be with friends, to feel proud about representing their school, and to do something to help the school' (p. 57).

Also with reference to Britain, Cashmore (1982) reports that many Black male Caribbean high school athletes believe that their academic life suffered because of their involvement in sport. However, despite this belief, a large number of the athletes who participated in the study went on, after high school, to do well academically. Cashmore argues that sport may have a stimulating effect in that it is able to transform the athlete's "understanding of his *(sic)* own capacities and inspiring him *(sic)* to greater objectives in other realms." There is a "spillover" effect in which the sense of achievement that the athlete gains from participation in sport spills over into academic life. This reflects the notion that "once exposed to the possibilities of achieving, the youth seeks to habitualize success" (Cashmore, 1982: 202).

In his examination of the cultural significance of sport in the school life of Black Caribbean students in Toronto, Solomon (1992) found that the student athletes or "jocks" expect school to help them realize their potential in athletics. For this reason, rather than dropping out, they would "shop around" for a school that would provide them with opportunities to play sports. Like Carrington (1983), Solomon also notes that athletic activities, and the space that these athletes occupy provide them with an opportunity to dominate a particular school activity, and resist the rules and regulations of the school, thus undermining the school's strategy of control.

In a recent article on how African Canadian students use sport to negotiate the barriers to school participation and educational achievement, James (1995) noted that Black youth view sport as a means of coping with a school system in which they are marginalized. Furthermore, by using sport to develop friendships, gain recognition, educate their white peers, challenge stereotypes, and assume leadership responsibilities within sport teams and associations, they felt that they were using sport to be active participants in their own schooling and to overcome the barriers to their academic success. James (1995) suggested that this was an indication that "these Black youth subscribe to the myth that through individual efforts, one can overcome socially constructed systemic barriers; and that sports, like education, are viable means by which to do so" (p. 29).

Generally, studies show that students from higher socioeconomic groups have a greater likelihood of participating in athletic activities, and in turn benefit from such participation (McNeal 1995; Fejgin 1995; Marsh 1993). As Fejgin (1995) explains: "Students from lower socioeconomic groups have fewer opportunities to participate in school sports because the schools they attend offer fewer such activities or do not encourage active participation" (p. 225).[8] However, as already mentioned, Black students from lower social class backgrounds attracted by the possibilities that participation in athletics provides, become heavily involved in their school's athletics activities (James, 1995; Solomon, 1992; Carrington, 1983; Cashmore, 1983); and as studies indicate Black student athletes, regardless of social class, are more successful academically, and are less likely to drop out of school than non-athletes (Fejgin 1995; McNeal 1995; Harris 1991).

Further, in exploring the extent to which high school athletic participation leads to college attendance, Snyder and Spreitzer (1990) found that Black middle class male student athletes with positive parental relations and high cognitive abilities were 17 percent more likely to attend college than non-athletes. Similarly, white athletes were 7 percent more likely to attend college than white non-athletes. On the other hand, Black male athletes from working class families with poor parental relations and high cognitive abilities were 3 percent more likely to attend college compared to their white peers in similar circumstances. Regardless of social class, then, students who participate in athletic activities tend to do better in school.

Studies also identified that gender is a major determinant of students' participation in athletic activities with males having a higher participation rate than females (James 1995; Fejgin, 1995; Marsh, 1993; Mirza 1992; Sabo, Melnick & Vanfossen, 1993; 1989; Carrington, 1983). In some cases the difference between males' and females' participation in high school athletic activities was as much as 12 percent (Fejgin, 1995). While the studies indicate that females are less likely to obtain the same degree and type of benefit from athletic participation as their male peers, there are cases in which female athletes do better than their male counterparts. For example, in their U.S.-based study, Yetman and Berghorn (1993) show that among Black basketball players, 29 percent of males and 43 percent of females earned college degrees. Not only did Black females do better than their male counterparts, but Black female athletes fared considerably better than the Black student body as a whole (p. 313).

Essentially, we have seen that participation in athletic activities is likely to benefit students. While social class, gender, teacher encouragement, parental support, self-concept, cognitive development, and educational and career aspirations are factors that affect the degree to which sports benefit Black students, the research evidence indicates that such participation helps students to gain recognition and respect, feel good about themselves, establish allegiance with their school and hence remain in school. Furthermore, successful athletes learn the discipline and drive needed to pursue success in their academic endeavours. How, then, can we create a school environment that capitalizes on the possibilities and opportunities of athletic participation for Black students while enhancing their academic performance? This question will be explored in the following section.

Athletic Participation: A Means of Ensuring Equal Opportunity and Academic Success

The evidence is clear that athletic participation positively affects students' academic performance and outcomes. The evidence also indicates that Black youth, more than others in similar social and economic circumstances, tend to participate in athletic activities, and have used these activities to negotiate the school environment. And insofar as participation in athletic activities affords them opportunities to gain recognition, enhance cultural identity, build self-confidence and self-esteem, cultivate peer support, and tolerate or accept school, then it is logical that they would be attracted to sport as an important school activity. It seems, therefore, that in our attempts to reverse the negative experiences of Black youth within the existing school system and improve their academic performance, we cannot ignore the salience of athletics in helping them to do so. But how would this address the concerns of parents, educators and community members, who have argued, correctly, that the inequalities, racism and discrimination within the education system are responsible for pushing Black students towards athletics, and away from academics?

A number of studies have shown that current school athletic activities are nondemocratic, opportunistic and oppressive; they legitimate inequalities related to race, social class and gender, as well as power relations between teachers, coaches and students (Lapchick, 1995; Marqusee, 1995; Fejgin, 1994; Solomon, 1992; Carrington, 1983). Fernandez-Balboa argues that the hidden curriculum in physical education and sport in school socializes students into "accepting particular modes of thinking and acting that support and legitimize power structures and social inequalities. Physical education lacks some fundamental human values, such as equity, freedom, cooperation, and self-actualization (cited in Fejgin, 1995: 224). From this, it is clear that encouraging Black students to participate in school athletic activities is not enough. If we expect these students to realize as much success in their academic work as in sports, then school values, policies and practices which sustain inequalities, racism, classism, sexism, and discrimination must also be addressed and the system transformed. It is particularly necessary to advocate for changes in the ideology of the school which has encouraged Black students to strive for success in sports at the expense of their academic work.

Before proceeding, it is important to establish what must be considered academic success, particularly with reference to Black student athletes who tend to be portrayed as "dumb jocks" (Sailes, 1993; Engstrom & Sedlacek, 1989). While the research (e.g. Fejgin, 1995; Marsh, 1993) evidence indicates that under similar circumstances, student athletes tend to do better academically (or are more successful) than non-athletes, what it means to do better is open to question (Leonard, 1993). Undoubtedly, a 80 percent grade in chemistry means something different from 80 percent in physical education. And from discussions I have had with students during the preparation of this paper, it seems that teachers and coaches give them passing grades in order to keep them on sport teams. The grades too, might be a reflection of arrangements between teachers and coaches; or special allowances that coaches give to team members to whom they teach academic courses. For their part, and with the knowledge or approval of school administration, students shop around for, and are encouraged to take, "easy" courses which might guarantee passing grades. Sometimes these courses bear no relation to their career aspirations; and in some cases, the grades reflect the level of achievement after students' second attempt at the subject. These practices contribute to the suspicions that persist about the academic success of student athletes. Hence, in examining academic success, consideration must be given to those systemic and individual practices which undermine the academic capability of student athletes, and call into question the role of the school in preparing these students for educational and occupational success.

Advocates for democratic changes within the school system tend to more often single the academic curricula, arguing for an anti-racism approach to address the negative ideology and practices that undermine the success of minority students. Since within this framework all school activities are understood to contribute to the educational process, physical education and extra-curricular athletic activities must be assessed for inherent biases like any other academic activity. Further, in terms of making education equitable, accessible and inclusive, it is important for educators to provide learning activities that take into account the diverse needs and interests of students. For this reason, athletic activities must be incorporated into the school program for they are activities to which students are entitled (Kidd, 1995) not only for health reasons, but also because they can help to meet the academic, psychological, social, and spiritual needs of students.

If students, and Black students in particular, are to benefit from their participation in athletic activities, then the environment in which they pursue their education and athletic interest must be one in which the students are valued equally for their academic and athletic abilities. This is crucial for, as Leonard (1993) points out, the most significant factors that determine the educational outcomes of athletes are the school's "value climate" (i.e.wherein athletic achievement is more highly valued than scholarship), and perceived peer status (i.e. whereby the perception of high peer status facilitates and creates a desire for continued recognition, perhaps through college attendance) (p. 322). This should not be surprising since, as many writers (e.g. Lapchick, 1995; Marqusee, 1995; Dei, 1993; Leonard, 1993) have argued, the school is a microcosm of a society in which race, class and gender stratification exist and are sustained by racism, sexism and classism. Hence, the school climate (i.e. the structure, the philosophy, the program, the policies) and everything that informs the teaching practices and the curricular and extra-curricular activities must be geared toward making equity, access and success a reality for all students, irrespective of backgrounds.

Because athletic activities serve as cultural resources and references, and play an important role in the lives of students of particular age, ethnic, racial, gender and immigrant back-grounds, educators, parents and policy-makers need to be aware of the potential and actual role that athletics play (see Karp, Stone & Yoels, 1991, Chapter 8). For instance, research shows that for some immigrant group members, participation in sports helps them to learn the norms and values of the host society (Solomon, 1992; James, 1990). In a diverse society in which teachers and administrators must seek ways of meeting the needs of *all* students, school administrators and teachers must diversify their approach to the educational process. They must know that to treat students equitably means teaching them differently, taking into consideration cultural differences, needs interests and abilities. Students who choose to partici-pate in sports should be able to do so to gain confidence, build self-esteem, and promote their connection with their schools, communities and society (Shilling, 1993), and not feel stereo-typed, side-tracked or trapped. It is important to enable stu-dents to either participate in sports or to opt out without feeling stigmatized.

As with all other educational activities, athletics can be used to transform the current unicultural school climate and make the diversity within the student body more evident in all the school's activities. In addition, sports can be the means through which students become aware of the educational structure and therefore develop the skills, confidence and commitment to ini-tiate changes in all areas of schooling that will benefit them. Indeed, James (1995) demonstrates that one of the ways in which Black Toronto students negotiate the hurdles of school is to take leadership positions in areas of school life where they are significantly represented and can exercise some control. For example, James tells of one student who relates his success in athletics to his popularity in school, and ultimately to his elec-tion as president of the school's Athletic Association. In that position, he managed to diversify the athletic activities of the school which in turn helped Black students to make a greater commitment to the school and their schooling

The support of educators, both teachers and coaches, is criti-cal in the transformation of the system where athletic activities serve as a control mechanism, as well as to re-enforce the physical abilities rather than the intellectual abilities of Black students. Teachers and coaches must change the current practices which tend to over-emphasize participation in athletic activities for competition and performance (Kidd, 1995; Hall et al, 1991). Rather, athletic activities should also be seen as educational and as a means of inculcating discipline, hardwork, and cooperation, communal values, and cultural respect. It also means that the "the win at all cost" philosophy must go. For too long it has been used to re-enforce stereotyping, and hence the over-representation of some racial and ethnic groups in some sport activities. This philosophy has contributed to conflicts between students, undermined their self-esteem and forced them to have doubts about their personal worth and commitment to school. It has producd great pressure even on the successful student athlete (Frey, 1994; Dodds, 1993; Hall, Slack, Smith and Whitson, 1991). Athletic activities then should be seen as providing spaces where students can gain some control of their schooling process (Thomas, 1988), and develop the skills that will enhance educational aspirations and commitment to academic endeavours.

Crossley (1988) argues that such control is not only learned by participating in organized sports. He suggests a move away from organized to unorganized sport and social recreation in order to provide young people with opportunities to exercise and develop capacities and abilities to become autonomous and participate in the construction of their success in life. According to Crossley, "unorganised sports afford the type of participation that not only enhances self-determination, but provides practical experience in deciding principles of social co-operation" (1988:190). Hence, unorganized athletic activities can be an effective part of after school programs where students can cultivate important social and political values.

In an earlier version of this chapter, a number of readers raised questions about what I have said of competition. They suggested that competition and performance are not necessarily bad. It is in this milieu that Black student athletes have succeeded, and if we remove competition and the perception that these youth have extraordinary skill, then we are removing Black youth competitive advantage. Furthermore, competition and excellence in performance are also to be found in the area of academics where white students are perceived to have the advantage. I have no problem with this argument. It is not that I think that competition should be eliminated. Indeed, we live in a capitalist society, hence competition cannot be avoided. However, teachers and coaches can use competition to instill in students confidence, self-worth and a sense of success. Students should be encouraged to apply competitive skills learned in the gym and playing field to their academic endeavours.

To provide equitable opportunities, coaches, teachers and administrators must be conscious of how students are represented in all school activities. To this end, coaches, teachers and administrators must ensure that school sport teams reflect the racial and ethnic composition of the school. Black students, therefore, should not be recruited only for the basketball or track teams, but also for the swim and the hockey teams. Further, as Hill (1993) argues: "it is healthier for young athletes to engage in a diverse set of activities in order to develop "alternative identities" as well as to have a "cushion" for the stress that is inherent in sport participation" (p. 113).

Encouraging athletes to diversify the sports in which they participate would not only broaden their athletic repertoire by allowing them to demonstrate their diverse abilities and skills, but also address "the volatile and divisive issue of sport specialization" (Hill, 1993: 113). Further, it would help to challenge the stereotypes and myths that exist around race and gender. For Black youth in particular, these stereotypes and myths have contributed to the expectation that they should excel in sports rather than academics. To do otherwise would be seen by their peers as "being white" (James, 1995; BLAC, 1994; Solomon, 1992) — peer pressure many youth wished they did not have to contend with. For instance, in a recent conversation with Steve, a fourth year university student, he recalled that during high school not only did his basketball coach "pressure" him to do well in basketball (sometimes leaving his English class early to practise), but his friends expected him to dominate the game. As Steve states: "If I do not play well, my friends are going to say 'what are you doing, you should be better.' Friends put pressure on you to excell because that is the expectation." Steve reported that he had to stop playing sports and concentrate on his academic work in order to fulfill his aspiration of going to university. But he also agrees that the skills he learned from sports, and the support he got from his friends continue to serve him well today in both his academic life and entrepreneurial endeavours.

Despite Steve's experience, sports is not necessarily antithetical to academic pursuits. Robert, a recent university graduate, provides an example of this. In his comments at a recent gathering to honour him and other university scholarship winners, he told the audience that he managed to get through school because of wrestling and the support of the Black coach. As a teenage immigrant form Jamaica, he found school boring and alienating. This caused him to get into trouble and at one time, he was suspended from school for two weeks. Upon his return, the wrestling coach, a Jamaican immigrant teacher, invited him onto the wrestling team. Robert asserts that this was his "hook," and with the support of the coach, whom he credits 'for where he is today,' he was able to complete high school and win the scholarship to university. Robert's story also illustrates the important role that coaches, particularly those from minority backgrounds, can play in making the schooling process pleasant for minority students.

The possibility of obtaining university sports scholarships has also been the "hook" for students to remain in school. The movie *Hoop Dreams* about two working class Black youth demonstrates both the possibilities and limitations in aspiring for, and achieving athletic scholarships. The movie illustrates the efforts and energies that student athletes must exert to remain top players. It also shows how the hard work and discipline can reward young people once they have the necessary peer, parental and school support. More importantly, the movie shows that as student athletes mature, they come to appreciate the importance of education in broadening their future career opportunities and to recognize the role racism plays in limiting their athletic and academic endeavours. Although Black athletes are more actively recruited for some sports, once on the team they must demonstrate greater skills and outperform whites in order to have an equal chance of remaining on the team

(Leonard 1993; Karp, Stone & Yoels, 1991). This indicates that sports do not secure upward social mobility, nor do they offer an escape from racism. However, they can strengthen racial identity and help to develop the skills to confront racism in other spheres of life. Parents have a significant role to play in supporting their children as they participate in school athletic activities. While it might seem appropriate for parents to discourage or limit their children's participation in athletic activities because they failed a test or do not do well in school, it is equally important that they pay attention to the systemic problems that are responsible for the students' lack of success in the first place. In discouraging athletic participation, parents must be aware that taking away "the hook," or that aspect of school life that contributes to the social, psychological and intellectual development of the student can be more detrimental to their educational process. For as Robert illustrates, sports, accompanied by responsible and supportive teachers, can make the difference between failing and succeeding academically. That sport did not serve Steve well, is not merely a reflection of insensitive teachers and coaches, but also the inability of parents to identify the systemic factors which contribute to some of the problems that students have in school.

There is ample evidence to show that Black and Caribbean parents expect their children to concentrate on their academic subjects because they see academics as the sole means of succeeding in a racist society (James, 1995; 1990; Harris, 1994; Brathwaite, 1989; Cashmore, 1982). Furthermore, parents discourage involvement in sports because they believe that relying on sports is problematic since an injury could easily limit future achievement. With this philosophy, parents are sometimes inflexible (Cashmore, 1982), and the children who adhere to their expectations are left without the necessary academic, social, psychological and political supports they might have received if they had participated in athletics. However, when parents do give support, they are in effect paying attention to the individual abilities and interests of their children, and encouraging them to apply themselves to their academic work in ways that will ensure success. Chris, a grade 6 teacher in Metropolitan Toronto, is an example of a student whose parents gave him the space to pursue his interest in football while ensuring that he concentrated on his academic work. In telling his story, Chris says that he has been able to 'transfer the value of discipline and hard work that he learned from sports to his education and teaching' (Pittaway, 1994).

The situation of female athletes deserves special consideration, as gender bias in school athletic activities tends to rob them of the opportunities, supports and benefits that males receive. Also, while males have other avenues (e.g. community and recreational centres, clubs, the street and other places) to participate in athletic activities, females, in many cases, must rely on the opportunities that schools provide. Attempts must be made to address this "malestream" orientation (Kidd, 1995). As Hall, Slack, Smith and Whitson (1991) contend, while males and females may have equal rights to access physical education or extra-curricular athletic programs in schools today, they do not have equal opportunities to learn, and benefit from these activities. The needs and aspirations of females are different from those of males and must be recognized as such. Hence teachers, coaches, and parents must make specific efforts to encourage females to get involved in athletic activities, taking into consideration their social circumstances and individual interests, abilities and experiences (Lenskyj, 1994; Williams, 1993; Talbot, 1993).

The Black community has a role to play in helping to reconceptualize the role and function of athletics as complementary to academic activities. By community, I refer not only to so-called leaders, community, youth and recreational workers, and "big brothers" and "big sisters" but also to athletes who are held up as role models (see Marqusee, 1995)and frequently called upon to give motivational speeches because they are regarded as people who have "made it." Often these "role model" athletes tell youth that they can become anything they want, they just have to work hard. Such misleading testimonials must be discouraged. As Arthur Ashe suggests, professional athletes have a responsibility to tell youth "the facts of life." They should know that "racial and economic discrimination forced us to channel our energies into athletics and entertainment. These were the ways out of the ghetto" — the ways to get that BMW automobile, Nike shoes, Rolex watch and Armani suit. The message that Ashe communicates is that there must be a healthy combination of athletics and academics, something that parents must instill. He goes on:

> I have often addressed high school audiences and my message is always the same. For every hour you spend on the athletic field, spend two in the library. Even if you make it as a pro athlete, your career will be over by the time you are thirty-five. So you will need that diploma ... (cited in Leonard, 1993: 186).[9]

Prominent African American sports sociologist, professor and former athlete, Dr. Harry Edwards concurs with Ashe, advancing the point that the African American community should not "discourage its youth from sport participation," for it has benefited the community in many ways:

> On a spiritual level, the performances of outstanding Black athletes have bolstered Black pride and self-esteem. On a practical level, sports have been means to higher education opportunities for many Black youths ... who have moved on to establish productive careers in other fields. Further, by virtue of their enormous accomplishments in sports, Black athletes have demonstrated that the greatest obstacle to Black achievement in all areas of American life has not been lack of capacity or competitiveness, but a lack of opportunity.

Capitalize on Abilities, Recognize Diversity, Provide Opportunities, Practise Equity

By way of concluding, let us return to Dane. Clearly, his experience in school is not unique. Like many other Black students, Dane's education is taking place within a school system that is white, middle class and Eurocentic (Ministry of Education and Training, 1993), run by white middle class teachers and administrators who are probably unaware of how school policies and practices alienate and silence Black youth (see James, 1994). It is a school system in which racist ideology, unless recognized and interrogated, contributes to teachers' expectations that Dane will do better athletically than academically. As such, school for Dane, and others like him, is not an especially hospitable place. Unable to compete easily in school and experiencing "status frustration," they seek "alternative ways to express a competent and valued self" (Karp, Stone and Yoels, 1991: 213). The "gym" and the playground are the few spaces in schools where these students can establish their sense of individuality and identity, enhance their status, and gain credibility. Should we not encourage students to participate in activities that make a difference, and provide opportunities that increase their chances of succeeding academically? The skeptic's answer may be: Would not this help merely to re-enforce existing stereotypes held by teachers? Would not teachers continue to use sport as a side-track and a coping strategy to deal with Black students, whom they do not understand, or do not wish to understand? Would the "success" or achievements (i.e. the "passing inflated grades?") of the Black student athlete continue to leave doubts about what they actually know?

Clearly, the argument I have advanced should leave little doubt as to the answers to these questions. The problem with Dane and other Black student athletes is not that sports is "too central to their schooling," or that they spend too much time in the gym or on the playground. Rather, it is the way in which the educational system, the curriculum content, and teachers' pedagogical approaches render Black students invisible and silent. It is this that must be addressed, not the ways in which these youth have sought to cope with schooling. Certainly, in looking for ways to reduce drop-out rates and achievement gaps between student groups, we also have to look at the benefits that athletic participation provides (Dei et al, 1995; Fejgin, 1995). Accommodating the needs, interests and aspirations of Black student athletes, and incorporating athletics into the school program may well help school to be less alienating, accessible and equitable for these students. But ultimately, for Dane and other such students who are caught within an educational system that values them more for their athletic skills and the fame they bring to the school, parents must make decisions that will benefit their children. This may mean prohibiting their children from participating in athletes.

Sports historian Bruce Kidd argues that physical activity and good health are basic human rights in Canada. Hence, students are "entitled" to participate in physical activities which provide them with opportunities to sustain good physical, cultural, social and psychological health needed for academic success. Schools, therefore, have the responsibility to facilitate the development of healthy students. This would mean that the focus of students' participation in athletic activities, would not only be to produce athletic competence or excellence, (Kerr, 1995), or help teachers cope with, or "side-track" students, but to provide students with opportunities that will contribute to their "empowerment," and instill confidence, dignity and pride in themselves and their community.

NOTES

1 The understanding here is that there is no biological basis for differences in abilities and skills in academics or athletics. Hence, Black students' interest and success in athletics must be seen as products of the extent to which they have internalized the social construction of race that has been imposed upon them.

2 BLAC was a committee of educators, lawyers, civil servants and community workers that were appointed by the Nova Scotia Government in 1990.

3 The Group was established to report on the situation of Black youth in Toronto after the 1991 "Yonge Street incident" in that city.

4 The researchers also explain that the inability of sport to hold urban students in school might be due to the fact that "the social and personal rewards cannot counteract the problems of city schools and the urban environment" (Sabo, Melnick & Vanfossen, 1989: 9).

5 I suggest that while it is meaningful to encourage students to participate in sport because of the social and psychological benefits that they can gain from doing so, the blind obedience that schools often expect of the student-athletes cannot go unchallenged.

6 It should be noted that Fejgin (1994), in her study on students' participation in high school competitive sport, found that "the effect of athletic participation is similar to the effect of participation in academic clubs for educational aspirations" (p. 219).

7 The study did not specify the activities in which the students are engaged. As these findings show it would be quite important to do so.

8 It is also fair to assume that work and familial demands that are placed on working class students limit their opportunities to participate in after school activities.

9 This was part of an article entitled "An Open Letter to Black Parents: Send Your Children to the Libraries" in the *New York Times* (February 6, 1977: Scetion 5, p. 2).

Chapter Fifteen

BEYOND SAMENESS
THINKING THROUGH BLACK HETEROGENEITY

RINALDO WALCOTT

Introduction: The Importance of Multidimensional Approaches to Blackness

Austin Clarke's (1980) memoirs *Growing Up Stupid Under The Union Jack* details how the type of colonial education that he received taught him everything about the "mother country" but little about the immediacy of his own environment. What Clark's memoirs demonstrate today is how what was constituted as "education" for him, was really a specific and particular exercise in the cultural study of middle class, white, (male) Britain. Clark's education then was an exercise in a particular and limited cultural study of Britain.

Such an observation as the one above is borne out by the research of the Caribbean historian and poet Kamau Brathwaite (1993) who has written that the British colonial education many Caribbean people received gave them the vocabulary to imagine and write about British environs and landscapes without having been there. Thus early Caribbean poets could write reasonably good poetry about England using specific metaphors and allegories for experiences they had never had. Such a practice was in contradistinction to writing poetry about their own environment. Brathwaite argues that much of the poetry about local landscape and environs (the Caribbean) was inadequate.

I offer those two related examples to demonstrate that education can be a form of cultural study and can have clearly defined borders for what is *in* and what is *out*. In the above two examples colonialism and imperialism dictated what aspects of culture would be deemed important for education and what specific elements of culture would be legitimated as knowledge. W.E.B. DuBois, a valiant fighter for legitimating Black cultural expression in his classic 1903 *Souls of Black Folk*, demonstrated the multidimensional aspects of Black people's lives. Dubois's text used history, sociology, fiction and music to attempt to narrate the lives of Black people in racist America. His text is a polyphonic testimony to Black complexity and can be considered a precursor to what is today called "cultural studies." He recognised that no single discipline could account for the complexity of Black life and therefore he wrote his text as an example of what might be required to make sense out of Black lives.

What I am going to suggest in this essay is that education might and can be about much *more* than what schools currently allow and I also want to suggest that current approaches in what is being called "cultural studies" might allow us to access the *more* of education. Cultural studies is an anti-discipline, trans-discipline, inter-discipline mode of analysis that is interested in everything from history, audience, audience reception, production both in terms of artistic production and the commercial dissemination of the finished product, aesthetics, identity formations, social and political identifications, the politics of representation, the analysis of significant events, products, performances and their effects (Grossberg, Nelson, Treichler, 1992). As well, cultural studies is concerned with disturbing the boundaries of what we think we know. Thus no-one is assumed to possess knowledge that they can transfer to others. In this way, cultural studies seeks to open up a discursive space so that a multiplicity of positions, ideas, opinions and interpretations might take place in the classroom.

The specificity of history (personal and collective), identifications and positionality come into play in recognising how representations and interpretations are made. Cultural studies begins with the assumption that all representations whether in novels, poems, films, music, advertisements, and so on are open to multiple interpretations but also have important historical narratives behind them that might reveal narrative intensions. However, intensions and outcomes can never be totally revealed nor predicted because readers read differently, bringing in and taking away different ideas and experiences from their engagement with cultural products. Critical or left cultural studies call into question and critiques enlightenment and humanist ideas as those ideas reproduce the structures of historical and contemporary forms of oppression. Cultural studies then as an approach raises many questions for multicultural societies.

In many Ontario classrooms today, multicultural education has been advocated as the panacea for correcting the historically structured inequalities of schooling for "minorities." Multicultural education is often presented as a text based exercise in which teachers can offer information on others who might not be imagined to be "original" Canadians (English and French). Instead teachers can now teach about the Others of the Canadian nation (Native people, Black people, Ukrainians, Japanese, and so on) by using the cultural products of the Others. The cultural representations of these Others have been infused into the curriculum through novels, plays, short stories, poetry and music created by and about them. But an important question still remains: How can the complex social, cultural and political lives of these Others be addressed without essentializing who they are? I want to suggest that understanding education as a form of cultural studies might provide some answers to this question, and raise new and important questions at the same time in schools.

To develop this point I want to do two different but related and complementary readings of M. Nourbese Philip's (1988) *Harriet's Daughter*. The first reading is done in the context of anti-racist education and Black difference and demonstrates what a cultural studies approach might allow us to see; the second reading situates a number of issues concerning the novel in terms of its author's history and the novel's publication in the context of white supremacy in Canada. What these two brief readings attempt to do is demonstrate the importance of multiple readings for the production of knowledge and therefore the enhancement of education.

The Politics of Black Difference

After the 1992 "riots" in Toronto on Yonge Street the Ontario NDP government commissioned Stephen Lewis to investigate Black community allegations of racism. The resultant Stephen Lewis Report documented that racism in the province of Ontario seems to be mainly anti-Black racism. Despite Lewis' report of virulent anti-Black racism and the urgent need for anti-racism strategies, the debates on and around what exactly constitutes anti-racism continue to rage. I believe we need to take stock around what anti-racism suggests and means[1] and we need to resist particularly any inclinations to interpret it primarily as a project about enabling Black folks to develop self-esteem. For anti-racism to be theoretically and practically strong, I contend that it should be understood as an attempt to take seriously *the politics of difference*. By this I mean to suggest that anti-racism as a pedagogical practice should be concerned with all forms of oppression and domination as constituted through social relations. Anti-racism as praxis should take heterogeneity (i.e. multiple differences) as the assumed underpinning of its praxis (i.e. practice based in theory). Recognition not only of Black difference but also the complex and shifting differences among visible minority and other marginalized groups is essential to anti-racism pedagogy. In this essay my first reading of *Harriet's Daughter* explores what a politics of difference would mean in light of secondary schooling initiatives to implement an anti-racism pedagogy that would support an anti-racism curriculum.

Drawing on McCarthy (1990) I want to begin by pointing to the importance of the concept non-synchrony — that is, not reducing differences or multiple characteristics to a single category. Black people, like any other people, live in varying socioeconomic classes, they live in or come from different geographical/cultural environments, they have varying sexual orientations, and so on. The importance of non-synchrony lies in the ways in which multicultural curricula have allowed the current organization of schooling to use "race" and "ethnicity" as synonymous with — or inclusive of—gender, sex, class, and so on, thus avoiding the need to address the ways in which difference and contradiction work in "minority" relations within state institutions like schools(p.83). For example using "race" as synonymous for other socio-cultural differences would not explain why it is that young Black women do better in schools than young Black men.[2] To further demonstrate the complexity of the issue I would suggest that in most cases systemic oppression for Black women is organized through what Himani Bannerji has called sexist racism. Also using "race" as inclusive of "sex" would not necessarily explain the experiences of gay and lesbian youth of colour in schools. If we assume non-synchrony, we can develop an analysis that does not reduce difference to a single category that then legitimates the neglect or exclusion of other important variables of social difference.

McCarthy argues that current approaches to anti-racism and multicultural education have produced a monolithic notion of Blackness. He further demonstrates that while Black people might have a common history of enslavement and oppression in the Americas, that oppression has been experienced differently for different people according to class, gender, sex and I would add colour. What those differences mean is that approaches to how Black people are treated in the school system should be understood as always complicated by a number of other variables that impact on how they live their lives. The ways in which certain forms of racism affect working-class Blacks can be and often is different from how it will affect middle-class Blacks who have more access to specific resources of the dominant culture (i.e., cultural access and privilege acquired through being a member of the preferred class, gender, sex, etc.). Thus the practice of anti-racism must avoid any attempt to synchronize (i.e., align the intergroup differences) or to make singular the experiences and histories of a heterogeneous group into a monolithic narrative of oppression.

I want to demonstrate by using *Harriet's Daughter*, a novel that has been taught to Grade 9 students in a number of Toronto schools, what the politics of difference approach would mean in light of secondary schooling initiatives to implement an anti-racism pedagogy.

In the novel, the two protagonists are our first encounters with a non-synchronous Blackness. Margaret is a Canadian born young Black girl and her friend Zulma is a recent immigrant from Trinidad and Tobago. While both of them share the history and legacy of slavery, there are also fundamental differences that separate them. Zulma speaks an English (or what Philip in other places has called a demotic) that is different from Margaret's; the latter knows little about the island that Zulma has come from and they share different cultural etiquette about what is acceptable to ask and what is not; Margaret has a cosmopolitan sensibility about her that Zulma does not. It is only through a game ("The Harriet Tubman Game" in which many of the historical roles are reversed: white kids play slaves and so on) as well as Margaret's growing awareness of the Black diaspora — that is, how Blacks have been scattered from their original community — that the two become good friends, able to communicate across their differences.

The differences that exist between Margaret and Zulma are important ones and should not be ignored. The experience of being an immigrant is quite different from being born in Canada, whether or not both persons are Black. Place as in geography, citizenship and nation are important to understanding Margaret's and Zulma's differences. The differences that exist between Zulma and Margaret raise crucial questions in terms of what emphases are given importance in the pedagogical choices of anti-racism in any North American school today. Are those choices going to focus on the experience and histories of migration? Are the practices of anti-racism pedagogy going to address the ways in which exclusionary practices have denied some members of the society their historical and contemporary claims to citizenship? Or is anti-racism as pedagogical practice going to address the ways in which all forms of domination work to exclude anyone who is positioned or imagined to be outside the structures of citizenship and normality?

Zulma's main problem is a feeling of exile from Tobago and her grandmother with whom she had grown up, during the time that her mother immigrated to Canada. Philip raises here the very complex issue of how some immigrant families have been separated for so long that they and their children have had to get to know each other again, sometimes with disastrous effects. That such problems (some of the effects of migration) do not affect all Black students in schools is one of the first differences that anti-racism pedagogy should take seriously. The ways in which Zulma's and Margaret's problems and informal education are resolved in Philip's novel point to the challenges that a politics of difference demands of anti-racism pedagogy.

Zulma's return to Tobago and a reunion with her grandmother is made possible through an inheritance that Margaret receives. The inheritance comes from Mrs. Blewchamp. Mrs. Blewchamp was a woman who Harriet (Margaret's mother) had worked for when she first came to Canada. Mrs. Blewchamp was Jewish and had escaped the Nazis during World War II. Philip as author in a work that appears to be ostensibly about Blackness and one immigrant child's experience, places on the pedagogical agenda questions of the Holocaust and Jewish otherness. Philip does this by revealing to us that Mrs. Blewchamp had numbers on her hand. Those tell-tale markers of Nazi terror make the pedagogy of anti-racism much more complex in relation to thinking about teaching Philip's work and the pedagogical choices one might make. By placing Mrs. Blewchamp in the story as essential to Zulma's "emancipation," Philip asks us to consider the complex relations of domination and subordination and their application across racial/ethnic differences.

To attempt to incorporate Philip's novel into existing school curriculum would mean that current definitions of anti-racism would have to take as important the complex relations of difference to the pedagogy of anti-racism. By that I mean that anti-racism would have to take all forms and histories of oppression as central to its practice. Mrs. Blewchamp symbolically represents other histories and forms of oppression that have been and continue to be markers of a diasporic or displaced people. Anti-racism as pedagogical practice should be fluid enough to shift between the various historically manifested forms of racism and oppression. As such anti-racism could produce analyses that do not dissipate past nor contemporary differences but attempt representations and inclusion of the complex nature of difference.

Many of us have been concerned about the recent discussion both in Canada and the United States about the relations between Blacks and Jews. Some readers may see my analysis as an attempt at diluting the focus of anti-racism on visible minorities. It is, however, the case that "jewishness" and "Blackness" are both social and cultural constructions that tend to produce narratives of "oneness." By that I mean that too often the ways in which Blackness and Jewishness are discussed produce a picture in which the cultural members of both groups are represented as if they do not have important and conflicting differences in and among themselves. Thus it remains important that those of us committed to social change recognize that it is a fiction when any of these cultures appear to be synchronized either from outside or inside the community. Both Blacks and Jews are differentiated by class relations, gender, sex and colour that have profound implications for how people live their lives in a discriminatory, hierarchized society (for example, we should all remember the debates about the evacuation of Ethiopian Jews to Israel that centred on whether or not they were really Jews).

If anti-racism is incapable of addressing the complex and shifting relations of domination, it will become what multicultural education has become. As mentioned earlier in this essay, multicultural education currently serves to only include static historical information about particular groups without having to make any major shifts in the ways in which schooling is currently organised. Those arrangements are based on liberal notions of inclusion that do not take seriously claims that old ways of doing schooling can not adequately address nor "manage" the incorporation of "new" information that requires "new" practices. Anti-racism on the other hand challenges the very fundamentals of schooling and suggests strongly that some rethinking needs to be done.

The challenge for those of us who advocate anti-racism is to understand and begin with the assumption of Black difference coupled with a complex reading and analysis of the practices of domination. Any attempt to synchronize Blackness will only result in piecemeal changes, and it is only by understanding anti-racism as the practice of a politics of difference that we can begin to practice a pedagogy that does not produce exclusions that reinscribe the practices of domination. Teachers must shift from the easy multicultural assumption of "tribal sameness" to an assumption of "difference within and without" as a first place to practice anti-racist pedagogy. Education as cultural studies can facilitate a politics of difference analysis that is so crucial to a more rigorous anti-racism pedagogy.

The Promise of Cultural Studies

Cultural studies disrupts categories of sameness by pointing to varying identifications and the ways in which individual and collective subjectivities are constituted and manifested. Thus cultural studies could encourage practices that challenge how we arrive at too easy conclusions and definitions concerning sameness through having us acknowledge and take account of the ways in which we are multiply constituted and positioned.

The author of *Harriet's Daughter* might be said to be multiply located or represent the complexity of difference. Philip is a Trinidadian/Tobago-Canadian Black woman. Those identities must be understood and addressed in relationship to the teaching of her work. Black, woman, immigrant and so on are identities that shape the kinds of choices and narrative decisions that she makes as an author. But to recognize those identities as having an impact on the art of Philip, readers would also have to address the history and cultural practices situated both within and outside the novel. For example the histories of Caribbean migration to Canada; Black North American history dating back to the 1600s and so on; those historical narratives play important roles in the themes of the novel. Zulma immigrates to Canada to live with her mother who had come some years before her.

The narrative of *Harriet's Daughter* demands that reading and teaching it goes beyond the "comfortable" confines of the novel and the traditional strategies of themes, metaphors, allegory and aesthetics to account for historical, social and political implications of the past and the contemporary period. The

"Underground Rail Road Game" or Harriet Tubman Game and other references to slavery are just examples of the imperative to move beyond the confines of the novel so that the meanings and complexity of its narrative can have a greater impact. If *Harriet's Daughter* is to be meaningful to students, links would have to be made between history, contemporary and past "migration" practices, as well as aesthetics, in particular Black diasporic aesthetics, audience, publishing practices and so on.

What raising these issues is meant to suggest is the complexity of Black lives and why pedagogical practices should begin with the assumption of Black difference. Unless Black complexity and difference is assumed, practices that hinder Black people's opportunities will continue to be sites of pain for the most disadvantaged Black people. DuBois's own ambivalent relationship to Black oral culture and its possibilities led him to revise his idea of the Talented Tenth. He realized that Blackness was too complex to have one program for addressing oppression. It is such insights that make cultural studies valuable as intervention in debates on Black peoples.

Cultural studies begins from a place of attempting to address all those issues and understands them as an integral part of what it means to read and derive meaning from a text. The inter-disciplinarity, anti-disciplinarity, trans-disciplinarity of cultural studies allow for the asking of all kinds of questions within the context of education. To further demonstrate the point that I am making some other issues might be considered in relationship to Philip's novel. The novel was reportedly rejected by major Canadian publishers because the publishers believed that there was no market for a novel about two Black girls. That a women's press published the novel should be an important consideration in light of the gender and racial issues involved in its earlier rejection, as well as the themes of the novel. Also that the novel won the *Casa De Las Americas* prize and was widely received in Britain, the Caribbean and Canada as an important children's book should be considered. Such issues could open up the space to discuss in school how processes of legitimation work, gender and racial discrimination, the politics of publishing, the dissemination of information and the exclusion of particular voices from the public sphere.

Cultural studies approaches only ask that we engage texts and their teaching more honestly. Cultural studies asks us to think about how our positions and practices are always already complex, contradictory, tension filled and ambivalent. If we recognize and explicitly address these qualities as informing what we do, we might do more interesting things with the various texts that we encounter. Thus we might move forward with the legacy that DuBois leaves by always remembering that Black people are a complex collectivity constituted of many differences.

Note: A portion of this paper was previously published in *Orbit: Anti-Racist Education: Working Across Differences*. George Dei [Ed.]. Ontario Institute for Studies in Education, vol. 25, No.2,1994. Other parts of this paper were presented at the meeting of the Ontario Council of Teachers of English Annual Conference, 1993. I wish to thank Mary-Jo Nadeau for her generous help.

NOTES

1. Barb Thomas (1987) lists three main points that she feels distinguishes anti-racist education from multicultural education. It is useful to paraphrase those points here. 1) The definition of the problem: anti-racist educators pay attention to the significance attached to differences; 2) anti-racism explores and places in up-front ways the various histories of racism in Canada as part of the curriculum to expose ways in which racism perpetuates unequal ralations and: 3) anti-racist education has emerged out of community organizations and institutions as opposed to multicultural education that has been state sponsored and instituted. For Thomas these three important points allow for the possibility of radical transformation of schooling, leading eventually to equity in schools and in the larger society.

2. For the development of this argument see Heidi Safia Mirza (1992). In a comparative study of second generation young Caribbean women in Britain and the United States, with background information on the Caribbean, Mirza argues that the notion that young Black women are underachievers is inaccurate. What she points out is that young Black women usually have the same or higher expectations than their male and white peers but the ideological forces (patriarchy and racism) in the society prohibit their acievements. Thus in the final analysis young Black women end up achieving less than their male and white peers but not because of their own lack of motivation.

Chapter Sixteen

RETHINKING 'AFRICAN-CENTRED' SCHOOLS IN EURO-CANADIAN CONTEXTS

George J. Sefa Dei

Introduction

Many educators, students and community workers in the African-Canadian community have drawn attention to the need for alternative pedagogic and communicative tools, resources and instructional strategies to deliver effective education to our youth. In this context there are many among us who are calling for the choice of 'African-centered' schools. This paper adds to the on-going debate by exploring the social, political and philosophical basis of such schools. Essays in this book provide a sound critique of conventional approaches to delivering education in Euro-Canadian/American contexts. The emerging call for 'African-centred' schools is a recognition of the importance of providing education that speaks to the lived material and social realities of peoples of African descent in a white-dominated society.

I will begin this discussion by stressing that our individual political assumptions do in fact impinge upon how we each structure our pedagogical and communicative ideas about educational alternatives. Our personal and collective journeys reflect and influence how we read and interpret the world around us. One cannot look at the "crisis" plaguing African-Canadian youth today "with respect to education and achievement" (RCOL, 1994) and claim political and academic neutrality. I therefore call on us all, educators, administrators, students, parents, community workers and caregivers to join forces by linking knowledge, social commitment and political action in our efforts to bring about educational change in Ontario.

Recently, I attended the annual meeting of the American Educational Research Association in San Francisco. In a round-table session about African-centred schools, one panellist (African-American educator, Gloria Ladson-Billings), poignantly asked whether as African educators we can function as advocates of African-centered schools, and at the same time examine critically the ideas and assumptions behind such schools. I would suggest that we cannot afford not to. Those who advocate for such schools should also be prepared to interrogate the underlying assumptions in order to ensure that the educational success of our students is of paramount concern. We may be approaching such schools in diverse and even opposing ways, but there must be room for mutual dialogue. We must also resist closure of debate, whether by those who are staunchly opposed to the idea of such schools or by those who are in favour and thus vehemently denounce any critique.

I need not reiterate here the reasons behind the push for such schools. In fact, one only has to read the countless research reports, academic studies and anecdotal comments on the education of African youths in Euro-American/Canadian contexts (Board of Education, 1988; Brathwaite, 1989; Solomon, 1992; CABE, 1992; Henry, 1992; Lewis, 1992; BEWG, 1993; OPBC, 1993; Dei, et al., 1995, James, 1994; RCOL, 1994; Calliste, 1994; Cheng, 1995) to understand the frustrations that has led to the cry for African-centered schools. There is a deep sense of frustration among many African-Canadian students, educators, parents and community workers regarding the education of students from minority backgrounds in Canadian schools. To make this comment does not by itself deny that there are many educational success stories in our community that make us all proud. However, our concern is that all our young people deserve an equitable and appropriate education.

To reiterate, there are some legitimate concerns being expressed by many African-Canadian youths, parents and community workers about the state of public schooling in this country. The important question is, how best can these concerns be addressed to meet the needs of all students? The idea of African-centred schools presents some challenges and questions for all advocates of an inclusive and equitable learning environment in our community. For example, can the concerns about African-Canadian youths' sense of identification with, and connectedness to, the school be addressed through the current school system? What sorts of systemic changes and structural transformations are required? What assurances can Canadian educators and administrators give to alienated youths, that the unfulfilled commitments made by the educational system in the past three decades will now be kept?

The idea of African-centered schools raises other pertinent questions. For example, do African-Canadian youth need a school that is owned and controlled by their community in order to feel more engaged with their schooling and less likely to drop out? How can it be ensured that the existence of African-centred schools would not distract from the legitimate pressures to force mainstream schools to change their Eurocentric focus? Do all African-Canadian students share a sense of a common ancestral heritage? If they do not, how can it be ensured that teaching about African heritage and cultures does not merely feed on Black students' already deep sense of alienation? How do we ensure that an African-centred school is not stigmatized by society? (see also Bancroft, 1994; Collins, 1994).

These are significant questions but they do not in any way diminish the importance of African-centred schools. The call for African-centred schools is an outward manifestation of the larger problems facing the Canadian public school system. The idea of such a school questions the fundamental objectives of public schools: what they are supposed to teach and how, who graduates from the system and with what accreditation, and whose interests are reflected in both the official and the "hidden" curriculum?

Let me reiterate what many advocates of African-centred schools have been saying: It is important to note that African-centred schools are not intended to romanticize or valorize everything African. These schools are not African versions of Eurocentric schools. They are not set up primarily to address any presumed and unfounded "deficits" in African-Canadian youths. In fact, I do not perceive such schools as exclusively for those youth who are failing, and/or who have been failed by, the public school system. As I have pointed out elsewhere, one only needs to talk to academically successful Black students to learn that they, too, feel marginalized in mainstream schools. The fact that some of our students do well in spite of feelings of social marginality and masked frustrations should not give comfort to anyone. Their survival strategies should not be presented as logical pathways for other students to follow. There must be unrelenting pressure on the educational system to remove all elements that make students feel marginalized and frustrated. African-Canadian parents have an important role to play in this struggle (and many will continue to play this role).

An important way to address issues of marginality, particularly for subordinated youth, is to centre individual and collective experiences and social knowledge in the organizational life, curriculum and pedagogies of the school. In fact, it is inherently problematic to argue that there should be no centering of cultures and experiences in the learning processes. Such an academic posture fails to take account of the asymmetrical power relations that govern the lives of minority students in the conventional school system. This should be the prism for an interrogation of the idea of African-centred schools, rather than the worn-out critiques about these schools going back to the days of educational segregation and social separation. Mixing students is not by itself a sufficient guarantee for integration and social acceptance.

In a piece to *Pride Magazine* (see June 8–14, 1995 issue) on this same subject, I discussed why debates about what is Black, what is African — which often crop up when one mentions the idea of African-centred schools — are misplaced and misguided. I indicated that an African-centred school is defined more by certain basic principles, rather than by who goes to such school or who teaches in such schools. It is not that these latter questions are unimportant. They are significant considerations. However, answers to these questions are guided more by the basic principles of an African-centred school. In fact, given the political and economic climate and contexts in which African-centred schools are being discussed, it is important that these schools be open to all those who share the same underlying cultural, ideological and philosophical principles and assumptions.

In effect, the issue is not racial solidarity so much as cultural solidarity. For, as Ladson-Billings (1995) pointed out, racial identity does not guarantee academic success for African-Canadian students. However, we cannot simply dismiss the fact that so far non-Africans have not had a tremendous amount of success in educating African-Canadian youths.

So, readers may be asking: What are these basic principles? In my view, the social, political, cultural and spiritual affirmation of Africa and her historical ties with the Diaspora, is crucial to the educational objectives of African-centred schools. Learning starts by centering the student in her or his experiential realities, cultures and heritage. Culture is not frozen, fixed or timeless, but dynamic and historical. All students must be culturally situated and grounded in order to learn effectively. The task of educating young people is made easier when the students are able to link issues of individual and group identities with what goes on at school. African-centred schools seek to emotionally and spiritually ground students' educational and social experiences. Notions of *community* and *social responsibility* are at the centre of schooling and education in the African-centred school. Individual learning is for both self-improvement and community upliftment and empowerment (see also Dei, 1995).

These schools would be guided by classroom pedagogical styles that stress holistic learning and teaching about African cultures as historically, ideologically, politically, and spiritually collective and communitarian. The school would be structured around the African traditional values of communality, co-operation, reciprocity and mutual interdependence. Dialogue, consensus, cooperative and egalitarian interactions would be encouraged among the teachers and students.

What will these schools be like? The idea of African-centred schools calls for imagining new forms of teaching, learning and administration. It calls for new ways of fostering student-peer and student-teacher interactions, as well as developing new and alternative strategies for inclusiveness in the curriculum. Students should be allowed to learn in diverse and multiple ways and to teach about their out-of-school cultures (street/home cultures). These cultures can be important pedagogic and communicative tools.

African-centred schools should be educational sites, organized around communal principles and non-hierarchical structures (see also Karenga, 1986; Asante, 1991). These schools would foster the social and academic learning of students. They would also open up broader definitions of students' success besides strictly academic ones. For example, the performance of civic duty and social responsibility should factor in the evaluation of students' academic and school success.

African-centred schools would place a high value on the teachings of parents, caregivers, community workers, and elders in the holistic education of the youth. The schools should create sites for parents, community elders, and workers to come in to teach and learn from students. This may require some form of adult education in that students and teachers would be part of the process of teaching and learning with parents and community workers. Teaching, learning and social interaction revolve around letting the child, adult and community see the social and natural worlds from viewpoints which ensure that community issues are the primary concern of all.

Admittedly, it still remains to be seen how African-centred schools can deliver on the many expectations we have of them. The idea has not yet been tried. African-centred schools could be alternative educational environments to cater to those students who cannot adjust to conventional schools, for a variety of reasons. The debate about the efficacy of such schools should not be conducted by an either-or argument. What is at issue here is trying multiple strategies to address the problem of educating our young people. The question is not whether African-Canadian youths should continue to be main-streamed or removed to ensure success. As African-Canadian educator, Vernon Farrell (1994), argued, the concepts of "alternatives" and "choice" are significant in debates about African-centred schools. Students should have the right to be exposed to alternative learning environments and parents must also retain the element of choice as to which schools to send their children.

It is not too far-fetched to assume that, for students and parents who opt for African-centred schools, making the choice to go to such a school may have positive effects on students' attitudes toward school and towards learning. Students usually learn better in an educational setting with which they can identify. Students who choose to leave mainstream schools to attend African-centred schools may develop a sense of identification with the school. African-centred schools could be established alongside conventional schools and both forms of schooling could work together to address the mutual concerns of parents, teachers, and community workers about the education of the youth. It is a false and twisted argument that one cannot continue to pressure mainstream schools to be more inclusive at the same time that one is engaged in educational advocacy for African-centred schools. Is it not arrogance at its highest pinnacle when even a well-intentioned education official insists, without giving any explanation, that the idea of 'African-centred' schools will never, ever be considered by a school board? The right of allowing a people to think out solutions to their problems must always be upheld. Let us in the African-Canadian community develop the political courage and commitment to back up the rhetoric of striving to make academic excellence equitable with meaningfull and concrete action, including the establishment of African-centered schools.

Note

DEAR HIGH SCHOOL TEACHER

December 1995

I am a new high school student and I am looking forward to these next years of my schooling. I feel the need to write this letter because I seek a different experience in high school from that of elementary school. One of the things I would like to see changed is the relationship between students and teachers. I feel that a relationship that places students on the same level as teachers should be established. By this I mean that students' opinions should be taken seriously and be valued as much as those of teachers, and that together with the teachers we can shape the way we learn and what we learn.

Currently, discussion about issues that affect us directly is so rare that school becomes for us boring and irrelevant. Teachers should ensure that students have access to a wide range of resources and encourage independence in study so that creativity may blossom. Teachers should listen to students with an open mind and speak on our behalf when we are not given the opportunity to express ourselves to the school authorities.

Our curriculum is one which breeds stereotypes and does not address the issues that affect our lives every day. What we need is a curriculum that all students can relate to and that will motivate us to be the best we can be by introducing people like us in all kinds of occupations. We need curriculum that will not shield us from reality but will prepare us for life.

Like all other students, Black students come to school with expectations that they will do well. But so much emphasis is placed on athletics for us that we are looked upon as athletes alone and teachers believe that we are more likely to succeed in sports than in academics. Let me relate an example of this. This happened when I was in elementary school. We were celebrating Black History Month for the first time. A student brought in a documentary about Malcolm X. We were told that the head office doesn't allow certain films to be shown in school, so we would have to settle for a video about the Harlem Globetrotters basketball team instead.

Apart from sports, whenever we discuss math, geography, science and even music, reference is constantly made to white Europeans such as Pascal, Newton and Mozart instead of Matthew Henson, George Washington Carver and Louis Armstrong . It is only when we discuss basketball or track and field that we hear about a Black person. By the end of that day many students left the class not knowing who Malcolm X was or what he did.

Occurences similar to this one went on throughout my years at elementary school. This probably didn't affect me as much as it did other students whose entire school years revolved around basketball and track, which was all right with the teachers.

I am interested in athletics but do not want teachers to assume that it will be my major interest in school or that I will be participating in every sport that comes along, because while I may participate in a sport, I am aware of the importance of a balance between sports and academics and will keep that in perspective.

After years of being ignored, what the students need, and what Black students in particular need, is curriculum that we can relate to and that will interest us. We need appropriate curriculum that will motivate us to be the best we can be. We need to be taught to have a voice, and have teachers who will listen to us with an open mind and not dismiss our ideas simply because they differ from what they have been told in the past. We need to be made aware of all of our options in life. We need to have time to discuss issues of concern to the students as well as the teachers. We must be able to talk about racism without running away from it, or disguising the issue. We must also be taught to recognize racism instead of denying it and then referring to those who have recognized it as "paranoid." We also need to be given the opportunity to influence our education and in turn our destinies.

We should also be given the right to assemble and discuss issues without having a teacher present to discourage us from saying what we need to say. Teachers must gain the trust of their students and students must be given a chance to do the same. We need teachers who will not punish us just because they feel hostile or angry. We need teachers who will allow us to practice our culture without being ridiculed.

The school office has been turned into a place that students dread. It is where we are sent for doing anything from fighting to expressing disagreement. It is a place where we are lectured to and made to feel like we are criminals. A place where we may speak only when we are apologizing to whomever we have hurt, which is in most cases a teacher. Instead, the office should be a place where we can be heard, a place where we have the opportunity to point out how a teacher could have dealt with the situation differently and a place where we are advised on how to handle future incidents.

My expectations of high school are that more issues will be open for discussion and that students will be given a more active role in the school community. I also trust that the changes I have proposed will be taken into consideration and that we will get the respect and recognition we deserve. I'm hoping that high school will be a change for the better from what I have experienced in elementary school. Hopefully, high school will be an opportunity to voice my opinion as someone who is as valuable to the school community as all other members, including the teachers.

This is a change I look forward to.

SINCERELY,
KAI JAMES

Bibliography

"A chance for 65 more Blacks." (1970, August 1–15). *Contrast*, p. 15.

"A chance to make good." (1970, December 18). *Contrast*, p. 1.

"Action must be coordinated." (1977). *The Black Liaison Committee*. Toronto.

Alexander, Livingston & Miller, John W. (1989). "The Recruitment, Incentive and Retention Programs for Minority Pre-service Teachers." In Garibaldi, Antione, M. (ed.) *Teacher Recruitment and Retention with a special focus on minority teachers*. Washington: National Education Association.

Allen, A. L. (1994). "On Being a Role Model." In Goldberg, D. T. (Ed.) *Multiculturalism: A Critical Reader*. pp.180–199. Cambridge: Basil Blackwell Ltd.

Anderson, Woosley & Grant, Rudolph W. (1975). *The New Newcomers*. North York: York University.

Anderson, W. W., & Grant, R. W. (1987). *The New New-Comers*. Canadian Scholars Press, First published 1975. Toronto

Anisef, P., Okihiro, N., & James, C. (1982). *The Pursuit of Equality: Evaluating and Monitoring Accessibility to Post-secondary Education in Ontario*. Toronto: Ontario Ministry of Education Ministry of Colleges and Universities.

Apple, Michael (1993). *Official Knowledge: Democratic Education in a Conservative Age*. New York: Routledge.

Arnold, G. (1978, March 15). "Education system a 'setback.'" *Chronicle Herald*.

Asante, M. (1980). "Afrocentricity and culture." In M. Asante and W. Asante (eds.), *African Culture* (pp. 3–12). Trenton: African World Press.

Asante, M. (1987). *The Afrocentric Idea*. Philadelphia: Temple University Press.

Asante, M. (1991). "The Afrocentric idea in Education." *Journal of Negro Education*, 60(2).

Bancroft, G. (1994). "One Step Forward, Three Steps Backward: Challenging The Concept of Black Focused Schools." *Pride Magazine*, January 20, p. 26.

Beauger, Dieujuste, Dorsaint, Antoine, & Turenne, Hilarion (1994). "Education Initiatives for Haitians Students in Quebec." In V. D'Oyley (ed.) *Innovations in Black Education in Canada*. Toronto: Umbrella Press, pp. 72–74.

BEP. (1976). *the Black Education Project*, 1969–1976. Mimeo.

"BEP announces expansion plan." (1971, December 20). *Contrast*, p. 5.

Berserve, Christopher (1976). "Adjustment Problems of West Indian Children in Britain and Canada: A Perspective and a Review of Some Findings." In V. D'Oyley and H. Silverman (eds.) *Black Students in Urban Canada*. Toronto: T.E.S.L. Talk. Ministry of Culture and Recreation.

Bickel, R., & Papagiannis, G. (1988.) "Post-High School Prospects and District-level Dropouts." *Youth and Society*. 20(2), pp. 123–47.

BLAC Report on Education. (1994, December). *Redressing Inequity – Empowering Black Learners*. Halifax.

"Black education project announces expansion plan." (1971, December 20). *Contrast*, p. 5.

Black Educators Working Group (BEWG) (1993). *Submission to the Ontario Royal Commission on Learning*. Toronto.

Black Learners Advisory Committee (1994). *The BLAC Report on Education: Redressing Inequality — Empowering Black Learners*. Volume 2. Halifax: The BLAC.

Black Learners Advisory Committee (BLAC) (1994). *BLAC Report on Education: Redressing Inequality — Empowering Black Learners*. Volume 3: Results of A Socio-Democratic Survey of the Nova Scotia Black Community. Halifax: Black Learners Advisory Committee.

——————————————— (1994). *BLAC Report on Education: Redressing Inequality — Empowering Black Learners*. Volume 1: Summary. Halifax: Black Learners Advisory Committee

The Black Man in Nova Scotia Teach-In Report. (1969, January). St. Francis Xavier University.

"Black parents want Heritage Programmes." (1982, February). *Caribbean Focus*, p. 2.

"Black school gets down to real problems." (1970, November 1). *Contrast*, p. 9.

"Black school opens June." (1970, June 1). *Contrast*.

Board of Education for the City of Etobicoke (1993). *Students' Perspectives on Current Issues*. Etobicoke (Ontario): Board of Education.

Board of Education, Toronto. (1988). *Education of Black Students in Toronto: Final Report of the Consultative Committee*. Toronto: Board of Education.

Bowles, S., & Gintis, H. (1976). *Schooling in Capitalist America*. New York: Basic Books.

Brathwaite, E. (1977). *The Black Liaison Committee*. Toronto.

Brathwaite, Keren (1989). "The black student and the school: A Canadian dilemma." In S. Chilungu and S. Niang (eds.) *African Continuities/ L'Héritage Africain*. Toronto: Terebi

Brathwaite, K. (1993). "A History of the Voice." *Roots*. Michigan: Ann Arbor Paperbacks, University of Michigan Press.

Brathwaite, K. (1995, June). "TYP as a Program to Address Institutional Transformation." Paper presented at the Canadian Sociology and Anthropology Association annual meeting, Montreal.

Bray, Cathy (1988). "Theoretical Approaches to the Study of Class and Gender with Respect to Sport." In S. Ross and L. Charette (eds.) *Persons, Minds and Bodies*. North York: University Press of Canada, pp. 41–49.

Bristow, Peggy et al (1994). *'We're Rooted Here and They Can't Pull Us Up.' Essays in African Canadian Women's History*. Toronto: The University of Toronto Press.

Broderick, D. M. (1973). *Images of the Black in Children's Fiction*, New York: R.R. Bowker Company.

Brown, Robert S. (1993). *A follow-up of The Grade 9 Cohort of 1987 Every Secondary Student Survey Participants*. Toronto: Toronto Board of Education.

Brown, R., Cheng, M., Yau, M., & Ziegler, S. (1992). *The Every Secondary Student Survey: Initial Findings*. Toronto: Toronto Board of Education.

Bruner, A. (1979). "The genesis of Ontario Human Rights Legislation." *University of Toronto Faculty of Law Review*, *37*(2), 234–255.

Burnet, Jean & Palmer, Howard (1989). *Coming Canadians: An Introduction to a History of Canada's People*. Toronto: McClelland and Stewart Inc.

Burnett, W. (1995). Personal Communication, Toronto.

Cadieux, P. H. (1991). "The Stay-In-School Initiative: A Call to Action." *Equation. The Newsletter of the Stay-In-School Initiative*. July 1991, Ottawa. Ministry of State for Youth.

Calliste, Agnes (1982). "Educational and Occupational Expectations of High School Students." *Multiculturalism*. *5*(3), pp. 14–19.

Calliste, Agnes (1993–94 Winter). "Race, Gender and Canadian Immigration Policy: Blacks from the Caribbean, 1900–1932." *Journal of Canadian Studies*, *28*(4).

Calliste, A. (1994). "Blacks' Struggle for Education Equity in Nova Scotia." In V. D'Oyley (ed.) *Innovations in Black Education in Canada*. Toronto: Umbrella Press.

Calliste A. (1994). "Anti-racist Educational Initiatives in Nova Scotia."

307

Orbit, 25(2).

Calliste, A. (1994). "African-Canadian Experiences: The Need For Inclusion in the University Curriculum." Paper read at the forum on: *Diversity in the Curriculum*, Hart House, University of Toronto, February 7.

Calliste, A. (1995). "Influence of the civil rights and Black Power movement in Canada." *Race, Gender and Class*, 2(3), pp. 123–139.

Canadian Alliance of Black Educators (CABE) (1992). *Sharing the Challenge I, II, III.: A Focus on Black High School Students*. Toronto.

Campbell, T. (n.d.). The Transitional Year Program.

Canada, House of Commons. (1953, April 13). *Debates*.

Canadian Alliance of Black Educators (n.d.). The objectives and purpose of the organization. Toronto.

Canadian Education Association (1992). *Teacher Recruitment and Retention: How Canadian School Boards Attract Teachers*. Toronto.

Carrington, Bruce (1983). "Sport as a Side-Track: An Analysis of West Indian Involvement in Extra-Curricular Sport." In L. Barton and S. Walker (eds.), *Race, Class and Education*. Sydney: Croom Helm Ltd, pp. 40–65.

Case, F. (1977). *Racism and National Consciousness*. Toronto: Plowshare Press.

Cashmore, Ernest (1982). *Black Sportsmen*. London: Routledge & Kegan Paul.

Cheng, M. (1995). "Black Youth and Schooling in the Canadian Context: A Focus on Ontario." Unpublished paper, Department of Sociology, OISE.

Cheng, M., Tsuji, G., Yau, M., & Ziegler S. (1987). *The Every Secondary Student Survey: Fall 1987. #191*. Toronto: The Toronto Board of Education.

Cheng, M. et al. (1989). *Every Secondary Student Survey: Fall 1987*. Toronto: Toronto Board of Education.

Cheng, M., Tsuji, G., Yau, M., & Ziegler, S. (1993). *The Every Secondary Student Survey, Fall, Part II: Detailed Profiles of Toronto's Secondary School Students*. Toronto: Toronto Board of Education.

Cheng, M., Yau, M., & Ziegler, S. (1993). *Every Secondary Student Survey, Parts 1, 2 and 3*. Toronto: Research Services, Toronto Board of Education.

Christensen, Juliette M., Thornley-Brown, Anne, & Robinson, Jean (1980). *West Indians in Toronto: Implications for Helping Professionals*. Toronto: Family Services Association.

"City negro veterans' association." (1947, October 10). *Campus*. Toronto: University of Toronto.

Cizek, G.J. (1995). "On the Limited Presence of African American Teachers: An Assessment of Research, Synthesis, and Policy Implications."

Review of Educational Research, 65(1), pp. 78–92.

Clairmont, D., & Magill, D. (1970). *Nova Scotian Blacks*. Halifax.

Clark, A. (1980). *Growing Up Stupid Under The Union Jack: A Memoir*. Toronto: McClelland & Stewart.

Clarke, G. (1994). "Summer Math Camp for Blacks." In V. D'Oyley (ed.), *Innovations in Black Education in Canada* (58–63). Toronto: Umbrella Press.

Coard, B. (1971). *How the West Indian Child is made educationally sub-normal in the British School System*. London: New Beacon Books.

Coelho, Elizabeth (1988). *Caribbean Students in Canadian Schools*. Book 1. Toronto: Carib-Can Publishers.

Cohen, J. (1983). *Class and Civil Society*. Oxford: Martin.

Collins, E. (1994). "Black Focused Schools: An Examination." *Pride Magazine*, 3, pp. 23–24. Toronto.

Conference Board of Canada (1991). *Profiles in Partnerships: Business-Education Partnerships That Enhance Student Retention*. Ottawa: Conference Board of Canada.

Congress of Black Women of Canada, Preston Chapter (1991). *First Annual Celebration for Black Women who have made a Difference*. Dartmouth.

Consultative Committee on the Education of Black Students in Toronto Schools (1988). *Final Report*. Toronto: Toronto Board of Education.

Coopersmith, S. (1967). *Antecedents of Self-Esteem*. San Francisco: Freeman Press.

Crichlow, W. (1994). "Understanding the World of the Black Child." *Orbit*, 25(2), pp. 32–34.

Crossley, David J. (1988). "Unorganized Sport as a Model of Political Values." In S. Ross and L. Charette (eds.) *Persons, Minds and Bodies*. North York: University Press of Canada, pp. 183–190.

Cruxton, Bradley & Wilson, Douglas (1978). *Flashback Canada*. Toronto: Oxford University Press.

Cummins, J. (1986). "Empowering Minority Students: A Framework for Intervention." *Harvard Educational Review*, 56(1), pp. 18–34.

Cummins, J. (1989). "Education and Visible Minority Youth." In Ministry of Citizenship, Ontario, *Visible Minority Youth Project*. Toronto.

Curtis, B., Livingstone, D., & Smaller, H. (1992). *Stacking the Deck: The Streaming of Working-class Kids in Ontario Schools*. Montreal: Our Schools/Our Selves Education Foundation.

Davis, Kortright (1990). *Emancipation Still Comin': Explorations in Caribbean Emancipatory Theology*. New York: Orbis Books.

Davis, M., & Krauter, J. (1971). *The Other Canadians*. Toronto: Methuen.

Dehli, K. with Ilda Januario (1994, October). *Parent Activism and School*

Reform in Toronto, Department of Sociology, OISE.

Dei, G.J.S., (1993, April). *(Re)Conceptualizing "Dropouts" from Narratives of Black High School Students in Ontario*. Presentation paper, Atlanta, GA: American Educational Research Association.

Dei, G.J.S. (1993). *The examination of high school dropouts among Black students in Ontario public schools. Preliminary Report*. Toronto: Ministry of Eduction and Training.

—— (1994). "Afrocentricity: A cornerstone of pedagogy." *Anthropology and Education Quarterly*, *25*(1), pp. 3–28.

Dei, George J. Sefa (1994a). "Reflections of an Anti-Racist Pedagogue." In L. Erwin and D. MacLennan (eds.), *Sociology of Education in Canada: Critical Perspectives on Theory, Research and Practice*. Toronto: Copp Clark Longman Ltd., pp. 291–310

Dei, G. (1994a, June). "Learning or leaving: The 'dropout' dilemma among Black students in Ontario public schools." Second preliminary report submitted to the Ontario Ministry of Education, OISE.

Dei, G. (1994b). "Anti-racist education." *Orbit*, *25*(2), pp. 1–3.

Dei, George (1994) "Anti-Racist Education: Working Across Differences." *Orbit*, *25*(2).

Dei, G. 1995. "Examining the case for 'African-centred' Schools in Ontario." *McGill. Journal of Education*, *30*(2), pp. 179–199.

Dei, G. (1995b). "Integrative anti-racism: Intersection of race, class and gender." *Race, Gender and Class*, *2*(3), 11–30.

Dei, George (1995). "Black/African-Canadian Students' Perspectives on School Racism." In I. Alladin (ed.) *Racism in Canadian Schools*. Toronto: Harcourt Brace.

Dei, George J. Sefa with Holmes, L., Mazzuca, J., McIsaac E., & Campbell, R. (1995). *Drop Out or Push Out? The Dynamics of Black Students' Disengagement from School*. Toronto: Dept. Of Sociology in Education, Ontario Institute for Studies in Education.

Dei, G.J.S. (1995a). "Black Youth and Fading Out of School." In J. Gaskell and D. Kelly (Eds.). *Debating Dropouts: New Policy Perspectives*. (Forthcoming).

—————————————— (1993). "Narrative Discourses of Black/African Parents and the Canadian Public school System." *Canadian Ethnic Studies*, *3*, pp. 49–64.

—————————————— (1994b). "Anti-Racist Education: Working Across Differences." *Orbit*, *25*(2), pp. 1–3.

——————————(1995b). "Examining The Case for 'African-centred' Schools in Ontario." *McGill Journal of Education*, *30*(2), pp. 179–199.

——————————, L. Holmes, J. Mazzuca, E. McIsaac & R. Campbell (1995). *Drop Out or Push Out?: The Dynamics of Black Students' Disengage-*

ment from School. Final report submitted to the Ontario Ministry of Education, Toronto.

Delpit, L. D. (1988). "The Silenced Dialogue: Power and Pedagogy in Educating Other People's Children." *Harvard Educational Review*, *58*(3), pp. 380–398.

Delpit, L.D. (1995). *Other People's Children: Cultural Conflict in the Classroom*, New York: The New Press.

Deosaran, Ramesh A. (1976). *The 1975 Every Student Survey: Program Placement Related to Selected Countries of Birth and Selected Languages #140*. Toronto: The Toronto Board of Education.

Department of Education and Science (DES) (1985). *Education for All*, (The Swan Report). London, H.M.S.O.

Dickson, K. (1994, September 19). "St.F.X. Ethnic Minorities and Multicultural Society to launch Mentoring Program." *Campus News*, pp. 13–14.

Dilworth, M.E. (1990). *Reading Between the Lines: Teachers and Their Racial/Ethnic Cultures*. ERIC Teacher Education Monograph No.11. Washington: Clearinghouse on Teacher Education.

Dodds, Patt (1993). "Removing the Ugly 'Isms' in Your Gym: Thoughts for Teachers on Equity." In J. Evans (eds.), *Equality, Education and Physical Education*, London: The Falmer Press, pp. 28–39.

D'Oyley, Vincent (ed.) (1994). *Innovations in Black Education in Canada*. National Council of Black Educators of Canada. Toronto: Umbrella Press.

D'Oyley, Vincent & Silverman, Harry (eds.) (1976). *Black Students in Urban Canada*. Toronto: T.E.S.L. Talk. Ministry of Culture and Recreation.

DuBois, W.E.B. (1903). *The Souls of Black Folk*. New York: Library of America.

Elster, C., & Simons, H.D. (1985). "How Important are Illustrations in Children's Readers?" *The Reading Teacher*, pp. 148–152.

EMMA. (1994). Mentor Program. Antigonish.

Emply, C. (n.d.). *Remedial Education Project Threatened*.

Engstrom, Catherine McHugh & Sedlacek, William E. (1991). "A Study of Prejudice Toward University Student-Athletes." *Journal of Counselling & Development*, *70*(1), pp. 189–193.

Epstein, B. (1990). "Rethinking social movement theory." *Socialist Review*, *20*(1), pp. 35–65.

Fanon, Frantz (1963). *The Wretched of the Earth*. New York: Grove Press, Inc.

Farrell, V. (1994, Jan. 6). "Support for Black Focused Schools." *Share*, p. 8.

Fejgin, Naomi (1994). "Participation in High School Competitive Sports: A

Subversion of School Mission or Contribution to Academic Goal?" *Sociology of Sport Journal*, *11*, pp. 211–230.

Ferris, J. A. (1992). "Disadvantaged Students in University: An analysis of Attrition Rates and Patterns at the University of Toronto." M. A. Thesis, University of Toronto.

Felker, D. (1973). *The Development of Self-Esteem in Young Children.*

Figueroa, Peter (1993). "Equality, Multiculturalism, Antiracism and Physical Education in the National Curriculum." In J. Evans (eds.), *Equality, Education and Physical Education*, London: The Falmer Press, pp. 90–102.

Fine, M. (1991). *Framing Dropouts: Notes on the Politics of an Urban Public High School.* New York: SUNY Press.

Finn, C. E., Jr. (1987). "The High School Dropout Puzzle." *The Public Interest*, *87*, pp. 3–22.

——————————. (1989). "Withdrawing from School." *Review of Educational Research*, *59*(2), pp. 117–142.

Ford, D. Y. (1992). "The American Achievement as Perceived by urban African-American Students: Exploration by Gender and Academic Program." *Urban Education*, *27*, pp. 196–211.

Forsythe, D. (ed.), (1971). *Let the Niggers Burn.* Montreal: Black Rose Books.

Foster, M. (1989). *Recruiting teachers of color: Problems, programs and possibilities.* Paper presented at the Fall Conference of the Far West Holmes Group, Reno, NV.

Foucault, M. (1980). *Knowledge/Power: Selected Interviews and Other Writings.* New York: Pantheon Books.

Found, Wm. C. (1991). *Who are York's undergraduates: Results of the University's 1991 comprehensive survey.* North York, Ontario: York University, Office of the Vice-President (Institutional Affairs).

Four-Level Government/African-Canadian Community Working Group (1992). *Towards a New Beginning: Report on Metropolitan Toronto Black Canadian Community Concerns.* Toronto.

Fram, I., Broks, G., Crawford, P., Handscombe, J., & Virgin, A. E. (1977). "'I don't know yet' — West Indian Students in North York Schools: A Study of Adaptive Behaviours." *Research Report.* North York: North York Board of Education.

Francis, R. Douglas & Smith, Donald B. (1990). *Readings in Canadian History: Pre-Confederation.* Toronto: Holt, Rinehart and Winston of Canada, Ltd.

Frey, Darcy (1994). *The Last Shot: City Streets, Basketball Dreams.* New York: Houghton Mifflin Company.

Fuller, Mary (1983). "Qualified Criticism, Critical Qualifications." In L. Burton and S. Walker (eds.) *Race, Class and Education.* London: Croom and Helm Publishing.

Garibaldi, A. M. (ed.) (1989). *Teacher recruitment and retention: with a special focus on minority teachers.* Washington, D.C. National Education Association.

Garibaldi, A. M. (1992). "Educating and Motivating African Americans to Succeed." *Journal of Negro Education, 61*, pp. 4–11.

Gewirtz, Deborah (1991). "Analyses of Racism and Sexism in Education and Strategies for Change." *British Journal of Sociology of Education, 12*(2), pp. 183–201.

Gill, Wali. (1989). "Who will teach Minority Youth?" In Garibaldi, Antione, M. (ed.) *Teacher Recruitment and Retention with a special focus on minority teachers.* Washington: National Education Association.

Gillborn, D. A. (1988). "Ethnicity and Educational Opportunity: Case studies of West Indian male-white teacher relationships." *British Journal of Sociology of Education, 9*(4), pp. 371–385.

Gilmore, P. (1992). "'Gimme Room': School Resistance, Attitude, and Access to Literacy." In P. Shannon *Becoming Political: Readings and Writings in the Politics of Literacy Education* (pp.113–127), Portsmouth, NH: Hienemann Educational Books Inc.

Gramsci, Antonio (1987). *The Modern Prince & other writings.* New York: International Publ.

Gramsci, Antonio (1971). *Selections from the Prison Notebooks.* New York: International Publ.

Green Paper on Immigration and Population. (1974). Vol. III.

Grossberg, L., Nelson, C., & Treichler, P. (1992). "Cultural Studies: An Introduction." *Cultural Studies.* L. Grossberg, C. Nelson, P. Treichler (Ed.). New York: Routledge.

Haber, L. (1970). *Black Pioneers of Science and Invention.* New York: Harcourt, Brace and World.

Hall, Ann, Slack, Trevor, Smith, Garry and Whitson, David (1991). *Sport in Canadian Society.* Toronto: McClelland & Stewart Inc.

Hargreaves, A. & L. Earl (n.d). *Rites of Passage: A Review of Selected Research about Schooling in the Transition Years.* Toronto: Ministry of Education.

Harris, Othello (1994). "Race, Sport, and Social Support." *Sociology of Sport Journal, 11*, pp. 40–50.

———— (1991). "Athletics and Academics: Contrary or Complementary Activities?" In G. Jarvie (ed.), *Sport Racism and Ethnicity.* London: The Falmer Press, pp. 124–149.

Harris, V. J. (1990). "African American Children's Literature: The First One Hundred Years." *The Journal of Negro Education*, pp. 540–555.

Harris, V. J. (1993). "Contemporary Griots: African-American Writers of

Children's Literature." In V. Harris *Teaching Multicultural Literature in Grades K–8*, Norwood, MA: Christopher-Gordon Publishers, Inc.

Head, F., & Lee, J. (1975). *The Black Presence in the Canadian Mosaic.* Toronto: Ontario Human Rights Commission.

Head, Wilson (1975). *The Black Presence in the Canadian Mosaic.* Toronto: Ontario Human Rights Commission.

Henry, A. (1992). "African-Canadian women teachers' activism: Recreating communities of caring and resistance." *Journal of Negro Education, 61*(3), pp. 392–404.

Henry, A. (1992). *Taking Back Control: Toward an Afrocentric Womanist Standpoint on the Education of Black Children.* Unpublished Ph.D. dissertation, Department of Curriculum, Ontario Institute for Studies in Education, Toronto, Canada.

Henry, Annette (1994). "The Empty Shelf and other Curricular Challenges of Teaching of Children of African Descent — Implications for Teacher Practice." *Urban Education, 29*(3), pp. 298–319.

Henry, F. (1978). *The Dynamics of Racism in Toronto.* Toronto: Department of Anthropology, York University.

Herstein, H. et al (1970). *Challenge and Survival: The History of Canada.* Scarborough: Prentice-Hall of Canada, Ltd.

Hill, Grant M. (1993). "Youth Sport Participation of Professional Baseball Players." *Sociology of Sport Journal, 10*, pp. 107–114.

Hurshman, B. (1978, April 20). Communication and education and education of parents aim of workshop. *Mail Star.*

Inter-University Committee on Access for Under-represented Populations. (1992, June). *Report to the Council of Nova Scotia University Presidents.* Halifax.

Irvine, Jacqueline, J. (1988). "An analysis of the Problem of Disappearing Black Educator." *The Elementary School Journal, 88*(5), pp. 503–13.

—— (1990). *Black students and school failure – policies, practices and prescriptions.* New York: Greenwood.

James, C. E. (1990). "I Don't Want To Talk About It." *Orbit, 25*(2), pp. 26–29.

James, C. E. (1990). *Making It: Black Youth, Racism and Career Aspirations in a Big City,* Oakville: Mosaic Press

—— (1994). *"Access Students": Experiences of Racial Minorities in a Canadian University.* Paper presented at the society for Research into Higher Education Annual Conference, The University of York, England, Dec. 21.

James, C. E. (1994). "I Don't Want to Talk About it: Silencing Students in Today's Classrooms." *Orbit, 25*(2).

James, C. E. (1994). Panel Discussion on How Black Students Experience

314

the Schools. African Studies Association Conference. Toronto.

James, Carl E. (1995). "Negotiating Schooling Through Sports: African Canadian Youth Strive for Academic Success." *Avante, 1*(1), pp. 20–36.

James, Carl E. (1995, Spring). "Multicultural and Anti-Racism Education in Canada." *Race, Gender & Class, 2*(3), pp. 31–48.

James, Carl E. (1995). *Seeing Ourselves: Exploring Race, Ethnicity and Culture*. Toronto: Thompson Educational Publishing, Inc.

James, Carl E. (1996). "Challenging the Distorted Images: The Case of African Canadian Youth." In C. *Green The Urban Challenge and the Black Diaspora*. New York: New York State University Press.

————— (1994). "I don't want to talk about it: Silencing Students in Today's Classrooms." *Orbit, 25*(2), pp. 26–29.

————— (1990). *Making It: Black Youth, Racism and Career Aspirations in a Big City*. Oakville (Ontario): Mosaic Press.

James, R., & Papp, L. (1988). "School system fails to education Black children, parents charge." *Toronto Star*.

Jenks, C. et al. (1972). *Inequality: A Reassessment of the Effects of Family and Schooling in America*. New York: Basic Books.

Karenga, M. (1986). *Introduction to Black Studies*. Los Angeles: University of Sankore Press.

Karp, David A., Stone, Gregory P., & Yoels, William C. (1991). *Being Urban: A Sociology of City Life*. New York: Praeger Publishers.

Karp, E. (1988). *The Dropout Phenomenon in Ontario Secondary Schools: A Report to the Ontario Study of the Relevance of Education and the Issue of Dropout*. Toronto: Queen's Printer for Ontario.

Kauffman, L. A. (1990). "The anti-politics of identity." *Socialist Review, 20*(1), pp. 67–80.

Kerr, Gretchen A. (1995). "The Role of Sport in Preparing Youth for Adulthood." Paper prepared for the National Research and Policy Symposium on Youth in Transition to Adulthood" (Draft). Kananaskis, Alberta. April.

Kidd, Bruce (1995). "Confronting Inequality in Sport and Physical Activity." *Avante, 1*(1), pp. 1–19.

Kiefer, B. (1983). "The Responses of Children in a Combination First/Second Grade Classroom to Picture Books in a Variety of Artistic Styles." *Journal of Research and Development in Education, 16*(3), pp. 14–20.

King, A.J.C., Warren, W. K., Michalski, C., & Peart, M. J. (1988). *Improving Student Retention in Ontario Secondary Schools*. Toronto: Ontario Ministry of Education.

King, S. H. (1993). "The limited presence of African American Teachers." *Review of Educational Research, 63*(2), pp. 115–150.

Klein, Gillian (1985). *Reading Into Racism:Bias in Children's Literature and Learning Materials*. Boston: Routledge and Kegan Paul.

Knowlton, K. (1995, June 7). "Questions About Remedial Education in a Time of Budget Cuts." *New York Times*, p. B8.

Laclau, E., & Mouffe, C. (1985). *Hegemony and Socialist Strategy*. London: Verso.

Ladson-Billings, G. (1992). "Liberatory consequences of literacy: A case of culturally relevant instruction for African-American students." *Journal of Negro Education, 61*(3), pp. 378–391.

Lamoureux, H., Mayer, R. & Panet-Raymond, (1989). *Community Action*. Montreal: Black Rose.

Langston, D. (1988). "Tired of Playing Monopoly?" In J. Whitehouse Cochran, D. Langston, and C. Woodward (eds.) *Changing Our Power: An Introduction to Women's Studies*, Dubuque, IA: Kendall-Hunt.

Lapchick, Richard E. (1995, April-June). "Race and college sport: A long way to go." *Race & Class, 36*(4), pp. 87–94.

Lawton, S. B., & Leithwood, K. (1988). *Student Retention and Transition in Ontario High Schools*. Toronto: Ontario Ministry of Education.

Lawton, S. B. (1992). "Dropping Out: A Literature Review, 1988–1992." Unpublished paper, Ontario Institute for Studies in Education, Toronto.

Larter, S., Cheng, M., Capps, S., & Lee, M. (1982). *Post Secondary Plans of Grade Eight Students and Related Variables*. Toronto: The Toronto Board of Education.

LeCompte, M. D., & Dworkin, A. G. (1991). *Giving Up on School:Student Dropouts and Teacher Burnouts*. Newbury Park, CA: Corwin Press, Inc.

Lee, E. (1985). *Letters to Marcia*. Toronto: Cross Cultural Communication Centre.

Lee, E. (1994). "On Any Given Saturday." Paper presented at Association of African Studies Conference. Toronto.

Lee, Enid (1994). "Anti-Racist Education: Panacea or Palliative?" *Orbit*, *25*(2), pp. 22–25.

Lenskyj, Helen J. (1994). "Jocks and Jills: Women's Experience in Sport and Physical Activity." In G. Finn (ed.) *Limited Edition*. Halifax: Fernwood Publishing.

Leonard, Wilbert M. (1993). *A Sociological Perspective on Sport*. Toronto: Maxwell Macmillan Canada.

Lewis, S. (1992). *Report on Race Relations*. Toronto: Government of Ontario.

Lewis, Stephen (1992). "Dear Bob." Letter to the Premier. Toronto.

Little, D. (1992). "The Meaning of Yonge Street: What do the Kids Say?" *Our Schools/Our Selves, 4*(1), pp. 16–23.

Loehr, P. (1988). "The urgent need for minority teachers." *Education Week*,

p. 32.

Loney, M. (1977). "A political economy of citizen participation." In L. Panitch (ed.), *The Canadian State*, pp. 446–472. Toronto: University of Toronto Press.

Lortie, D. (1975). *Schoolteacher: A Sociological Study*. Chicago: University of Chicago Press.

Lovell, Tessa (1991). "Sport, Racism and Young Women." In G. Jarvie (ed.), *Sport Racism and Ethnicity*. London: The Falmer Press, pp. 58–73.

Lundy, J. E., & Lawrence, D. (1993). *Equity in Access to Teacher Education: Issues for Visible Minorities, Physically Challenged and First Nations Candidates*. A Paper presented at the CSSHE Conference, Carleton University, Ottawa.

MacCann, D., & Woodard, G. (1985). *The Black American in Books for Children: Reading in Racism* (2nd ed.) Metuchen, NJ: The Scarecrow Press Inc.

Mackay, R., & Myles, L. (1989). *Native Student Dropouts in Ontario Schools*. Toronto: Ontario Ministry of Education.

Macleod, J. (1987). *Ain't no making it: Leveled aspirations in a low income neighborhood*. Boulder: Westview Press.

Maguire, Joe (1991). "Sport, Racism and British Society: A Sociological Study of England's Elite Male Afro/Caribbean Soccer and Rugby Union Players." In G. Jarvie (ed.), *Sport Racism and Ethnicity*. London: The Falmer Press, pp. 94–123.

Mannette, J. (1987). "'Making something happen': Nova Scotia's Black Renaissance, 1968–1986." Ph.D. thesis, Carleton University.

Manski, C. F. (1989). "Schooling as Experimentation: A Reappraisal of the Postsecondary Dropout Phenomenon." *Economics of Education Review*, *8*(4), pp. 305–312.

Marcuse, Herbert (1969). *An Essay on Liberation*. Boston: Beacon Press.

Marqusee, Mike (1995, April-June). "Sport and stereotype: From role model to Muhammad Ali." *Race & Class*, 36(4), pp. 1–29.

Marsh, Herbert W. (1993). "The Effect of Participation in Sport During the Last Two Years of High School" *Sociology of Sport Journal*, *10*, pp. 18–43.

Martinez, R., & Dukes, R. (1991). "Ethnic and Gender Differences in Self-esteem." *Youth and Society*, *22*(3), pp. 318–338.

Maslow, A. (1980). *The Further Reaches of Human Nature*.

McAndrew, Marie (1991). "Ethnicity, Multiculturalism, and Multicultural Education in Canada." In R. Ghosh and D. Ray (eds.) *Social Change and Education in Canada*. Toronto: Harcourt Brace Jovanovich.

McCarthy, C. (1990.) *Race and Curriculum: Social Inequality and the Theories and Politics of Difference in Contemporary Research on Schooling*.

317

London: The Falmer Press.

McLaren, Peter (1994). *Life in Schools: An Introduction to Critical Pedagogy in the Foundations of Education.*" Longman Publishing.

McNeal, Jr., & Ralph B. (1995, January). " Extracurricular Activities and High School Dropouts." *Sociology of Education, 68,* pp. 62–81.

Melucci, A. (1980). "The new social movements." *Social Science Information, 19*(2), pp. 199–226.

Meta, Fernando G. (1989). *The Black Youth of Toronto: Exploration of Issues.* Ottawa: Policy & Research, Multiculturalism & Citizenship. Government of Canada. December.

Millar, H., & Reviere, R. (eds.) (1993). "Towards anti-racist teaching in Nova Scotia's universities." Proceedings from the second Workshop on Anti-Racist Teaching, Halifax, April 27.

Ministry of Citizenship (1989). *Visible Minority Youth Project. Child, Youth and Family Project.* Research Centre. Toronto: Ontario, Ministry of Citizenship.

Ministry of Education and Training (1993). *Antiracism and Ethnocultural Equity in School Boards: Guidelines for Policy Development and Implementation.* Toronto: Queen's Printer for Ontario.

Mirza, Heidi Safia (1992). *Young, Female and Black.* London: Routledge.

Mock, K. R., & Masemann, V. L. (1990). *Implementing race and ethnocultural equity policy in Ontario school boards.* Ontario: Ministry of Education.

Mooers, C., & Sears, A. (1992). "The 'new social movements' and the withering away of state theory." In W. Carroll (ed.), *Organizing Dissent,* pp. 52–68. Toronto: Garamond Press.

Moreau, B. (1982). *Programme Innovation: The Transition Year Programme at Dalhousie University.* M.A. thesis, Dalhousie University.

National Film Board. (1993). *Speak It.* Halifax.

New England Board of Higher Education (1989). *Equity and Pluralism: Full Participation of Blacks and Hispanics in New England Higher Education.* Boston, Mass.: New England Board of Higher Education.

Nova Scotia Department of Education and Culture (1995, June). *Response to the BLAC Report on Education.* Halifax.

Offe, C. (1985). "New social movements." *Social Research, 52*(4).

Ogbu, J. U. (1974). *The Next Generation: An Ethnography of Education in an Urban Neighborhood.* New York: Academic Press.

Ogbu, J. U. (1978). *Minority Education and Caste: An Ethnography of Education in an Urban Neighbourhood.* New York: Academic Press.

Ogbu, J. U. (1988). "Cultural Diversity and Human Development." In D. Slaughter (ed) *Black Children and Poverty: A Developmental*

Perspective, pp. 11–28. San Francisco: Jossey Bass

Okafor, V. O. (1992). "A Reevaluation of African Education: Woodson Revisited." *Journal of Black Studies*, 22, pp. 579–592.

Oliver, Jules (1972). "The Black Child and White Education." In N. Byrne and J. Quarter (eds.) *Must Schools Fail?* Toronto: McClelland and Stewart Ltd.

O'Malley, M. (1972). "Blacks in Toronto." In W. E. Mann (ed.), *The Underside of Toronto*, p. 136. Toronto: McClelland and Stewart.

Ontario Multicultural History Society (1991). *Many Rivers to Cross: The African Canadian Experience*. Toronto: Primetype.

OPBC. (n.d.). Presentation to the Congress of Black Women on the implementation of curriculum and the Black Student Report.

OPBC. (1992, June 29). Memorandum to the Director, Toronto Board of Education.

Organisation of Parents of Black Children Papers (1980–1985).

Organisation of Parents of Black Children (OPBC) (1990). *Tenth Anniversary Celebration Booklet*: "Ten Years of Involvement, Struggle, Achievement."

Organization of Parents of Black Children (OPBC) (1993). Oral Submission to the Ontario Royal Commission on Learning. October.

Organisation of Parents of Black Children (OPBC) (1994). Submission to the Ontario Royal Commission on Learning.

Orlikow, Lionel and Young, Jon. (1993). "The Struggle for Change: Teacher Education in Canada." In Verma, Gajendra (ed.) *Inequity and Teacher Education: An International Perspective*, London: Falmer Press.

Osborne, Ken (1995). *In Defence of History*. Montreal: Our Schools/Ourselves Education Foundation.

Pachai, B. (1990). *Beneath the Clouds of the Promised Land*. Halifax: Black Educators Association.

Parris, J. (1995). *Access Initiative Program Report*. Faculty of Education. York University, North York.

Parry, Jose & Parry, Noel (1991). "Sport and the Black Experience." In G. Jarvie (ed.), *Sport Racism and Ethnicity*. London: The Falmer Press, pp. 150–174.

Patai, D. (1991). "Minority status and the stigma of surplus visibility." *The Chronicle of Higher Education*, Oct. 30, p. A. 52.

Perry, C. (1994). "Saturday Morning Tutorial Programmes of the Canadian Alliance of Black Educators." In V. D'Oyley (ed.), *Innovations in Black Education in Canada*. Toronto: Umbrella Press.

Peter, K. (1984). "The myth of multiculturalism and other political fables." In J. Dahlie and T. Fernando (ed.), *Ethnicity, Power and Politics in Cana-*

da, pp. 56–67. Toronto: Methuen.

Philip, M.N. (1988). *Harriet's Daughter*. Toronto: Women's Press.

Phinney, J. S. (1989). "Stages of Ethnic Identity in Minority Group Adolescents," *Journal of Early Adolescence*, *9*, pp. 34–39.

Phinney, J. S. (1990). "Ethnic Identity in Adolescence and Adults: Review of Research." *Psychological Bulletin*, *108*(3), pp. 499–514.

Pieterse, J. N. (1992). *White on Black: Images of Africa and Blacks in Western Popular Culture*, London, England: Yale University Press.

Pike, R. M. (1970). *Who Doesn't Get to University and Why: A Case Study on Accessibility to Higher Education in Canada*. Ottawa: Association of Universities and Colleges in Canada.

Pinar, William (1993). "Notes on Understanding Curriculum as a Racial Text." In C. McCarthy and W. Crichlow (eds.) *Race, Identity and Representation in Education*. New York: Routlegde.

Pittaway, Kim (1994). "Scoring a touchdown in the Classroom." *Home & School*. November.

Pollard, D. S. (1989). "Against the Odds: A Profile of Academic Achievers from the Urban Underclass." *Journal of Negro Education*, *58*, pp. 297–308.

Pratt, S. (1972). *Black Education in Nova Scotia*. M.A. thesis, Dalhousie University.

Prince, Althea, Taylor Caldwell, (forthcoming). *On Making Herstory*.

"Racism inherent in our education system" (1969, December 19). *Contrast*, p. 5.

Radwanski, G. (1987). *Ontario Study of the Relevance of Education, and the Issue of Dropouts*. Toronto, Ontario: Ministry of Education.

Radwansky, G. (1988). *Ontario Study of the Relevance of Education and the Issue of Drop-outs*. Toronto. Ministry of Education.

Ralston, M. (1990). "Using Literature in a Whole-Language Program." In V. Froese *Whole-Language Practice and Theory*, pp. 47–85. Scarborough, ON: Prentice-Hall Canada Inc.

Ramcharan, Subhas (1982). *Racism: Nonwhites in Canada*. Toronto: Butterworth & Co.

Ramcharan, Subhas (1975). "Special Problems of Immigrants Children in the Toronto School System." In A. Wolfgang (ed.) *Education of Immigrant Students*. Toronto: Ontario Institute for Studies in Education.

Ramsay, J. G. (1993, November). "Resignation and Pretest: How Children's Picture Books Depict Poverty." Paper presented at the American Educational Studies Association Annual Meetings, Chicago, Il.

Ratteray, J. D. (1992). "Independent Neighbourhood Schools: A Framework for the Education of African Americans." *Journal of Negro Education*,

61, pp. 138–147.

Richardson, George (1994). "Education Innovations: The Montreal Experience." In D'Oyley, V. (ed.), *Innovations in Black Education in Canada*. National Council of Black Educators of Canada. Toronto: Umbrella Press.

Richardson, R. C., & Skinner, E. F. (1991). *Achieving Quality and Diversity: Universities in a Multicultural Society*. Toronto: Collier MacMillan Canada.

Ross, S. I., & Jackson J. M. (1991). "Teachers' expectations for Black males' and Black females' academic achievement." *Personality and Social Psychology Bulletin, 17*(21), pp. 78–82.

Royal Commission on Learning (1994). *For the love of learning: Report of the Royal Commission on Learning*. Ontario: Royal Commission on Learning.

Royal Commission on Learning (1994). *For the Love of Learning: Make It Happen*. Volume IV. Toronto: Publications Ontario.

Royal Commission on Learning (1994). *For the Love of Learning: Report of the Royal Commission on Learning*, Toronto: Ministry of Education

Royal Commission on Learning (1994). *For the Love of Learning*. Toronto: Queen's Printer of Ontario.

Sabo, Don, Melnick, Merrill, & Vanfossen Beth (1993). "High School Athletic Participation and Postsecondary Educational and Occupational Mobility: A Focus on Race and Gender." *Sociology of Sport Journal, 10*, pp. 44–56.

——————————— (1989). *Minorities In Sports: The Effect of Varsity Sports Participation on the Social, Educational, and Career Mobility of Minority Students*. New York: The Women's Sports Foundation.

Sailes, Gary A. (1991). "The Myth of Black Sports Supremacy." *Journal of Black Studies*, 21(4), pp. 480–487.

Samuel, J. (1992). *Visible Minorities in Canada: A Projection*. Toronto: Canada Advertising Foundation.

Schallert, D. L. (1980). "The Role of Illustrations in Reading Comprehension." In R. Spiro, B. Bruce & W. Brewer, *Theoretical Issues in Reading Comprehension*, pp. 503–524. Hillsdale NJ: Lawrence Erlbaum.

Schenke, A. (1993). "Being 'Access.' Doing change: Confronting Difference in Teacher Education." Unpublished Research Report. Faculty of Education, York University.

"Schools for Black children" (1970, April 17). *Contrast*, 2.

Schreiber, Jan (1970). *In the Course of Discovery: The West Indian Immigrants in Toronto Schools*. Toronto: The Toronto Board of Education.

Schuller, Robert H. (1984). *Possibility Thinkers Bible*. The New King James Version Thomas Nelson Inc. New York: U.S.A.

Shannon, P. (1992). "Overt an Covert Censorship of Children's Books." In P. Shannon, *Becoming Political: Readings and Writings in the Politics of Literacy Education*, pp. 67–71. Portsmouth, NH: Hienemann Educational Books Inc.

Shapson, S. M. (1994). "Emerging images for Teacher Education" In D'Oyley, V.R. (ed.), *Innovations in Black Education in Canada*. Toronto: Umbrella Press.

Shilling, Chris (1993). "The Body, Class and Social Inequalities." In J. Evans (eds.), *Equality, Education and Physical Education*. London: The Falmer Press, pp. 55–73.

Simic, Marjorie, McClain, Melinda, & Shermis, Micheal (1992). *The Confident Learner*. Indiana: Grayson Bernard Publishers.

Sims, R. (1983). "Strong Black Girls: A Ten Year Old Responds to Fiction About Afro-Americans." *Journal of Research and Development in Education, 16*(3), pp. 21–28.

Sims, R. (1993). "Multicultural Literature for Children: Making Informed Choices." In V. Harris *Teaching Multicultural Literature in Grades K–8*, Norwood, MA: Christopher-Gordon Publishers, Inc.

Sium, B. 1987. "Streaming in Education and Beyond: Black Students Talk." *Orbit, 18*(1), pp. 20–21

Skillington, Richard & Morris, Paulette (1992). *'Race' in Britain Today*. London: Sage Publications Ltd.

Smerdon, G. (1976). "Children's Preferences in Illustration." *Children's Literature in Education, 20*, pp. 97–131.

Solomon, R. P. (1992). *Black Resistance in High School: A Separatist Culture*. Albany: State University of New York Press.

Solomon, R. P (1994). "Academic Disengagement: Black Youth and the Sports Subculture form a Cross-National Perspective." In L. Erwin and D. MacLennan (eds.), *Sociology of Education in Canada: Critical Perspectives on Theory, Research and Practice*. Toronto: Copp Clark Longman Ltd., pp. 188–199.

—— & Riviere, P. (1993). *The Access Initiative Research Project*. Faculty of Education, York University, North York.

—— , Dippo, D.;, Schenke, A., & Fullerton, O. (1994). "Creating diversity in teacher education: York University's Access Initiative." Presented at the Ethnography and Education Conference, Philadelphia.

Stage, F. K. (1989). "Motivation, Academic and Social Integration, and the Early Dropout.' *American Educational Research Journal, 26*(3), pp. 385–402.

Stasuilis, D. (1982). "Race, Ethnicity and the State." Ph.D. dissertation, University of Toronto.

Statistics Canada (1991). *School Leavers Survey*. Ottawa: Education Culture and Tourism Division, Statistics Canada.

Stewart, Anne-Marie (1975). *See Me Yah: Working Papers on the newly-arrived West Indian child in the Downtown School.* Toronto: The Toronto Baord of Education.

Stories from Bolans Village Oral Tradition, Antigua, The Caribbean. (Collected from two Morissey and Sebastian-Prince women, b. 1884 and 1902, respectively).

Talbot, Margaret (1993). "A Gendered Physical Education: Equality and Sexism." In J. Evans (eds.), *Equality, Education and Physical Education,* London: The Falmer Press, pp. 74–89.

Taxel, J. (1993). "The Politics of Children's Literature: Reflections on Multiculturalism and Christopher Columbus." In V. Harris *Teaching Multicultural Literature in Grades K–8,* Norwood, MA: Christopher-Gordon Publishers, Inc.

"The Black child in Ontario" (1970, April 4). *Contrast.*

"The plan to educate youths" (1970, July 18). *Contrast, 10.*

The Stephen Lewis Report (1992). *Recommendations for dealing with issues on Race in Ontario.* To Premier Bob Rae, June 16.

Thomas, Barb (1987). "Anti-Racist Education: A Response to Manicom." In J. Young (ed.) *Breaking the Mosaic: Ethnic Identities in Canadian Schooling.* Toronto: Garamound Press, pp. 104–107.

Thomas, Carolyn E. (1988). "Criteria for Athlete Autonomy in a Paternalistic Sport Model." In S. Ross and L. Charette (eds.) *Persons, Minds and Bodies.* North York: University Press of Canada, pp. 191–202.

Tomlinson, S. (1972). *Ethnic Minorities in British Schools: A Review of the Literature.* London: Heineman Educational Books.

Toronto Board of Education (1979, May). *Final Report of Sub-Committee on Race Relations.*

Toronto Board of Education (1987). *Draft Report: Consultative Committee on the Education of Black Students in Toronto Schools.* Toronto: Toronto Board of Education.

Toronto Board of Education (1988). *Education of Black Students in Toronto Schools*: Final Report of the Consultative Committee.

Toronto Board of Education (1991). *Every Student Student Survey*, Parts 1, 2, 3. Research Services.

Toronto Board of Education (1993). *Report on 1991 Toronto Every Secondary Student Survey.* Toronto: Toronto Board of Education.

"Towards a New Beginning": The Report and Action Plan of the Four-Level Government/African Canadian Community Working Group. Toronto: City of Toronto.

Transitional Year Program is success (1971, August 16). *Contrast, 1.*

323

Transitional Year Programme (1995). *Transitional Year Programme, University of Toronto Calendar 1995–96*. Toronto: Transitional Year Programme.

Trueba, H., Spindler, G., & Spindler, L. (eds.) (1989). *What Do Anthropologists Have to Say About Dropouts?* Basingstoke: Falmer.

Tullock, H. (1975). *Black Canadians*. Toronto: N. C. Press.

Ture, K., & Hamilton, C. (1992). *Black Power*. New York: Vintage Books.

"Universities waive admission requirements for Blacks" (1969, October). *Contrast*.

University Affairs (1991, August). "The High School Dropout Rate," p. 5. Ottawa: Canadian Association of University Teachers.

Urry, J. (1981). *The Anatomy of Capitalist Societies*. London: Macmillan Press.

Van Galen, J. A. (1993). "Caring in Community: The Limitations of Compassion in Facilitating Diversity." *The Urban Review*, 25(1), pp. 5–24.

Walker, James (1980). *A History of Blacks in Canada: A Study Guide for Teachers and Students*. Quebec: Canadian Government Pub. Centre.

Walker, J. (1981). *A History of Blacks in Canada*. Ottawa: Ministry of State-Multiculturalism.

Walker, S. S., & Rasamimanana, J. (1993). "Tarzan in the Classroom: How 'Educational' Films Mythologize Africa and Miseducate Americans," *Journal of Negro Education*, 62(1).

Waterhouse, P. (1990). *Qualitative Research on School Leavers. Summary Final Report*. Ottawa: Employment and Immigration Canada, and Statistics Canada.

Weis, L., Farrar, E., & Petrie, H. G. (eds.) (1989). *Dropouts From School*. New York: State University of New York Press.

Wiggan, L. (1992). *Organizing Teacher Education for Change: A Report on Equity and Inclusion*. Unpublished Report. Faculty of Education, York University.

Williams, Anne (1993). "Who Cares About Girls? Equality, Physical Education and the Primary School Child." In J. Evans (eds.), *Equality, Education and Physical Education*. London: The Falmer Press, pp. 125–138.

Winks, R. (1971). *Blacks in Canada*. Montreal: McGill-Queen's University Press.

Winks, R. W. (1971). *The Blacks in Canada: A History*. New Haven: Yale University Press.

Wood, E. (1986). *The Retreat from Class*. London: Verso.

Woodson, C. (1933). *The miseducation of the Negro*. Washington, DC: Associated Press.

Working Group. (1992). *Towards a New Beginning: The Report and Action*

Plan of the Four Level Government/African Canadian Community Working Group, Toronto: Metropolitan Toronto Government.

Wright, E. N. (1971). *Programme Placement related to selected Countries of Birth and Selected Languages #99*. Toronto: Toronto Board of Education.

Wright, E. N., & Tsuji G. K. (1984). *The Grade Nine Student Survey, Fall, 1983*. Toronto: Toronto Board of Education. No. 174.

Wright, E. N., & Tsuji G. K. (1983). *The Grade Nine Student Survey, Fall, 1982*. Toronto: Toronto Board of Education. No. 173.

Yau, M., Cheng, M., & Ziegler, S. (1993). *The 1991 Every Secondary Student Survey, Fall, Part III: Program Level and Student Achievement*. Toronto: Toronto Board of Education.

Yetman, Norman R., & Berghorn (1993). "Racial Participation and Integration in Intercollegiate Basketball: A Longitudinal Perspective." *Sociology of Sport Journal, 10*, pp. 301–314.

Yon, Daniel (1994). "The Educational Experiences of Caribbean Youth." In F. Henry *The Caribbean Diaspora in Toronto: Learning to Live with Racism*. Toronto: University of Toronto Press.

Youth Affairs Branch of Employment and Immigration (1990). *Tackling The Dropout Problem*. Ottawa, Ont.

Ziegler, S. (1987). *The Effects of Parent Involvement on Children's Achievement: The Significance of Home/School Links*. Toronto: Toronto Board of Education.

Educating African Canadians is part of *Our Schools/Our Selves* subscription series, which consists of three journals and three books a year. For subscription information, please see the subscription card in the back, or call toll-free 1-800-565-1975. For a book catalogue please write to:

> Our Schools/Our Selves
> 107 Earl Grey Road
> Toronto, Ontario
> M4J 3L6

Contributors

Keren Brathwaite is a founding faculty member in the Transitional Year Programme, University of Toronto, where she teaches and co-ordinates the English programme. She is chair and founding member of the Organization of Black Children (OPBC) which she helped to establish in 1980 as an advocacy group for African Canadian parents and students. She is the author of "The Black Student and the School: A Canadian Dilemma" and edited and introduced *Stories from Life*.

Carl E. James teaches in the Faculty of Education at York University. A former youth worker, he teaches courses in foundations of education and urban education. His research areas include anti-racism education and sports and racial and ethnic minorities. He is the author and editor of several books, including *Making It: Black Youth, Racism and Career Aspirations in a Big City*.

Andrew M. A. Allen is a primary school teacher in a metropolitan Toronto school board. He holds a Master's degree in Education from York University.

Keith Allen is Associate Director of the Transitional Year Programme, University of Toronto, and is a former school principal in Jamaica. His research interests include access to university education for underrepresented groups.

Wendy Brathwaite is a music and cultural studies specialist in Toronto who works with Black youth in schools and in the community. She has been an instructor in the Black Heritage Program at the Toronto Board of Education for several years.

Agnes Calliste is Associate Professor and chair of the Department of Sociology and Anthropology at St. Francis Xavier University in Nova Scotia. Her research is in the area of anti-racism, the education of African Canadians as well as in African Canadian social history of struggles against discrimination. Her most recent works have been on nurses and domestic workers.

Frederick Ivor Case is the Principal of New College, University of Toronto, and a professor in the Department of French. His research contribution to race, African and Caribbean literature and culture has been outstanding and his works include *Racism and National Consciousness*.

Muriel Clarke is former Chair and founding member of the Organization of Parents of Black Children (OPBC), and supports parents who are experiencing difficulties with the school system.

George J. Sefa Dei is Associate Professor in the Department of Sociology, Ontario Institute of Education, University of Toronto and teaches in the areas of anti-racism, international development and development education. He is the principal author of the 1995 study *Drop Out or Push Out? The Dynamics of Black Students' Disengagement from School.*

Venetta E. Goodall is a former vice principal in the Toronto Board of Education who has developed some strategies for involving parents in education. She is the owner of Goodall's Counselling, which provides counselling in education, careers and relationships.

Nancy Hoo Kong is a history graduate and a certified teacher, currently pursuing her Master's degree in education at York University.

Kai James is a high school student, who attends school in the greater metropolitan Toronto area. He is a member of his school's basketball team and chess club, and represents his school in both activities.

Bernard Moitt is Assistant Professor in the Department of History, Virginia Commonwealth University, USA. He specializes in the history of Africa and the African Diaspora, and has published numerous articles on Africa and the Caribbean with a particular focus on gender and slavery. He is former co-ordinator of African Studies at the University of Toronto, and executive member of the Organization of Parents of Black Children.

Althea Prince is a writer of adult fiction and children's stories. A sociologist by training, she teaches in the Faculty of Arts, and is academic advisor in Calumet College, York University. Her area of research is African Caribbean epistemology.

Marc A. Proudfoot is a parent and an occasional teacher and is currently pursuing his graduate degree in education at York University.

Gloria Roberts-Fiati is an Associate Professor in the School of Early Childhood Education at Ryerson Polytechnic University. She is a researcher with the Better Beginnings, Better Futures Project, and is also engaged in research evaluating the educational experiences of minority children.

R. Patrick Solomon is an Assistant Professor in the Faculty of Education, York University where he teaches foundations courses in education and courses in minorities and schooling. His research interests include race and ethno-cultural equity in teacher education. He is the author of *Black Resistance in High School: Forging a Separatist Culture*.

Rinaldo Walcott is an Assistant Professor in the Division of Humanities at York University, where he teaches in the area of Black North American culture.

Subscribe Today

OUR SCHOOLS / OUR SELVES

Bringing together education activists in our schools, our communities and our unions...*with your help* !

Please enter my subscription for 6 issues of OUR SCHOOLS/OUR SELVES starting with issue number_____. Please check one:

INDIVIDUAL

_____ Regular rate $38.00

_____ Student/Unemployed/ Pensioner rate $32.00

_____ Outside Canada Cdn $50.00

ORGANIZATION

_____ In Canada $50.00

_____ Outside Canada Cdn $60.00

SUSTAINING

_____ $100 _____ $200 Other $_____

OR send me issue number(s) _____ at $9.00 per single and $16.00 per double issue

TOLL FREE ORDER NUMBER 1-800-565-1975

Name_____

Address_____

City_____Prov_____Code_____

Occupation_____

_____ Cheque enclosed   _____VISA/Mastercard

Card No_____Expiry date_____

Signature_____

Pass to a friend

OUR SCHOOLS / OUR SELVES

Bringing together education activists in our schools, our communities and our unions...*with your help* !

Please enter my subscription for 6 issues of OUR SCHOOLS/OUR SELVES starting with issue number_____. Please check one:

INDIVIDUAL

_____ Regular rate $38.00

_____ Student/Unemployed/ Pensioner rate $32.00

_____ Outside Canada Cdn $50.00

ORGANIZATION

_____ In Canada $50.00

_____ Outside Canada Cdn $60.00

SUSTAINING

_____ $100 _____ $200 Other $_____

OR send me issue number(s) _____ at $9.00 per single and $16.00 per double issue

TOLL FREE ORDER NUMBER 1-800-565-1975

Name_____

Address_____

City_____Prov_____Code_____

Occupation_____

_____ Cheque enclosed   _____VISA/Mastercard

Card No_____Expiry date_____

Signature_____

MAIL ⮞ **POSTE**

Canada Post Corporation / Société canadienne des postes

Postage paid
if mailed in Canada

Port payé
si posté au Canada

Business Reply

Réponse d'affaires

0110253299   01

0110253299-B3H1G4-BR01

OUR SCHOOLS/OUR SELVES

5502 ATLANTIC STREET
HALIFAX NS   B3H 9Z9

MAIL ⮞ **POSTE**

Canada Post Corporation / Société canadienne des postes

Postage paid
if mailed in Canada

Port payé
si posté au Canada

Business Reply

Réponse d'affaires

0110253299   01

0110253299-B3H1G4-BR01

OUR SCHOOLS/OUR SELVES

5502 ATLANTIC STREET
HALIFAX NS   B3H 9Z9